# THE FOREIGN VISION OF CHARLOTTE BRONTË

# THE FOREIGN VISION
# OF
# CHARLOTTE BRONTË

ENID L. DUTHIE

BARNES & NOBLE

BOOKS

10 East 53d St., New York 10022
(a division of Harper & Row Publishers, Inc.)

*First published 1975 by*
THE MACMILLAN PRESS LTD
*London and Basingstoke*

Published in the U.S.A. 1975 by
HARPER & ROW PUBLISHERS, INC.
BARNES & NOBLE IMPORT DIVISION
ISBN: 0-06-491846-7

*Printed in Great Britain*

To my Sister

KATHLEEN FORDYCE PHILCOX

# Contents

# Acknowledgements

I should like to thank:

The Brontë Society for permission to use material from the Society's *Transactions* and also to include in the first chapter of this book material from my article in *Transactions* in 1959 on 'Charlotte Brontë's translation of the first canto of Voltaire's *Henriade*' (BST XIII, pt 69).

The family of the late C. K. Shorter for permission to use unpublished manuscripts by Charlotte Brontë in the Bonnell Collection, the Brontë Parsonage Museum and also the privately printed edition by C. K. Shorter of Charlotte Brontë's translation of the first canto of the *Henriade*.

Basil Blackwell for permission to quote from the Shakespeare Head Brontë.

The *Contemporary Review* for permission to use material from my article on 'Charlotte Brontë and Constantin Heger' (Mar 1955).

The British Museum, Bradford City Libraries and the Pierpont Morgan Library, New York for photocopies and other documents.

The Bibliothèque Royale Albert I$^{er}$, Brussels, for photocopies of M. Heger's speeches and for allowing quotation from them.

My thanks are also due to: Mr Norman Raistrick, Custodian of the Brontë Parsonage Museum, for much help in sending photocopies and supplying information; Mr H. L. Schollick, O.B.E., and Miss Ann Wormald for the loan or gift of valuable texts; Miss Elizabeth Suddaby, Miss Hilda Swinburne, Dr J. D. Biard, Mr H. W. Stubbs and Professor P. J. Yarrow for tracing references or answering queries.

Finally I should like to express my sincere thanks to the staff of the University Library, Exeter, without whose assistance this study could not have been completed.

E.L.D.

# Abbreviations

| | |
|---|---|
| AB | Anne Brontë |
| BM | British Museum |
| BPM | Brontë Parsonage Museum |
| BST | *Brontë Society Transactions* |
| CB | Charlotte Brontë |
| EJB | Emily Jane Brontë |
| EN | Ellen Nussey |
| Gaskell | *The Life of Charlotte Brontë* * |
| Gérin | *Charlotte Brontë. The Evolution of Genius* (Clarendon Press) |
| MT | Mary Taylor |
| PBB | Patrick Branwell Brontë |
| SHB | Shakespeare Head Brontë, *The Brontës, their Lives, Friendships and Correspondence*, 4 vols |
| SHBMU | Shakespeare Head Brontë, *The Miscellaneous and Unpublished Writings of Charlotte and Patrick Branwell Brontë*, 2 vols |
| SHBP | Shakespeare Head Brontë, *The Poems of Charlotte and Patrick Branwell Brontë* |

# Introduction

Ever since Mrs Gaskell published her *Life of Charlotte Brontë*, studies on the Brontës have continued to appear. As might be expected, the approach to the subject has undergone significant variations as new light has been shed on it from different sources. Mrs Gaskell's masterpiece established the validity as well as the charm of the biographical approach. The next contribution of major importance came when Clement Shorter, after visiting Mr Nicholls in Ireland, published *Charlotte Brontë and her Circle* and *The Brontës, Life and Letters*, based on the fresh biographical material he had acquired. Then came the publication of the four letters to M. Heger, another landmark in the story. A new dimension was given to that story with the discovery by Professor Fannie Ratchford of the significance of the juvenilia, which she spent many years deciphering and collating. At the same time the biographical approach continued to prove valuable with the acquisition of new background material and new insights. Margaret Lane's *Brontë Story* was offered 'as a sort of footnote to Mrs Gaskell', based on Mrs Gaskell's own text but putting the reader in possession of material still unknown to her. More recently Winifred Gérin's studies of the Brontës, particularly her comprehensive *Charlotte Brontë. The Evolution of Genius,* have made a massive and illuminating contribution to our understanding of this unique family.

There is now a growing interest in the direct analysis of the novels themselves, shown in critical articles and in full length studies. Yet where such highly personal writers are concerned, references to their individual experience will continue to be necessary. It seems therefore an appropriate moment to consider in more detail one area of Charlotte Brontë's experience which had far-reaching repercussions on her artistic creation.

It is well known that Mrs Gaskell, in her work published only two years after Charlotte's death, refrained from giving the Brussels period the significance which she knew from the letters shown her by M. Heger it had really possessed. Clement Shorter, writing forty years later, found it necessary to consider the position in more detail but rejected as unfounded the suggestion, largely due to the autobiographical interpretation of *Villette,* that she was in love with M. Heger. The publication in 1913 of her four letters to him naturally concentrated attention on the emotional drama. It was then generally recognised that the Brussels period was in fact of crucial importance and subsequent biographers have treated it in that light.

Its main interest, however, remained for most Brontë students on the emotional plane and its fertilising influence on Charlotte Brontë as an artist did not receive the attention it deserved. Mrs Humphry Ward had already drawn attention to its significance in this respect in her admirable introductions to the Haworth edition of the novels. And Clement Shorter himself, in *The Brontës, Life and Letters* (1908), had stressed the importance of M. Heger's teaching for Charlotte Brontë's development as an author. But the publication of the letters in 1913 diverted attention from this aspect of the Brussels period, and Brontë critics since have not considered it in any detail, though some, in particular Phyllis Bentley and Kathleen Tillotson, have made very discerning comments.[1]

To begin with, the stay in Brussels needs to be seen against a background which had prepared Charlotte Brontë to receive its impact. Her knowledge of French went back to childhood, and since childhood France had both attracted and repelled her. As the country of Napoleon, it was antipathetic to the worshipper of Wellington, but it had the attraction of all foreign countries for the creator of Angria, and its literature was connected in her mind with names like Mme de Staël, representative of the wider culture for which she longed. Brussels itself was as important for her intellectual and artistic maturation as for her emotional development. Some of her French essays have been reprinted from time to time in the *Brontë Society Transactions,* but the total achievement they represent and the comments of M. Heger deserve a place in Brontë criticism they have not yet been accorded. Without knowledge of them it is impossible to understand the full meaning of Charlotte's declaration that she would have liked to write a book which would have been dedicated 'à mon maître de littérature, au seul maître que j'ai jamais eu . . .'

But it is the novels themselves that provide the ultimate criterion for the value of the Brussels experience to Charlotte Brontë as a creative artist. And here above all it has not been appreciated as it deserves. It did not awaken her genius, for that genius had already expressed itself in the Angrian cycle, begun in childhood and continued throughout adolescence. But it provided material peculiarly suitable for her creative powers to work on; it enlarged the scope of her vision, giving a new dimension to her delineation of character and milieu; it influenced her style, and no aspect of her art has been so underrated as the new and constructive use she made of French words and phrases in her narration and dialogue; and it strengthened the ties that linked her art with European culture, making her not only a great English novelist but one of the most eloquent representatives in nineteenth-century literature of the undying heritage of the Romantic movement.

# 1 Before Brussels

The dark colours in which Mrs Gaskell painted the Brontës' childhood are now seen to have been considerably darker than the reality. Not only was the gift of the creative imagination their birthright but they grew up in circumstances exceptionally suited to its development. The drama of the Napoleonic wars which had already passed into legend was still recent history, the Romantic movement had revivified the arts, the world of elemental nature could be reached by 'the little and the lone green lane' that led from the parsonage to the moors. From all these sources they drew sustenance for their developing genius and created, while still children, an artist's paradise of their own.

The full significance of the Brontë juvenilia was realised only when it was discovered that the minute booklets, first seen by Mrs Gaskell, were part of a vast cycle, extending ultimately far beyond the childhood years. The origins of this cycle go back, as is well known, to a childhood play suggested by a box of wooden soldiers. To Charlotte, eldest of the surviving children, this instantly became an opportunity for the glorification of her hero, Wellington. In one of the earliest of the microscopic fragments, written in 1829, she tells how she snatched up one of the wooden soldiers, 'the prettiest of the whole, and the tallest, and the most perfect in every part', exclaiming: 'This is the Duke of Wellington! This shall be the Duke!'[1] Emily and Anne chose less ambitious names for the toys of their selection, but Branwell called his soldier 'Buonaparte'. The background to the children's play was the vast pageant of recent history, dominated by the victor of Waterloo.

But something else was needed to satisfy their ardent imagination. They wished to create an environment worthy of their heroes. The play of 'The Islanders' was a first attempt to effect this, but the real islands they chose were too near the coasts of their own land to satisfy them for long, and the scene was shifted by Charlotte to a fictitious Island of Dreams. In time this, too, lost its attraction, but they could not be satisfied by imagining adventures that took place in a familiar environment, for they had the Romantic's vision of a more vivid existence in a land distance enough to be another world. It took shape as an imagined Africa, representing the exotic at its most colourful. The wooden soldiers were sent on a voyage which resulted in shipwreck on the coast of Guinea and the building of a city which was to become the nucleus of a new kingdom. The material of Glass Town was a disparate medley of reality and dreams, which the Brontës' imagination resolved into a unity. It was Goldsmith's *Grammar of General Geography* which suggested the voyage of the twelve heroes to the Guinea coast. But Glass Town, in its earliest stage, took its exotic colouring predominantly from the *Arabian Nights*. The landscape undergoes transformations which are the work of the presiding Genii — in fact the four Brontë children — and it is thanks to their help that in a short time the city rises from the plain, beside the glass-like harbour from which it takes its name.

The charm of the exotic is not allowed to dim the cult of Wellington. Both Charlotte and Branwell make this clear in their accounts of the early history of the colony. They imagine its actual foundation as having taken place more than thirty years before, so that 'Arthur Wellesley' on his first appearance as one of the original twelve adventurers was only at the beginning of his career. In her 'Romantic Tale', written in 1829, Charlotte explains how his exploits in Africa were interrupted by more than twenty years in Europe, and how he returned in 1816 as 'His Grace the Duke of Wellington . . . the conqueror of Bonaparte . . .'[2]

Glass Town rapidly becomes the capital of a confederacy partitioned into four kingdoms, one of which belongs to Wellington. A map drawn up by Branwell of the confederacy shows that it includes several islands off the coast.[3] One of these is named Frenchland, supposed to be peopled with

French and has 'Paris' as its capital. Its presence constitutes a tangible reminder of the importance of the Napoleonic Wars in the genesis of the Brontës' imaginary kingdom.

Glass Town soon acquires a life of its own. It has its politics, its social round and, thanks to Charlotte and Branwell, its own literature. Inspired by *Blackwood's Magazine,* much admired at the parsonage, Branwell started in 1829 'The Young Men's Magazine' which lasted till December 1830, the later numbers being edited by Charlotte. The scope of the early Glass Town literature reflects the width of their interests. They read Shakespeare and Milton and eighteenth-century authors, but were naturally most affected by the Romantics of their own century; the poetry of Byron, whom Charlotte first read in 1829, and the novels of Scott were to be lasting influences on the whole Angrian cycle. And through *Blackwood's* and the newspapers they were also in touch with contemporary topics.

In this eclectic world the Wellington cult continues to provide a focal point. It is the Duke who heads Charlotte's list of 'Characters of the Celebrated Men of the Present Time'. The 'time' is 1829 and the Duke is now described as 'equally irresistible in the Cabinet as in the field'.[4] The political crisis leading to the Reform Bill was followed with keen interest at Haworth parsonage, but it is his victory over Napoleon which is still Wellington's greatest title to fame in the eyes of Charlotte Brontë.

For Branwell, Buonaparte still has his attraction. Scott's *Life of Napoleon Buonaparte,* published in 1827, was in his father's library, and it was from one of Napoleon's marshals that he took the pseudonym of 'Young Soult'. It was not that he had a cult of Napoleon in any sense comparable to Charlotte's adoration of Wellington. The Titan with whom he afterwards identified was his own creation, Northangerland. In spite of his 'arts and abilities' Buonaparte is referred to in his 'History of the Young Men' as 'the usurper', 'the Tyrant Napoleon'.[5] If he, or rather the puppet who represents him, is transported by Branwell to 'Frenchland', it is primarily to ensure future trouble for the adjacent territory of Glass Town and to stage the Wellington-Napoleon conflict over again in a new and exotic setting.

But, even at this early stage, there are indications that the young Brontës' approach to France is not conditioned entirely by recent history but that echoes of French literature and culture have penetrated to the parsonage. The poems Branwell writes under the pseudonym 'Young Soult' are provided with notes stated to have been supplied by 'Monsieur De La Chateaubriand, Author of Travels in Greece, the Holy Land, etc . . .'[6] The Heatons' library at Ponden House, to which the Brontës had access, contained a translation of Chateaubriand's *Itinéraire de Paris à Jérusalem,* and Branwell's interest in travellers' tales, as well as in things French, must have attracted him to this account of his Near Eastern journey by the ancestor of French Romanticism. Charlotte herself is not indifferent to the cultural attractions of Paris. The hero of her tale 'The Swiss Artist' is 'transported with joy' when a patron offers to take him to the French capital, for he has often heard of 'the magnificence of that great city, the splendour of the Tuilleries and the grand collection of paintings and statues which adorned the Louvre gallery . . .'[7] In 'A Frenchman's Journal' she includes an account of an evening at the theatre which begins satirically but becomes enthusiastic as the play follows its predictably melodramatic course to the 'dreadful *dénoument'.*[8]

The growing association in Charlotte's mind between France and cultural qualities is seen clearly in the description of the heroine's rival, Lady Ellrington, in her first love story 'Albion and Marina'. Her intellectual qualities at once suggest a comparison with Madame de Staël. In the preface she had already been referred to sarcastically as 'Marina's Frenchified rival', a term indicative of the dichotomy in Charlotte's attitude, for in the story itself she is an impressive figure: 'For some time she entertained him with a discourse of the most lively eloquence, and indeed Madame de Staël herself could not have gone beyond Lady Zelzia in the conversational talent.'[9] The name was always to furnish a criterion of intellectual brilliance in Glass Town. After Glass Town has become Verdopolis Lady Ellrington, splendid in 'velvet robes, dark plume and crown-like turban', is called 'the most learned woman of her age, the modern Cleopatra, the Verdopolitan de Staël . . .'[10]

It is significant that it is in 1830 that Charlotte first uses Verreopolis — which soon becomes Verdopolis — as an alternative for Glass Town. She explains that the new name means 'the Glass Town, being compounded of a Greek and French word to that effect'.[11] The prominence given to a French word is understandable, for she was now actively engaged in studying the language. This might be surmised from her attempts to introduce it into 'A Frenchman's Journal'. But conjecture is not needed, for the proof exists that in 1830 she was studying the language seriously. It was in August of that year that she completed her translation into English verse of the first canto of Voltaire's *Henriade*.

A result like this cannot be achieved at fourteen without some preliminary knowledge of the language. How and when she learnt it is an interesting question. Her only regular schooling at that date had been the unhappy ten months at Cowan Bridge, which she left at the age of nine in 1825. In the school curriculum French, Music and Drawing ranked as 'Accomplishments', for which an additional charge was made, but there is no record of Mr Brontë's paying extra fees for his younger children. He did, however, pay '£3 for French and Drawing for Maria'. It is more than probable that Charlotte admired her beloved sister's superior knowledge and longed to emulate it. It is worth noting also that Maria could read French *before* coming to the school, for the record of 'acquirements on entering' states that she has 'made some progress in reading French, but knows nothing of the language grammatically'.[12] This suggests some possibility of learning French at the parsonage. Clement Shorter thought that the children's aunt, Miss Branwell, must have known some French and that it was from her that Charlotte gained her early knowledge.[13] Ellen Nussey's account, however, is that she had taught herself 'a little French' before going to school for the second time at Roe Head in January 1831. It seems most likely that Charlotte at this time was in fact self-taught.[14] She had the intelligence to achieve this, as Maria seems to have done before her, and the drawbacks of such a method of learning a language would explain the gap between her facility as a translator and the uncertainty of her efforts when she tries to write in French herself.

If there must be some conjecture as to how she first learnt French, there must also be conjecture as to why she showed such increased interest in the language in 1830. Here the mental climate of the parsonage at the time suggests an answer. The collaboration between Charlotte and Branwell was very close — a collaboration which, as their writings show, was also a healthy rivalry. It was Branwell who, as the only son, had the privilege of being taught by his father the languages which Mr Brontë did know, Latin and Greek. Charlotte must have admired and perhaps envied her brother's newly acquired classical knowledge. It may well have awakened in her the ambition to excel in her turn in a modern language. The transformation at this period of Glass Town into Verreopolis, 'compounded of a Greek and a French word', suggests that she hopes to enrich their imaginary world with an eclectic culture to which they can both contribute.

The translation of the first canto of *La Henriade* is signed by Charlotte Brontë with her own name and not one of the pseudonyms such as 'Captain Tree' or 'Lord Charles Wellesley' which she constantly used. No doubt availability had something to do with her choice of the work. The *Henriade,* now one of the least read of Voltaire's works, enjoyed wide popularity in England, as well as in France, in the eighteenth and early nineteenth century. There had been several translations before 1830. Charlotte possessed her own copy, bought, according to the inscription inside the cover, in May 1830.

Her translation, though not faultless, is on the whole remarkably accurate and there is no need to ask for any special indulgence for its author on the grounds of her youth. The subject — the struggle which opposed the last Valois and Henry of Navarre to the League — was in tune with her natural love of drama, and the rôle accorded to England in the first canto of the *Henriade* must have been a particular attraction. Above all, the *Henriade* is centred round a hero and politics for her centred round the great man, be he a Wellington or a Henry of Bourbon. But the real interest of her translation lies in the way in which she has infused it with her own romanticism. Colours become more vivid, passions more intense. She has chosen to write her version in rhyming couplets, and she shows the same skill as a versifier she had already displayed, by August 1830, in a number of original poems. But her verses belong to a different emotional climate from the crisp alexandrines of Voltaire. His initial invocation to Truth and her translation of the couplet reflect, at the start, the difference between the two texts:

> Descends du haut des cieux, auguste Vérité,
> Répands sur mes écrits ta force et ta clarté . . .

becomes, for Charlotte Brontë,

> Come awful Truth descending from on high
> Shed power and splendour on this history . . .

The end of the year 1830 saw her temporarily obliged to abandon her imaginary kingdom of 'Verreopolis', though not the study of French. It was decided she should go to Miss Wooler's school at Roe Head, near Mirfield. To Branwell was left the responsibility of continuing the Verdopolitan chronicles, unsupported by the two other 'chief Genii', Emily and Anne, who initiated about this time their own independent realm of Gondal. On her arrival at Roe Head Charlotte at first found herself at a disadvantage because of her lack of regular schooling, but her intelligence soon gave her the leading place in class. Among the subjects in which she quickly began to distinguish herself was French. 'She soon began to make a good figure in French lessons.'[15] When she returned to Haworth at the end of her schooldays in July 1832, she brought back with her, among other acquisitions, a sounder knowledge of the language. In her anxiety to practise it she did her best to initiate a correspondence in French with Ellen Nussey, when she wrote to her after a visit to her home in September 1832. The letter, first quoted by Mrs Gaskell, is still far from perfect, as far as grammar is concerned — though haste in writing may have had something to do with this — but it contains graphic touches: 'Mes petites soeurs couraient hors de la maison pour me rencontrer aussitôt que la voiture se fit voir . . .'[16] In a postscript in English, Charlotte implores her friend to write to her in 'the universal language'.

No doubt French was among the subjects in which she was now instructing her own sisters, one of her duties after her return from Roe Head. But her enforced absence from her imaginary world had only made her more anxious to return to it, and her collaboration with Branwell became again her chief interest. The period from 1832 to 1835 — when Charlotte returned to Roe Head, this time as a teacher — was a prolific one for them both, in which the rapid development of the Glass Town cycle mirrored that of their own creative gifts.

Political upheavals were frequent in the Verdopolitan Confederacy during these years. They were caused chiefly by the rivalry between its two leading figures, the young Marquis of Douro, elder son of the Duke of Wellington, and his father-in-law Alexander Percy, Earl of Northangerland. The Confederacy also had to repel invaders, and among its enemies the French played a major part. When it was attacked by the Ashantees and Napoleon invaded it from the east, it was Douro who repelled them. He demanded in return that the territory he had saved should be ceded to him. As a result he became king of Angria — the name he gave to the new kingdom of the Confederacy — and also took the title of Duke of Zamorna.

There is still much in the military part of these adventures reminiscent of the struggle between Wellington and Napoleon. The titles of Zamorna and his infant son, the Marquis of Almeida, recall places made famous in the Peninsular War. It is Napoleon himself who is responsible for the invasion of the eastern provinces. He also appears episodically in Branwell's story 'The Pirate',[17] and in Charlotte's 'Napoleon and the Spectre', an episode in her tale 'The Green Dwarf'.[18] Supposed to be told by a French traveller at 'the Genii's Inn' in the early pioneer days of the colony, it is not itself connected with events in Verdopolis. The 'spectre' is that of General Pichegru, who was involved in a plot against the life of the First Consul and found strangled in prison. The main emphasis of the story is on the ghost's warning of coming disaster and this is delivered in a not unsympathetic tone. Charlotte seems to be preoccupied here with the dangers of Napoleonic ambitions rather than with their ethics. She is also concerned with the macabre possibilities of her theme.

The taste for the macabre blends with reminiscences of the sinister Frenchman Pigtail, still surviving from early Glass Town days, to produce some highly coloured incidents in the life of Verdopolis. Pigtail and his companion wander about 'without any other end than that of picking up stray children and selling them to owners of mills or torturing them to death to amuse themselves in their solitary rambles'. Here the legend of French cruelty to children, no doubt dating from the Napoleonic wars, is combined with a reference to child labour in mills, highly topical in 1832. Charlotte makes more graphic use of Pigtail's unpleasant activities in her story 'The Foundling'.[19]

The creation of Angria in 1834 marks the final expansion of the imaginary world. It remains, physically as well as politically, a complex one. Angria itself has seven provinces and remains part of the whole Verdopolitan Confederacy, which retains its separate kingdoms. Both Charlotte and Branwell describe its variety of landscape. They are no longer content to borrow their 'exotic' colouring chiefly from the *Arabian Nights*. They have drawn on their reading and their observation, and the result is a curious amalgam to which Scott and Ossian, their familiarity with their native moors and their father's nostalgic memories of Ireland have all contributed. But the fertile valleys in the south owe much to the sunny Mediterranean landscapes that delighted Charlotte in Byron's poetry. It is essential that their 'Africa' should remain 'an almost Utopian colony . . . rising like a new Albion under a brighter sky and sunnier climate'.[20]

Angria is rich not only in natural beauty but in cultural life. This ideal world is not a primitive Utopia but a highly sophisticated civilisation. It was not only in quest of brighter skies but of wider mental horizons that Charlotte Brontë was later to cross the sea. Neither she nor Branwell would have thought their 'bright and far continent' complete if it had not possessed a brilliant artistic life. Architecture, painting, music, literature all flourish on this favoured soil. Magnificent music accompanies the great Angrian ceremonies. Mrs Siddons plays at the Theatre Royal in Verdopolis. The Marquis of Douro owns 'one of the most splendid, select and extensive libraries now in possession of any individual'.[21]

The culture of Angria is an eclectic one, and it seems appropriate that the chief landmark in the capital city of the Confederacy should be the 'tower of all Nations'. English literature and art naturally have a prominent place in Angrian life, but the cosmopolitanism the Brontës had savoured as children both in Romantic writers and in the Napoleonic era are very much a part of Angria, and the two elements, French and Greek, which combined to form the name of the federate capital are still present. France still plays a part in Angrian politics, and French phrases are used in society to give an impression of sophistication.[22] The Greek influence is more diffused. It dominates Angrian architecture. The portico of the Zamorna palace suggests 'Ionia in her loftiest times'.[23] And there are echoes of Greek literature. Lady Ellrington reads Aeschylus in the original, even when her own situation bears an alarming similarity to the domestic tragedies of antiquity. The persisting rôle of Greece in Angrian culture is no doubt due at this stage as much to Byron's poetry as to Branwell's classical studies. Describing a portrait of the Duchess of Zamorna, Charlotte writes: 'As Byron says, her features have all the statuesque repose, the calm classic grace that dwells on the Earl's.'[24]

In this period of Angrian history, the Duke of Zamorna is at the zenith of his career. He had long since become more prominent in the Angrian saga than his father. Originally a sensitive and gifted youth, he had rapidly evolved into the brilliant Byronic figure whom Charlotte idolised and at the same time, writing under the pseudonym of Lord Charles Wellesley, his younger brother, severely censored. As Duke of Zamorna and King of Angria he has added the role of military conqueror to his other distinctions. There is a suggestion of almost oriental despotism about Zamorna now. By a curious reversal of rôles, the elder son of the Duke of Wellington seems to be acquiring Napoleonic characteristics. He has demanded the cession of the conquered provinces to himself, as king, and when his twin sons are born, they are presented to the Angrian people with the maximum of splendid ceremonial.

This over-brilliant period in the fortunes of Angria coincided with what was probably the happiest time in Charlotte Brontë's youth. '. . . in one delightful, though somewhat monotonous course my life is passed',[25] she wrote, rather misleadingly, to Ellen Nussey, who knew nothing about the imaginary kingdom. But this halcyon period came to an end in July 1835, when she returned to Roe Head to teach in the same school where she had been a pupil. In a different strain, she writes to Ellen now: 'My life since I saw you last has passed on as monotonously and as unvaryingly as ever, nothing but teach, teach, teach, from morning till night.'[26]

In the holidays she returned to her chronicles of the imaginary kingdom. Its history, in her absence, had been continued by Branwell. He too had encountered frustration, of a different sort, for in the Autumn of 1835 he had made his abortive journey to London, from which he returned without having been admitted, or even felt able to seek admission, to the Academy schools. His bitter disappointment coloured the Angrian story, into which he threw himself with renewed vigour. Zamorna does not reign long undisturbed. Northangerland intrigues against him and eventually Civil War breaks out. Zamorna's speedy defeat is really due to the foreign 'Allies', principally the French and the Ashantees, who are called into the country by his enemies, instigated by the treacherous Northangerland. The French led by Masséna and Marmont take a major part in the war. Zamorna is captured and sentenced to exile on Ascension Isle, a fate which inevitably recalls that of Napoleon exiled to St Helena. But this is the lowest ebb in the Angrian fortunes. They begin to recover when Zamorna escapes on his way into exile and, after hiding for some months in 'France', returns to Angria, rallies the remnant of his army and defeats his enemies in a decisive battle. Northangerland leaves the country and he is reinstated as king.

For Charlotte, Branwell's incessant wars are the backcloth against which, in the holidays from Roe Head, she stages the personal dramas that interest her more. She is not concerned with military matters in themselves, but with the light in which they show her characters. Zamorna in defeat is still an impressive figure. The fact that he takes refuge temporarily in the island originally called 'Frenchland' and later 'France' makes some reference to his stay there inevitable. But by using exclusively in this context the names of real places, Charlotte makes the usual Angrian compromise between imagination and reality less satisfactory than usual. Mina Laury, who was with Zamorna in his exile, says: 'I have followed his steps from Rousillon (sic) to Normandy . . .',[27] and he himself refers, even more disconcertingly, in a narrative poem, to the 'storied walls of old Provence'.[28]

Charlotte is more justified in referring to the varying racial characteristics of the Angrians in terms of European counterparts, since Europe provided the original colonists. According to Branwell, in his new version of the 'History of the Young Men', the majority came from England, Ireland and Scotland and a minority from Spain and Italy, while to the island of 'France', after the fall of Napoleon, 'all true Parisians flocked with eager wing . . .'[29] Racial characteristics, exaggerated no doubt but often by no means unconvincing, give an added interest to her rapidly developing powers of characterisation. Mina Laury belongs to 'the West, the sweet West' and refers to herself more than once as Irish. The Duke of Fidena has 'pride that could no more be thawed than . . . the snows of his own Highland-hills'.[30] Charlotte's view of the French is still strongly coloured by association with the Napoleonic Wars. They are the enemies of Angria. The few who make an individual appearance have little to recommend them. They are either domesticated in Angrian service like Eugene Rosier, Zamorna's valet and one of the few servants who risks impertinence to his master, or else, like Madame Lalande, they are frivolous and immoral. But however superficial such sketches may be, they show Charlotte's consciousness of the interest and the significance of racial characteristics.

It is for the same reason that she takes trouble to make her characters express themselves at times in their native idiom, whether it is a dialect or a foreign language. Her use of dialect is already impressive; not for nothing has she read Scott and Burns and listened herself to local speech. General Thornton would not be the convincing character he is if he did not constantly lapse into his 'beloved Doric'. And it is principally in the attempt to make the episodic characters more authentic that she introduces an occasional French word or phrase into the conversation of Rosier or Lalande.

After Zamorna's return there is a change in the mood of the Angrian cycle. There is less accent on military conquest or disaster, and Zamorna is seen as much on his country estates as in his capital city or Verdopolis. Northangerland, allowed to return from banishment on condition he avoids political intrigue, is no longer a Lucifer-like figure but an ageing rake and irritable hypochondriac. In this last phase of the cycle characters come into prominence who are in keeping with its more disillusioned mood. Branwell dramatises the clouding of his brilliant youth through the career of Captain Henry Hastings. The tragic disintegration of the same career is the subject of Charlotte's 'Henry Hastings'. By the time she wrote it, she had given up her teaching post in Miss Wooler's school — in May 1838 — and was temporarily at liberty to live once more in the world of Angria. 'Caroline Vernon', written at the same period, shows how the promise of youth is blighted in different circumstances. Here Zamorna bears the chief responsibility, but other factors come into the tragedy of Caroline Vernon, and these include a visit to 'France' at the most impressionable stage of her development.

Caroline is the daughter of Northangerland and the dancer Louisa Vernon, who had often appeared in Angrian tales. Louisa had been left in Zamorna's power when Northangerland fled the country. He gave her young daughter Caroline the sort of careless affection he gave all children and supervised her education. Northangerland, after his return from exile, realises she is growing up and considers she is now old enough to be introduced into society. To prepare her for this, he decides to take her to 'Paris', 'the only place to give her what he wished her to have, the tone, the fashion'.[31] Zamorna in vain criticises the plan, for he is convinced Caroline is too young and too susceptible to be plunged into a sophisticated society.

Ardent and impulsive, she is quick to respond to the influence of the new milieu. 'She changed fast in the atmosphere of Paris. She saw quickly into things that were dark to her before. She learnt life and unlearnt much fiction . . .'[32]

But it is not long before she encounters the corrupting influence Zamorna had foreseen though, ironically, he had not foreseen the direction it would take. One of her father's former boon companions, living since the war as a prescribed refugee in 'Paris', enlightens her as to Zamorna's reputation. And Caroline, already half in love with him since childhood, ceases to think of him as a rather remote and awe-inspiring character and realises how vulnerable he is to feminine beauty, just at the moment when she has first become conscious of her own. From this point the dénouement is foreseeable, though Northangerland accelerates it by sending Caroline, when they return, to an isolated country house with the intention of preventing her from seeing too much of Zamorna. Miserable in solitude and learning that he is staying in the same region, she rushes off impulsively to see him. Zamorna, realising her infatuation, does not send her back. Unlike Jane Eyre, she yields to her passion for him and becomes his mistress. The corrupting influence of 'Paris' certainly helps to bring about this result, though the main responsibility rests with Zamorna and with Caroline herself.

The time had now come when Charlotte Brontë, at the age of twenty-three, felt obliged to emerge from the world of Angria and acclimatise herself to a more temperate region whose quieter colours were nearer those of ordinary life. But her 'Farewell to Angria' reads rather like the farewell of someone reluctantly turning their back on a lost paradise: '. . . Yet do not urge me too fast, reader; it is no easy theme to dismiss from my imagination the imges which have filled it so long . . .'[33] It is not disillusionment with the dream world that motivates her but the imperative need of the extended imagination to relax its tension: '. . . Still, I long to quit for a while that burning clime where we have sojourned too long . . .'

During the period that followed, she tried, in the intervals of her two experiences as governess, to operate the transition from Angria to a more sober climate. One of the fragments surviving from this period shows the filiation between the Yorkshire social scene she describes and the unforgotten Angria.[34] Alexander Percy, the heroine's father, is the older Northangerland; Marian Fairburn, 'diffident and what the

French call *craintive'*, recalls Marian Hume, the first wife of Zamorna; Percy's daughter resembles his second wife and the young Arthur West is recognisably Zamorna himself in youth, in a country house setting. From the dialogue it seems that he, too, has had the opportunity of completing his social education in Paris, though he has not profited from it, according to one outspoken critic who says: 'You ought to take a few lessons in the science of *petits soins* . . . I should have thought your travels on the continent and your six months' residence in Paris might have taught you the elements of politeness, at least'. To which he retorts: 'It has taught me some pretty sentimental ways . . .'

It is evidently not only a social but a sentimental education that, in Charlotte's opinion, one receives in France. An exaggerated emotionalism seems as certain a result of it as the more desirable qualities of social flair and wit. The dichotomy in her attitude, evident in the Angrian cycle, was strengthened at this period, and her interest in France increased, by a new factor, the reading of contemporary French novels on a wide scale. This new contact with France came to her through the family of her schoolfriend Mary Taylor. The Taylors of Gomersal introduced her to a milieu very different from any she had known. Joshua Taylor, a cloth manufacturer whose family had been established in the district for generations, was a Radical in politics and also a man of strong cultural interests, who had travelled widely and could speak fluent French and Italian, as well as broad Yorkshire. He kept in touch with current French literature, and it was through the intermediary of the Taylor family that it reached the parsonage: 'I have got another bale of French books from Gomersal — containing upwards of 40 volumes,' wrote Charlotte to Ellen Nussey in 1840. 'I have read about half — they are like the rest clever wicked sophistical and immoral — the best of it is they give one a thorough view of France and Paris — and are the best substitute for French Conversation I have met with.'[35]

It was in part a practical motive that attracted Charlotte to these ambiguously described works. A good knowledge of spoken French was one of the first requirements of the profession on which she had reluctantly embarked. But it was the opportunity of contact with French life and thought that attracted her most. She believed she found it here at second hand. What she found was obviously conditioned by the choice of books sent from Gomersal. She mentions no titles but where 'upwards of forty volumes' are concerned, current popularity and availability must have been primary considerations in making the selection. It is safe to assume that the authors included some well-known figures. One would have expected Balzac to be among them but she did not, by her own account. know anything of his work till 1850.[36] But immense success was also enjoyed, at the time, by the popular novelist Eugène Sue. Charlotte later included him, as well as the earlier best-seller Paul de Kock, among the French novelists in the library of Yorke Hunsden in *The Professor,* a character partly suggested by Joshua Taylor. It seems probable that both were represented in the selection sent to the parsonage from Gomersal.

A much more significant name also figures among the authors in Hunsden's library, that of George Sand. She was certainly not like Balzac an 'unknown author' to Charlotte in her youth.[37] Her acquaintance with George Sand's novels must have begun prior to the composition of *The Professor,* finished in 1846. It is highly probable that some of them were included in the selection sent from Gomersal, and that this was her first introduction to them. In view of Charlotte's admiration of her work, it is natural to ask what qualities attracted her in this French author, in spite of her declared mistrust of French novels in general.

By 1840 George Sand had already expressed the turbulent romanticism of her youth in the pages of *Indiana, Valentine, Jacques* and *Lélia.* Their individualism and their intensely personal feeling could not fail to appeal to Charlotte Brontë, nor the fact that they express the Romantic's accusation against society from the woman's point of view. In *Lélia,* the protest of George Sand goes deeper still: Lélia is in revolt not only against social institutions but against life itself. But adultery, death and suicide are the most frequent results of the individual's revolt, unless, as in the dénouement of *Indiana,* free love in an extra-social setting is offered as a solution. Such views were not likely to be endorsed by

Charlotte Brontë, in spite of her indulgence to the Byronic heroes of the Angrian saga. But George Sand achieved a less despairing romanticism in *Mauprat,* of all her early novels the one likely to have had the deepest appeal for Charlotte Brontë.[38] Its moderate optimism stems partly from its author's growing interest in humanitarian beliefs. But it is the study of the much-tested love of Bernard de Mauprat for his cousin Edmée, 'la fée qui m'a transformé', rather than the Rousseauesque side of the novel, which must have had most attraction for the future author of *Jane Eyre.* In *Mauprat,* too, George Sand shows even more clearly than in the earlier works her outstanding narrative and descriptive gifts, as well as the strong vein of poetry in her fiction.

All this, however, does not alter the fact that George Sand's novels, if, as seems most likely, they were included in those sent from Gomersal, did not cause Charlotte to modify her verdict on French novels in general. Criticism of George Sand was indeed strongly expressed in some English reviews,[39] though by 1840 English opinion was becoming more favourable to her.[40] But it was her own judgement rather than the climate of critical opinion that dictated Charlotte's verdict. She believed the novels to be in general 'clever, wicked, sophistical, and immoral'. But, as Mrs Humphry Ward points out, she read them.[41] And her reading of them was the first stage in that closer contact with French literature which was shortly to become more complete and discerning under the direction of an excellent guide.

If it was through the medium of the novels sent her by the Taylors of Gomersal that Charlotte renewed her contact with France, it was a letter from Mary Taylor, then in Brussels, which in 1841 provided the impetus which was finally to take her across the Channel. By then she and her sisters felt that to open a small private school would be preferable to the drudgery of teaching among strangers. But they had no diplomas and few accomplishments. Charlotte knew that, in spite of her reading, her knowledge of languages was still insufficient. But it is significant that she does not seem to have thought definitely of going abroad till the letter from Mary Taylor fired her imagination as it had been fired before by dreams of Angria: 'Mary's letter spoke of some of the pictures and cathedrals she had seen — pictures the most exquisite — and cathedrals the most venerable — I hardly know what swelled to my throat as I read her letter — such a vehement impatience of restraint and steady work. Such a strong wish for wings — such wings as wealth can furnish — such an urgent thirst to see — to know — to learn — something internal seemed to expand boldly for a minute — I was tantalized with the consciousness of faculties unexercised — then all collapsed and I despaired.'[42] But she did not despair, for she now had the necessary impetus to cope with practical obstacles, and she persuaded her aunt, Miss Branwell, to lend enough money for herself and Emily to spend half a year at a school in Brussels.

Brussels was chosen because Mary Taylor and her younger sister Martha were there. After their father's death at the end of 1840, the family had dispersed and the sisters were staying at a finishing school, the Château de Koekelberg. Its terms put it out of reach of the Brontës but eventually Charlotte heard, through the wife of the chaplain to the British Embassy, of a less expensive school, the pensionnat kept by Madame Heger in the Rue d'Isabelle. In February 1842, accompanied by their father and by Mary and Joe Taylor, Charlotte and Emily left Haworth and, after a few days in London, crossed the Channel for the first time and arrived in Brussels.

Charlotte, the instigator of the journey on which her sister accompanied her from duty rather than inclination, took with her a sound knowledge of French, if little fluency in speaking it, and an attitude of mind in which anticipation and prejudice were curiously blended. In her eyes the foreign milieu stood for culture, for the breadth of interests and depth of experience she envied in writers like Madame de Staël and George Sand, as well as for a brighter climate, the novelty of another language and a more colourful way of life. But it was also associated in her mind with the Napoleonic ambitions which her hero Wellington had been called on to resist in the name of freedom, and with the immoral tendencies she considered characteristic, no less than their wit and brilliance, of the French novels which had reached the parsonage in such quantities shortly before her journey to Brussels.

What she did not seem to anticipate was the impact which the difference of religion in a predominantly Catholic (Roman) milieu would make on her. Religion had not been a primary concern in Angria. Only in 'The Spell', written in 1834, do differences of religion have a certain importance, which no doubt stemmed from the interest felt at the parsonage a few years before in the question of Catholic Emancipation and the passing of the Bill. But the leaders of Angria, with the sole exception of the serious-minded Warner, were too preoccupied with passion and ambition to have much time to spare for religious concerns. Their creator herself was never indifferent to them, but she was quite unprepared for the strength of the reactions which the difference of religion in a foreign country would provoke in her. Had she had any premonition of the isolation which she and her sister would feel as almost the only Protestants in their new milieu, she might have felt some hesitation in fixing on a school where Catholicism was recognised as the basis of the community and of the educational programme. But neither she nor perhaps more surprisingly her father seem to have known any apprehension on this score. And it was predominantly in a spirit of joyful expectancy that Charlotte at least, if not her sister, arrived at the pensionnat Heger.

# 2 Brussels

When Charlotte Brontë arrived in Brussels in 1842, she came to a kingdom whose origins, like those of her own Verdopolitan confederacy, were intimately connected with the aftermath of the Napoleonic Wars. But, unlike the imaginary colony, the area that was now Belgium had been shaken by political convulsions for centuries. The land was steeped in history, though the kingdom was of recent creation. The southern Netherlands had known the splendours of the Burgundian period, the oppressions of Spanish rule, the rule of the Austrian Hapsburgs and occupation by Napoleon, before the Congress of Vienna united the Belgian province to Holland in 1815. By the revolution of 1830 they had emancipated themselves from Dutch rule and founded a new state, but one which was heir to the traditions and the tensions of a rich and stormy past.

The pensionnat itself stood on historic ground. A flight of steps led up from the Rue d'Isabelle to the Rue Royale and the fashionable quarter with the park and the Palace. The street itself, skirted for part of its length by portions of the original city wall, was built on what had once been the exercise ground for the powerful Guild of the Arbéletriers. It had been constructed in 1625, under the government of the Infanta Isabella, to provide a nearer way to the cathedral of Ste Gudule. The house itself, however, had been built at the end of the eighteenth century and its architecture was of the formal classic style.

This house on a historic site was inhabited by a family whose own history had been partly shaped by the events of the more recent past. Claire Zoë Parent, later Madame Heger, who bought the house in 1830 and set up a school in it, was the daughter of an émigré from the French Revolution who had fled to Brussels in 1789 and settled and married there. His children were educated by their aunt Anne-Marie Parent, a nun whose convent at Charleville was disestablished at the Revolution and who escaped to her brother's home in Brussels. She had a natural aptitude for teaching which she showed first in educating her brother's family and later in founding a successful pensionnat.[1] Her example was followed by her niece Zöe, who had a similar aptitude for teaching and started the pensionnat in the Rue d'Isabelle after her aunt's death. She married Constantin Heger in 1836 and her school was officially described, in the prospectus sent to the Brontës, as 'sous la direction de Madame Heger-Parent'. Her husband had also experienced the effect of political upheavals, in his case at first hand, for he had taken part in the fighting during the Belgian Revolution of 1830.

But long before the political crisis family misfortune had shadowed his youth.[2] His wealthy father suffered a crippling financial loss while he was still in his teens and he was sent to Paris to earn a living. After four years as secretary to a solicitor, he returned to Brussels in 1829 and obtained a teaching post at the Athénée Royal. He married at twenty-one, shortly before the outbreak of the Revolution, during which his wife's brother was killed at his side. In 1833 he lost his young wife and child on the same day during the cholera epidemic. His second marriage in 1836 was to give him the stable background and family affection which he had never till then been able to enjoy without the sudden irruption of disaster. In February 1842, when the Brontës arrived in Brussels, the Hegers had a family of three children and a fourth, their first son, was born in March. They were still a relatively young couple, Constantin Heger thirty-two and his wife, his senior by five years, thirty-seven. But their experience of life, including their present position at the centre of a flourishing pensionnat, had given them a maturity which is reflected in the kindness with which they responded to Charlotte's anxious enquiries about terms and their sympathy with her desire for further study.

They realised, as M. Heger later told Mrs Gaskell, that these daughters of an English pastor, of moderate means, were 'anxious to learn with an ulterior view of instructing others,'[3] and they respected the determination which made two young women of twenty-five and twenty-three willing to return to school with this end in view. Naturally, at their ages, any real integration of the Brontës into the schoolgirl community was not possible, and would hardly have been so had they been as extrovert in temperament as they were the reverse. But they had the support of each other's companionship; above all, they had the satisfaction of finding that they had come to a place where their primary aim could be fully achieved. 'They wanted learning. They came for learning. They would learn.'[4]

For Charlotte, at least, their new position was not merely tolerable, but intensely exhilarating. The founding of a school was still her declared objective; but the preparation for it now involved, instead of the drudgery of teaching, what she had always desired: a widening of cultural contacts, a chance at last to develop those 'faculties unexercised' which she was so conscious of possessing. Her satisfaction finds vigorous expression in a letter to Ellen Nussey:

> I was twenty-six years old a week or two since, and at this ripe time of life I am a schoolgirl, a complete schoolgirl, and, on the whole, very happy in that capacity. It felt very strange at first to submit to authority instead of exercising it — to obey orders instead of giving them; but I like that state of things. I returned to it with the same avidity that a cow, that has long been kept on dry hay, returns to fresh grass. Don't laugh at my simile. It is natural to me to submit, and very unnatural to command.[5]

It was natural to her to submit, but only to an authority whom she thoroughly respected. Till then she had been largely self-educated. At Roe Head, in spite of her deficiency in formal schooling, she impressed the critical Mary Taylor as knowing 'things that were out of our range altogether', and, after eighteen months, she was considered, at the age of sixteen, to have learnt all the school could teach her. The Taylors opened wider horizons for her, especially through their father's contacts with the Continent, but it was not until she met M. Heger that she encountered a teacher whose intellectual power she could at once acknowledge. That his was no ordinary intelligence she realised from the first: 'There is one individual of whom I have not yet spoken – M. Heger, the husband of Madame. He is professor of rhetoric, a man of power as to mind, but very choleric and irritable as to temperament . . .'[6] Quoting this sentence in the *Life*, Mrs Gaskell prudently stopped there, but Charlotte went on to criticise M. Heger's appearance and manner in trenchant terms, describing him as 'a little black ugly being, with a face that varies in expression. Sometimes he borrows the line-aments of an insane tom-cat, sometimes those of a delirious hyena; occasionally, but very seldom, he discards these peril-ous attractions and assumes an air not above 100 degrees removed from mild and gentleman-like'. The family group by Ange François in 1847[7] shows that this does very much less than justice to Constantin Heger's appearance in his thirties; Charlotte gives a caricature rather than a portrait but it brings out, through its very exaggeration, the dynamism that charac-terised him, and which contributed to his effectiveness as a teacher.

For he was a highly gifted teacher, whose teaching was based on a personal relationship with his pupils. Intensely individual himself, he was well aware that the pupil's indivi-duality must also be studied. In the case of the Brontës, their mature age and their different nationality made this all the more essential and so, as this acute observer soon discovered, did their temperaments and their gifts. 'M. Heger, who had done little but observe, during the first two weeks of their residence in the Rue d'Isabelle, perceived that with their unusual characters, and extraordinary talents, a different mode must be adopted from that in which he generally taught French to English girls.'[8]

As far as their previous knowledge of French was con-cerned, he did not rate it highly. 'M. Heger's account,' says Mrs Gaskell, 'is that they knew nothing of French.'[9] She adds: 'I suspect they knew as much (or as little), for all conversational purposes, as any English girls do, who have never been abroad, and have only learnt the idioms and pronunciation from an Englishwoman.' She was no doubt right as far as their spoken French was concerned, but it is certain that Charlotte could not have made the progress she did in Brussels without a sound preliminary knowledge of the language. She was aware of this, and of her advantage over Emily in this respect: 'Emily works like a horse, and she has had great difficulties to contend with, far greater than I have had . . .'[10]

During the Brontës' first weeks at the pensionnat, the Hegers were no doubt concerned to find out how much French they actually knew. It is unlikely that M. Heger, who was Professor of Literature in his wife's school and also had his own teaching post at the Athénée Royal, had much to do with teaching the rudiments of French grammar. Probably this was the province of the French mistress, Mlle Blanche. Charlotte Brontë's first exercise book at the pensionnat shows that she did in fact begin her studies there on an elementary level.[11] The 'cahier' simply contains exercises based on a passage in English, followed by the translation into French. That the original text was French is indicated by the 'English' of phrases like 'Jeanne, though still young, had a general rheumatism . . .' or 'The robust peasant, climbing up the boughs, his double sack upon his back, sang gaily . . .' The corrections on Charlotte's 'cahier' are minimal and make it obvious that she had outgrown the need for this kind of exercise.

Fortunately, this preliminary stage was of short duration. M. Heger soon decided that a more advanced method of study must be adopted with these unusual pupils: '. . . some weeks ago, in a high-flown humour, he forbade me to use either dictionary or grammar in translating the most difficult English compositions into French.'[12] Instead of the formal grounding in grammar, his aim became to attune them to the spirit and rhythm of the language. He decided, as he afterwards explained to Mrs Gaskell, to read them passages from French authors, pointing out 'in what such or such an author excelled, and where were the blemishes.'[13] Impressed by their skill in composition he believed these exceptional pupils would then be capable of 'catching the echo of a style, and so reproducing their own thoughts in a somewhat similar manner'.[14]

Such a method obviously depended for its success not only on the ability of the pupils but on the passages chosen. M.

Heger was too discerning a teacher not to consult their taste as well as his own. He chose texts which he considered likely to appeal to the Brontës. It was in ignorance of this that Emily Brontë objected that his plan was inimical to originality. He usually left it to them to decide what subject they would choose for similar treatment. 'It is necessary,' he told them, 'before sitting down to write on a subject, to have thoughts and feelings about it. I cannot tell on what subject your heart and mind have been excited. I must leave that to you.'[15] With a teacher like Heger and pupils like the Brontës, such a method produced results very different from the *devoirs* of the ordinary classroom. The chosen passage frequently acted as a catalyst. The *devoirs* written by Charlotte and Emily show their increasing power of expressing feelings and ideas which have taken clearer shape by being formulated in a different medium. In reading Emily's, one has the impression that she half resented the fact that 'the classroom forced her ideas into the open.'[16] Charlotte, on the other hand, uses the exercise partly as an instrument for communicating her own personality; her *devoirs* chart the course of her emotions as well as her ideas during the Brussels period.

There is naturally no direct reference in the *devoirs* to the preliminary readings, but M. Heger himself, in his talk with Mrs Gaskell, mentioned some of the passages he read with the Brontës. There also still survives an exercise book in which Charlotte made a number of transcriptions from French authors.[17] She did not herself possess the background necessary for making such a selection; it clearly reflects M. Heger's choice. Such passages were a part of her Brussels experience. Some of them have obvious links with the surviving *devoirs,* and another was years later to find an echo in one of her novels. The literature to which M. Heger introduced her was on a different plane from the majority of the French novels which had reached the parsonage in such quantities. Nineteenth-century Romanticism is represented by Hugo, Lamartine, Nodier and the ancestor Chateaubriand. There are also poems by Millevoye and Soumet, and a passage from the historian Michaud. Nineteenth-century literature has the largest share in the selection. The eighteenth century is represented by Buffon and the Abbé Barthélemy and the seventeenth by Bossuet and Massillon. Several of the chosen passages are poems, and it is noticeable that most of the prose extracts have, in varying degree, a poetic quality.

The early *devoir* 'La jeune fille malade' was written by Charlotte when she had been at the pensionnat just over a month.[18] In treatment as well as subject it is strikingly similar to the first of her transcriptions, Alexandre Soumet's poem *La Pauvre Fille,* which had made its author celebrated when it appeared in 1814. In itself this first *devoir* is rather a halting production. Its interest lies less in any intrinsic merit than in the fact that it announces a theme that was to become a dominant in Charlotte's novels, starting with *The Professor.* The illness from which the girl is suffering seems to be largely a neurosis caused by loneliness. In the case of Soumet's heroine, her loneliness stems primarily from destitution: there was no type of social victim for whom the French Romantics felt more sympathy than for the forsaken child. In Charlotte's *devoir* this additional cause of misery is absent, but in her novels, from *The Professor* onwards, she was to choose a heroine who was not only lonely but singularly alone in the world.

Her 'Portrait de Pierre l'Hermite' dates from several months later.[19] Like Emily's companion piece, 'Le Roi Harold avant la bataille de Hastings', it too has a source among the Brussels transcriptions. M. Heger told Mrs Gaskell these *devoirs* were written after he had read with the Brontës Victor Hugo's portrait of Mirabeau. 'Mais, dans ma leçon,' he explained, 'je me bornais à ce qui concerne *Mirabeau orateur.*'[20] Just how skilfully he did this can be seen from Charlotte's transcription with the title 'Mirabeau à la Tribune'. From the crowded pages of Hugo's dense and brilliant *Étude sur Mirabeau*[21] he has extracted exactly what he wanted for his purpose. The Brontës were fortunate to find, at a time when French Romanticism was still liable to be excluded from the curriculum, a teacher who was liberal enough to admire its greatest master, and who could read such passages as they demanded to be read. Constantin Heger had a striking gift of dramatic interpretation, which had been encouraged by his opportunity for seeing as a young man some of the finest acting in Paris. While he was working there, 'the only pleasures he could allow himself were to go to the Comédie Française as a paid *claqueur* and to study declamation in this manner at second-hand.'[22]

The portrait of Mirabeau, of whose name Charlotte had made unflattering use in the Angrian saga, did not inspire her to choose another subject with a revolutionary background. She went to the Middle Ages for her portrait and chose Peter the Hermit. Her 'Portrait de Pierre l'Hermite' was one of the *devoirs* reproduced by Mrs Gaskell, with M. Heger's marginal comments. It is very likely that the subject was suggested by another of her Brussels transcriptions, 'Prise de Jérusalem par les croisés,' taken from Michaud's *Histoire des Croisades,*[23] which ends with a reference to the 'Hermite Pierre', hailed by the Christians in Jerusalem as their real liberator. There is still a stiffness in her use of French and M. Heger's corrections show he has tried to lighten the rather heavy style, but the real defect of the *devoir* lies deeper than that: she has not succeeded in painting a great religious enthusiast as Hugo painted a great orator. What she has done is to show her passionate and romantic admiration for the quality of genius in itself.

In choosing Peter the Hermit, Charlotte selected a hero whose crusading zeal was likely to appeal to her teacher. It was perhaps with the consciousness that her choice would be less congenial to M. Heger that Emily wrote on 'Le Roi Harold avant la bataille de Hastings'.[24] It is ironic that her *devoir* should be, as Mrs Gaskell noted, superior to Charlotte's in force and originality. Her Saxon hero, silhouetted against a sky lit by enemy fires, has a certain tragic grandeur which emerges even through the medium of her hesitant French. The sombre conclusion of her essay is in stark contrast to the determined optimism of her sister's 'la bataille ne sera livrée que demain, mais la victoire est décidée ce soir . . .'

One wonders if it was partly with Emily's *devoir* in mind that Charlotte later chose a Saxon theme for the essay in *The Professor* which first reveals Frances Henri's unusual gifts to her teacher. It was perhaps of the outstanding qualities of her sister's early *devoirs* as much as of her own that she was thinking when she made Crimsworth give his opinion of

Frances' essay in terms which may reflect similar views once expressed by M. Heger: 'There were errors of orthography, there were foreign idioms, there were some faults of construction . . . it was mostly made up . . . of short and somewhat rude sentences, and the styles stood in great need of polish and sustained dignity; yet such as it was, I had hitherto seen nothing like it in the course of my professorial experience.'[25]

The whole episode in *The Professor* where the hidden powers of Frances Henri are revealed through her *devoir* is developed with a detail that suggests the immediacy of recent experience. Crimsworth's verdict on the essay when giving it back to his pupil is an astringent blend of denigration and qualified praise: it has numerous faults, but he sees in it 'some proofs of taste and fancy'.[26] The response of Frances to this qualified encouragement is as unexpected as it is authentic:

> . . . on looking up, I saw the sun had dissevered its screening cloud, her countenance was transfigured, a smile shone in her eyes — a smile almost triumphant; it seemed to say — 'I am glad you have been forced to discover so much of my nature; you need not so carefully moderate your language. Do you think I am myself a stranger to myself? What you tell me in terms so qualified, I have known fully from a child.[27]

Crimsworth soon discovered that in crediting his pupil merely with 'taste and fancy' he had done her less than justice, and that 'judgment and imagination' would have been a more accurate description of her gifts. M. Heger's opinion of the Brontës' abilities must have increased with corresponding rapidity, for in a remarkably short space of time their *devoirs* showed a striking development in scope and depth. They again treated similar themes in 'La Chenille' and 'Le Papillon', both written, like their previous essays, in the summer of 1842.[28] The chief interest of the subject for the Brontës was in its symbolic implications. Both treat the metamorphosis of the insect as part of the pattern of creation. Charlotte traces the analogy between the larva and the limitations of human existence, and her essay culminates in an exploration of the affinities between the chrysalis and the tomb. In style, form and rhythm it is much superior to anything she had yet written in French. The breadth and dignity of her treatment reflect something of the manner of Chateubriand.[29] But it no doubt owes its personal accent chiefly to her own experience — the memory of her sisters' deaths and of the graveyard seen from the parsonage windows. The grounds of her final optimism are those of the *Génie du Christianisme:* 'Le corps est semé corruptible, il ressuscitera incorruptible'.[30] Emily's view of the pattern of the universe is a far starker one: she sees cruelty and mutual destruction operating in the whole creation. But her essay, too, terminates with the vision of a new creation in which the enigma of suffering will be resolved.

In addition to the *devoirs* written after the reading of French authors, M. Heger later introduced another teaching method. This 'more advanced plan' was intended, as he explained to Mrs Gaskell, to train these unusual pupils in synthesis as well as analysis. He read them accounts of the same person or event from various sources, made them notice the differences and then showed them how to find the origin of these differences in the 'character and position' of each separate writer. This concern to give relativism its due place in criticism is another indication of the modernity of his teaching. It was a need which was being increasingly recognised by literary critics like Villemain, who features among the 'sundry modern authors' in Hunsden's library in *The Professor.*[31] In illustration of this method M. Heger told Mrs Gaskell he had taken the different estimates of Cromwell given by Bossuet, Carlyle and Guizot. The choice was an apt one, for Carlyle and Guizot, at that time both a well-known historian and the leading minister of Louis Philippe, represented contemporary if widely different estimates of Cromwell's career.[32] It is noticeable that M. Heger recognised elements of truth in all the different views and believed in the possibility of a final synthesis. Such a method was calculated to encourage an open mind in his pupils, as well as to provoke lively discussions, and Charlotte at least seems to have responded to it with enthusiasm.[33]

It is not surprising that such teaching made this a halcyon

period for her. In July she wrote to Ellen Nussey: 'I don't deny that I sometimes wish to be in England or that I have brief attacks of home-sickness but on the whole I have borne a very valiant heart so far — and I have been happy in Brussels because I have always been fully occupied with employments that I like . . .'[34] The strongest proof of her happiness at this time is the information in the same letter that Mme Heger has invited her and Emily to remain for another half year, herself to teach English and Emily to give music lessons, and that the prospect attracts her.

Unfortunately there was another side to life in Brussels. On her arrival Charlotte had remarked that she and Emily were isolated in the midst of numbers because of the difference of country and religion. She decided at an early stage that the Belgians disliked the English, but her own conviction of English superiority to the foreigner was not calculated to help matters. In the same letter of July 1842 where she speaks so gratefully of the Hegers' kindness, she remarks: 'If the national character of the Belgians is to be measured by the character of most of the girls in the school, it is a character singularly cold, selfish, animal and inferior.' But the religious difference went deeper still. The Brontës' father was an Irish Protestant from Ulster, their mother a Methodist, and they had been brought up in an Anglican parsonage. They knew when they went to Brussels that they were going to a Catholic school where, as the prospectus made clear, the teaching programme was 'basé sur la religion', but, as Margaret Lane says, 'they seem to have been unprepared for the emotional hostility which Catholic practice aroused in them when they came in contact with it.'[35] Probably the fact of living in a house where they were almost the only Protestants sharpened their sense of isolation. 'All in the house are Catholics except ourselves, one other girl and the *gouvernante* of Madame's children . . .'[36] Mary Taylor at the Château de Koekelberg, where English and German pupils were in the majority, though just as insular in her views, did not express the same hostility to Catholic practice as Charlotte. Yet she was too honest not to recognise that Catholics of the stamp of M. Heger were as good Christians as any Protestants. Her verdict on the situation, biased and emotionally charged as it is, ends with a reservation:

People talk of the danger which Protestants expose themselves to in going to reside in Catholic countries — and
thereby running the chance of changing their faith — my
advice to all Protestants who are tempted to do anything
so besotted as turn Catholic — is to walk over the sea on to
the continent — to attend mass regularly for a time to note
well the mummeries thereof — also the idiotic, mercenary
aspect of *all* the priests, and *then* if they are still disposed
to consider Papistry in any other light than a most feeble
childish piece of humbug let them turn Papists at once
that's all — I consider Methodism, Dissenterism,
Quakerism, and the extremes of high and low Churchism
foolish, but Roman Catholicism beats them all. At the
same time allow me to tell you that there are some good
Catholics — who are as good as any Christians can be to
whom the bible is a sealed book and much better than
scores of Protestants.[37]

Her bias on the score of nationality and still more of
Catholicism was an obstacle to friendly relationships not only
with the much younger Belgian pupils at the pensionnat but
with the three woman teachers who were nearer in age to the
Brontës. Outside the classroom any contacts they had were
with those of their own nationality, and these were very
limited. The wife of the British Chaplain, on whose recommendation they had come to the pensionnat Heger, ceased to
invite them when she saw that their shyness made their visits
more of an ordeal than a pleasure. Their meetings with the
Taylors were naturally in a different category. As the
Taylors' school was outside Brussels, they could not be
frequent but the friends occasionally met, to their mutual
satisfaction. In July their solitude among numbers at the
pensionnat was mitigated by the arrival of five English girls as
day-boarders. They were the young daughters of Dr
Wheelwright, who had come to settle in Brussels. It was by
her evident consciousness of superiority to her foreign environment that the eldest, Laetitia, then fourteen, attracted
the amused but sympathetic notice of Charlotte Brontë.

When, in mid-August, the school broke up, the Brontës,
who had accepted Mme Heger's offer to remain for another
half year, stayed on during the 'grandes vacances'. The pen-

sionnat was empty except for a few other boarders, but they had each other's company, and for Charlotte at least the chance to see more of the artistic treasures of this continental capital was precious. Brussels she had from the first admitted to be a 'beautiful city'. It abounded in historic buildings of many periods and in rich art collections. She had always been passionately interested in art and she was fortunate, as Winifred Gérin has pointed out, in the fact that her visit to Belgium coincided with a 'Salon'.[38] Some of the pictures she saw in the Brussels Salon of 1842 were to reappear, in the form best suited to her purpose, in *Villette*.[39]

When the new school half year began in September, the Brontës were still happy in their new milieu. Mary Taylor, when she saw them again, could write: 'Charlotte and Emily are well; not only in health, but in mind and hope. They are content with their present position and even gay, and I think they do quite right not to return to England . . .'[40] But, even when she wrote this, the first of the series of deaths had occurred that was to darken their horizon so suddenly. William Weightman, their father's curate, who had made a place for himself in their life at Haworth by his kindness of heart as well as his charm of manner, had died of cholera after a short illness. In October the young, gay and lovable Martha Taylor died, like him, of cholera in a fortnight. Charlotte and Emily later went with Mary Taylor to visit her sister's grave in the Protestant cemetery outside Brussels, a memory that was to echo like an elegy in the novels.

These tragic events did not interrupt the normal course of life at the pensionnat for the Brontës. Charlotte's first *devoir* in the new school half year, 'La Justice Humaine', was in fact written before she heard of Martha Taylor's illness.[41] It seems likely that in this case M. Heger presented her with an abstract theme and left her to treat it as she wished. Her initial reaction was probably not unlike that of Lucy Snowe, presented with the identical theme: 'Human Justice! What was I to make of it? Blank, cold abstraction, unsuggestive to me of one inspiring idea . . .'[42] Like Lucy, she avoided dialectics, but instead of using a personification to illustrate her views she chose a concrete example: an innocent man is wrongly accused, has to face imprisonment before trial and

even when legally acquitted returns home to find his family
in want and himself a social pariah. Human sympathy is the
mainspring of this *devoir,* and perhaps it was primarily this
quality that earned for it the approval expressed in the
marginal comments of M. Heger. It is interesting to compare
the emotive tone of this essay with the trenchant irony of
Lucy Snowe's presentation of the 'red, random beldame,
with arms akimbo' whose misdirected blows no longer arouse
in her the sorrowful indignation evident in the Brussels essay.

Less than a fortnight later, and only a few days after the
death of Martha Taylor, she and Emily both wrote *devoirs* on
the same theme. This time it was a set subject, a fable,
entitled, by an ironic coincidence, 'Le Palais de la Mort.'[43]
There were no doubt various versions of this fable.[44] Both
essays start with an outline of the material presumably supplied by the version given by M. Heger: in former times only
Old Age furnished the kingdom of Death with subjects, but
now they have become so numerous that a 'premier ministre'
is needed to deal with them and, from the candidates for the
post, Death selects Intemperance as the vice which brings him
the greatest number of victims.

Out of this at first sight recalcitrant material the Brontës
have each constructed their 'Palace of Death'. There is no
doubt about the most arresting quality of Charlotte's *devoir;*
it is the descriptive power. Its ideological content is inferior
to Emily's. But when she paints Death's ice palace, one
cannot wonder that M. Heger has scored the margin of the
page with a long line of approval. 'Idée très bonne,' he
comments, when she writes that winter has been the architect
and has drawn his materials from the depths of an icy sea. In
this way she communicates the attributes of death, coldness,
rigidity, pallor, with all the immediacy of sensation. The
Court of Death awaits in utter silence for the appearance of
the rival claimants: '. . . jamais on n'a vu une assemblée si
sage; les statues qui peuplent une église ne sont ni plus
immobiles ni moins causeuses.' On to this silent stage she
brings three claimants for the post of Death's viceroy. Ambition, who speaks first, is the least effective of the three
figures and her Gothic train of 'gloomy phantoms', reminiscent of the appearance of the Genii in the early Angrian tales,

strikes a discordant note. But War the Huntress, holding in leash her hounds, 'Massacre' and 'Carnage', is drawn with bold strokes, full of movement. Intemperance, the last figure to appear, has the least to say, but she dominates the centre foreground in her tragic splendour. With a sure sense of perspective, the artist shows her at close range, so close that one can glimpse the serpent coiled among the flowers in her hair.

Emily approaches the subject from a different angle. She keeps to the stark outlines of allegory. The rival claimants are more numerous than in her sister's picture. Their names constitute a grim indictment of human history: Rage and Vengeance, Envy and Treason . . . But all give way before the three most powerful candidates. Ambition speaks first, followed by Fanaticism who, in Emily's version, takes the place of War. Last to appear is Intemperance. She claims to possess an ally whose power will increase with every century and at the same time increase her own: Civilisation. The association between civilisation and intemperance is not in the original. With her fundamentally philosophical mind, Emily Brontë felt its force for herself and makes of a moralising fable the diagnosis of a modern sickness. In the use of French, her essay is still inferior to her sister's. In content, both interpretations of the original 'matière' are equally striking; one catches the very chill of the atmosphere of the Palace of Death, the other investigates the conditions that have produced it.

It was an ironic coincidence which gave the Brontës this subject for *devoirs* written so soon after the death of their two friends. Only a fortnight later came the news of the serious illness of their aunt, Miss Branwell, followed next day by that of her death. This time the situation was one which made it imperative for them to return home as soon as possible, since their father and Branwell were alone at the parsonage. Their decision to leave at once was completely understood by the Hegers, though it could not have been a convenient one for them, since Charlotte was now English teacher at the pensionnat. By early November the sisters were back again at Haworth. Charlotte, at least, must have regretted, though she did not question, the necessity for leaving

Brussels. The period of unclouded progress and content at the pensionnat was at an end.

The change brought about by Miss Branwell's death made it necessary to revise their plans for the future. Their aunt had left her small property to be divided among her nieces and this would help them if they were ultimately able to proceed with the school project. The problem lay in their immediate situation. One of his daughters at least must remain with Mr Brontë, and this could not be Anne, as she had a post as governess. There was the further problem of Branwell, whose future, after his dismissal from Luddenden Foot, was problematical, though his family still believed in his gifts.

An important factor in the decision ultimately made was the letter of sympathy written to Mr Brontë by M. Heger.[45] In it he spoke in the highest terms of the progress made by Charlotte and Emily and expressed his regret that it should be interrupted at such a crucial stage. He referred to their progress not only in study but in learning to teach, a science in which they were still to some extent novices. His knowledge of their characters is seen in his remark that Emily by receiving piano lessons and giving them herself to young pupils would lose 'à la fois un reste d'ignorance et un reste plus gênant encore de timidité,' and that Charlotte was beginning to acquire 'cette assurance, cet aplomb' so necessary to the teacher. In his opinion another year at most would see all this satisfactorily accomplished. Speaking for his wife, as well as himself, he made it clear that if the sisters, or at least one of them, returned, it would be on a more profitable basis, financially, than before. He spoke of the 'affection presque paternelle' they had come to feel for their 'cheres élèves' and, with obvious sincerity, of their desire to continue to help them in their efforts to achieve independence. The effect of this letter was reinforced by another from Madame Heger to Charlotte, which made it clear that they were both genuinely anxious for her to return.[46]

There was enough in these letters to make it very understandable that Charlotte should wish to return to Brussels for another year, if conditions at home permitted. The problem of Branwell's employment was unexpectedly solved by the willingness of Anne's employers, the Robinsons, to take him as tutor to their son. Emily was prepared to stay and keep house at the parsonage. It did not seem unreasonable that Charlotte should decide to return to a position which held out both practical and cultural advantages. Yet she herself, when she reviewed her decision in retrospect, saw it in another light. Three years later, in a letter to Ellen Nussey, she said: 'I returned to Brussels after Aunt's death against my conscience — prompted by what then seemed an irresistible impulse — I was punished for my selfish folly by a total withdrawal for more than two years of happiness and peace of mind — I could hardly expect success if I were to err again in the same way.'[47] This admission has to be considered in its context. In 1846 it was Ellen who was thinking of taking pupils and was anxious to enlist Charlotte's help. Her friend replied that she could not leave home at present, and then referred to the parallel case in the past when she felt she had made the wrong decision. In view of this, it is clear that part of her self-reproach stemmed from the sense of having failed her family when her presence was really needed, however plausible the reasons for returning to Brussels might seem. But it is doubtful if she would have returned, if nothing more than the chance to help with a school project had been in question. Just how much the 'irresistible impulse' owed to her longing for a wider cultural life and how much to her emotional response to M. Heger himself, it is impossible to say. What is certain is that she went back to Brussels in a state of mind different from the elation she had felt on her first visit.

In the circumstances it seemed an unhappy omen that her journey should begin with a train delay that involved her in embarking on the Ostend packet alone in the dark of a winter night, though the experience was to undergo artistic trans-position in *Villette*. But there was nothing to complain of in her welcome when she finally arrived at the pensionnat: 'Madame Heger received me with great kindness.'[48]

Her position in the pensionnat was now that of teacher, not pupil. This was a change for the worse rather than an advancement, as far as her own inclination was concerned, but it was a change that had been begun during her second, interrupted, half year in Brussels. The difference in her situation that she no doubt felt most keenly at first was the loss of Emily as companion. That it would have an adverse effect was feared by Mary Taylor, then in Germany, who wrote in February to Ellen Nussey: 'I have heard from Charlotte since her arrival; she seems *content* at least, but fear her sister's absence will have a bad effect.'[49] The absence of Mary Taylor herself meant that Charlotte was also deprived of the chance of an occasional meeting with a friend in whom she could confide without reserve. There was some compensation, however, for Mary's absence in the fact that her cousins, the Dixons, who were then in Brussels, proved good friends to Charlotte as well. She also saw much more of the Wheelwright family than she had done when Emily, whom they found less congenial, was with her. With the other teachers at the pensionnat she felt as little in common as before, but her relationship with the Hegers themselves was still a happy one, and it was at this time that she started giving English lessons to M. Heger and his brother-in-law M. Chapelle.

In March she wrote to Ellen Nussey explaining both the advantages and the disadvantages of her present situation:

> ... I am not too much overloaded with occupation ... and if I could always keep up my spirits, and never feel lonely, or long for companionship, or friendship, or whatever they call it, I should do very well. As I told you before, M. and Madame Heger are the only two persons in the house for whom I really experience regard and esteem, and, of course, I cannot always be with them, nor even often. They told me, when I first returned, that I was to consider their sitting-room my sitting-room also, and to go there whenever I was not engaged in the school-room. This, however, I cannot do ... Thus I am a good deal by myself, out of school hours; but that does not signify. I now regularly give English lessons to M. Heger and his brother-in-law, M. Chapelle ... They get on with wonderful rapidity, especially the first. He already begins to speak English very decently. If you could hear and see the efforts I make to teach them to pronounce like Englishmen, and their unavailing attempts to imitate, you would laugh to all eternity ...[50]

The fact that Charlotte was giving English lessons to M. Heger meant that they now sometimes met on a different footing. Her conversational French was no doubt still too limited to allow her much freedom of expression, but when talking in English she must have been able to express her real opinions with far more ease than previously. He, on his side, must have found it possible to talk more freely than he could have done in any exchange between master and pupil. The increase in real communication between them is reflected in the closing sentences of her letter to Ellen. Speaking of Mary Taylor's present position, she says: 'She has nobody to be as good to her as M. Heger is to me; to lend her books, to converse with her sometimes, etc.'[51]

At longer intervals than before, Charlotte, though no longer his pupil in the former sense, still wrote *devoirs* which she submitted to him for criticism. They were no doubt intended to perfect her written French, but, as before, they were also a means of expressing her own feelings and they show her increasing need for an outlet of this kind during her second stay in Brussels. It was a poem, Millevoye's *La Chute des Feuilles*[52] which gave her the material for the first essay after her return.[53] It was one of the passages she had transcribed and the only one on which she had made a few marginal comments; opposite the lines where the young poet first speaks directly of his own coming death she had written: 'profondément touchant'. The essay was intended to be a 'devoir de style', but at an early stage it becomes clear that what interests the writer is not so much what Millevoye has achieved as what an intending artist may learn from him. The essay soon develops into a discussion of the creative process. This brief elegy evidently owed its immortality primarily to the intense feeling that inspired it. This leads her to state her own belief in personal experience as the basic element in art.[54] This belief is approved by M. Heger as 'très juste'. What interests her most, however, is the nature of genius, and she expresses her conviction that it owes very much less to the intellect than to the heart, so that an author of authentic genius needs no guide other than his own inspiration.

This conclusion was not allowed to pass without criticism by M. Heger, in spite of his appreciation of the essay in

general, and he took the trouble to supplement it by some
lines of cogent argument. He was no rigid classicist, but he
knew that genius itself cannot dispense with study, primarily
the study of technique. He chose to illustrate this by the
analogy between genius and force: work does not make a
genius, any more than machinery creates force, but just as
force can be regulated and centupled by the use of machinery, so the scope and effect of genius can be increased by
study and the knowledge of technique. Genius without
study, without art, is force without the lever . . . In his determination to press home the argument, he constantly varies
the choice of metaphor, until he finally discards all imagery
for the uncompromising simplicity of his conclusion: 'Poète
ou non étudiez donc la forme . . .'

'La Chute des Feuilles' shows that, though Charlotte
Brontë's present occupation is teaching, she still has an intense interest in the process of artistic creation. From the
assurance with which she speaks of the nature of genius, even
while relegating herself to the ranks of the 'novices on littérature', it is clear that she was very far from having lost
confidence in her own potential as an artist. It must also have
been clear to M. Heger that her interest in the creative
process was in essence a personal one. He recognises as much
in his 'Poète ou non . . .', but he avoids expressing any
definite opinion as to her gifts, contenting himself with
pointing out that study is needed to appreciate art fully, as
well as to achieve lasting masterpieces.

By this time he had seen examples of her versifying ability.
In February, she had translated into English verse *Les Or-
phelins* by Louis Belmontet.[55] The subject, like that of
Soumet's *La Pauvre Fille,* was one with a lasting appeal for
Charlotte Brontë, the sufferings of the child neglected by an
indifferent society. But Belmontet's now forgotten verses are
rhetorical where simplicity would have been more effective,
and it is not surprising that the translation has the same
defects. A very different original produced a very different
result when in March she translated Auguste Barbier's
*l'Idole.*[56] It is the most famous of the *Iambes* in which he
expressed his disillusionment with the results of the July
Revolution of 1830, one of which was a renewal of the cult

of Napoleon. He saw in the current worship of the Napoleonic legend a sort of deification of war, and attacked this mirage with the full force of his powerful imagery. His sustained metaphor of revolutionary France as the noble, unbroken horse the young Corsican masters and drives so unsparingly across the battlefields of Europe that at last she stumbles and throws her rider was calculated to appeal to the Romantic imagination. By a curious coincidence the mastering of a horse had already featured twice in the French passages transcribed by Charlotte Brontë, once when used by Bossuet as an illustration of his argument, and once when Buffon praised it as one of man's finest achievements.[57] But both the seventeenth-century preacher and the eighteenth-century naturalist had thought of the process as a humane one — in the Romantic poem it becomes an image of violence, which retains its deliberate brutality in the translation. It conforms to another of the archetypal patterns of Charlotte's art, that of the victim, in this case a willing one, who is finally driven to breaking-point.

The skill in versifying as well as the accuracy of these translations are not surprising in view of the fact that at fourteen Charlotte had already been capable of translating a canto of *La Henriade*. By this time she had also written a considerable amount of original verse, most of it in connection with the Angrian saga. On her return to Brussels in 1843, she brought back with her from Haworth some at least of these poems, for two of them, *Parting*[58] and *Life*[59], later included in her published verse, are known to have been copied at the pensionnat. They were short lyrics, whose quality could be appreciated without reference to Angrian subjects. It is highly probable that M. Heger saw these poems, in which case he would have added evidence of the literary aspirations implied in her *devoir* 'La Chute des Feuilles'. It is also very probable that she told him herself of the amount of writing she had been doing from childhood onwards, and that she showed him some of the prose manuscripts as well. If she did confide in him on the subject of her writings, it is most likely to have been at this time. A group of Angrian stories, bound together in a volume with the title 'Manuscrits de Miss Charlotte Brontë (Currer Bell)', were found by Professor

Ernest Nys on a second-hand bookstall in Brussels in 1892.[60] They are in the minute handwriting of the juvenilia, and it seems most likely that they were originally among the manuscripts taken to Brussels and were given to M. Heger to be read by him. They date from 1834 to 1835 and consist of two completed tales, 'The Spell' and 'High Life in Verdopolis', and 'The Scrapbook', a collection of miscellaneous fragments.

But it was not long before she found life at the pensionnat increasingly difficult. She did not enjoy the teaching, though she was not a full-time teacher and acknowledged that she had all the leisure she needed. In addition to her study of French, she was determined to perfect her German, but this never held the same attraction for her, though she admired Schiller and translated several of his poems. Her letter to Ellen Nussey at the beginning of April marks the start of the rapid decline of her happiness. She complains of the monotony of her life, of the constant sense of solitude — '. . . the Protestant, the Foreigner is a solitary being whether as teacher or pupil . . .'[61] — and in scornful reply to the gossip repeated by Ellen that it was in the hope of marrying she had returned to Brussels, declares: '. . . I never exchange a word with any other man than Monsieur Heger and seldom indeed with him.'[62] It is clear from this that the English lessons had ceased. A month later she wrote to Branwell, though she knew he was now an unreliable correspondent, perhaps because in a letter to him she felt she could give full rein to her impatience with her situation. She continues to find the inhabitants of the pensionnat, apart from the Hegers, totally uncongenial, but even Madame Heger is now referred to, for the first time, in a way that implies criticism. 'They (the others in the pensionnat) are very false in their relations with each other . . . and friendship is a folly they are unacquainted with. The black swan, M. Heger, is the only veritable exception to this rule (for Madame, always cool and always reasoning, is not quite an exception). But I rarely speak to Monsieur now, for not being a pupil I have little or nothing to do with him. From time to time he shows his kind-heartedness by loading me with books, so that I am still indebted to him for all the pleasure or amusement I have.'[63]

The letter to Branwell is significant, not only because it contains the first criticism of Madame Heger but because it contains the first nostalgic reference to Angria in Charlotte's correspondence from Brussels: 'It is a curious metaphysical fact that always in the evening when I am in the great dormitory alone . . . I always recur as fanatically as ever to the old ideas, the old faces, and the old scenes in the world below.'[64] It should be remembered that her 'farewell' to Angria had been made several years before she came to Brussels. It had represented a move towards maturity undertaken at her own volition. During the first year at the pensionnat the need to qualify for a teaching career had apparently become dominant, but the writing of the *devoirs* inevitably stimulated the artist in her. The themes on which M. Heger encouraged her to write were, however, constants of human experience. Her confession at this stage of a hidden but persistent nostalgia for Angria was really an admission that she still felt a nostalgia for a dream world whose demands on the artist were less stringent. The escapist longing for 'the world below' to which she confesses in her letter to Branwell is a gauge of her unhappiness at this stage of the Brussels period.

'La Mort de Napoléon', her next *devoir*, written at the end of May, is the first to have a subject with, for her at least, Angrian overtones.[65] Mrs Gaskell thought that, in writing it, she must have remembered the childish disputes at Haworth over the merits of Napoleon and Wellington. Probably more recent disputes were also in her mind. The cult of Napoleon had been intensified when his body was brought back from St Helena and reinterred in the Invalides in 1841. A former pupil at the pensionnat has recorded her memory of an argument about the conduct of England towards the Emperor, for which her school-fellows seemed to hold Charlotte personally responsible until she intervened to point out with much truth that 'Miss Brontë n'y était pour rien . . .'[66]

Although the essay is called 'La Mort de Napoléon', it is concerned with his captivity on St Helena rather than his death. Charlotte compares Napoleon on this barren island to Prometheus chained to the rock of the Caucasus: the one stole fire from Heaven to animate the body he had made, the other sacrificed entire nations to give life to the empire he had created. The analogy might have been continued, as M. Heger suggests, by a comparison between the torture inflicted on Prometheus by the vulture and the sufferings of the Emperor during his exile. Instead, Charlotte Brontë speaks of the misery of exiles in general, and in particular of one humiliation they may have to endure — overtures of friendship inspired by no warmer motive than charity or pity, which they owe it to their own self-respect to repulse. It is not difficult to see why such a situation, real or imagined, should occupy her thoughts at the time, but it adds nothing to her argument: on the contrary, it weakens it, since her own view of the Emperor is that he was motivated entirely by ambition and impervious to other feelings. She therefore finds herself obliged subsequently to make a sharp distinction between Napoleon and other more vulnerable exiles. Once this is established, she can proceed to the chief part of her argument, which is a vindication of the justice of sending Napoleon to St Helena, put into the mouth of Wellington. It is doubtful whether, when she began her essay, she meant it to develop into a eulogy of the hero of her childhood, but from the moment he appears, he occupies the centre of the stage. In his speech there is no denigration of his great adversary, but he is convinced there can be no temporising with Napoleon, Emperor of the French, if Europe is to have the chance to recover from the long years of war. Not England but the island of St Helena must be his place of captivity, however harsh this decision may appear. Wellington's speech gives Charlotte an opportunity to praise one of the qualities she most admired in him, his indifference to public opinion, which she contrasts with Napoleon's constant concern with it. The essay ends not with a return to the tomb at St Helena but with a reference to the ancestral home of the Wellesleys on the banks of the Shannon, and the prophecy of ever increasing fame for Wellington.

This *devoir* is less interesting as an ethico-political judgement than as a pointer to Charlotte Brontë's own opinions. Her admiration of Napoleon's greatness is sincere, but she prefers the young Corsican, the soldier of fortune, to the Emperor. It is noticeable that she sees the crown and royal robes of Napoleon as 'masking' the uniform of Bonaparte. The fallacy of her essay lies in her argument that Bonaparte, when he became Emperor, lost all human warmth, and became dominated by a cold and calculating ambition. Such a theory is inconsistent with her own introduction, where she had defined genius as excessive by its very nature, rash and daring. It was the demonic nature of Napoleon's genius that made him a legendary figure for the French Romantics. Charlotte herself had not been insensitive to it in her juvenilia. Zamorna's career of conquest was in fact much more reminiscent of Napoleon's than of Wellington's and he, too, knew disaster and exile. But she now sees the Emperor as coldly ambitious, incapable of deep feeling even in his isolation and separation from his family. Her portrayal of Napoleon is evidently coloured by prejudice, but her early bias against the rival of Wellington had certainly been strengthened by disputes of more recent origin than those of Haworth, and by an increasing sense of exile in a foreign milieu.

She is happier in speaking of Wellington than of his great opponent. The picture she gives shows her admiration both of the conqueror of Waterloo and of the uncompromising Tory aristocrat. Some of Wellington's salient characteristics emerge from her portrait: his lack of personal hostility towards his adversary and his recognition of Napoleon's genius, his belief in his own judgement and his unswerving determination in following what he believed to be the right course. When, however, she speaks with obvious admiration of his pride, which she exaggerates into 'la morgue de Wellington', and paints a dramatic but anachronistic picture of the hero defying the mob on the steps of his 'palais ducal d'Apsley', at the period of the Reform crisis, she is nearer the emotional climate of Angria than her subject warrants. To compare him with Coriolanus strikes a discordant note in a portrait of the victor of Waterloo.

But if the matter of the essay is open to some criticism, there can be no question of the quality of the style. There is still an occasional 'barbarisme', but the French is usually correct, and often it is far more than that — dynamic, flexible, persuasive, already the language of an artist. M. Heger's appreciation of this is evident in the care he takes to supply, from time to time, slight modifications of word or phrase whose function is simply to throw into relief an original thought or a vivid image. This sort of correction is almost a collaboration. One of Charlotte's most striking ideas was to oppose, within the framework of a single sentence, the two islands of Corsica and St Helena, birthplace and tomb of Napoleon. The similarities between the two rocky islands, and the vastness of the space between, she saw as symbolic of the tragedy of a career which covered so much space to arrive at a destination so like its starting point: 'Napoléon naquit en Corse et mourut à St Hélène; entre les deux îles il n'y a qu'un vaste continent et l'océan immense . . .' As alternative to 'un vaste continent', M. Heger suggested 'un vaste et brûlant désert'. In the margin beside her sentence he wrote the comment: 'Opposition remarquablement belle'. It was, consciously or not, almost a homage to genius.

Unfortunately, while she continued to write such outstanding essays, she was becoming increasingly unhappy at the pensionnat. In a letter at the end of May she voices for the first time her conviction that Madame Heger does not like her: 'I am convinced that she does not like me — why, I can't tell, nor do I think she herself has any definite reason for the aversion; but for one thing, she cannot comprehend why I do not make friends of Mesdames Blanche, Sophie, and Haussé.'[67] For the first time she wonders whether M. Heger shares his wife's disapproval:

> M. Heger is wondrously influenced by Madame, and I should not wonder if he disapproves very much of my unamiable want of sociability. He has already given me a brief lecture on universal *bienveillance,* and, perceiving that I don't improve in consequence, I fancy that he has taken to considering me as a person to be let alone — left to the error of her ways; and consequently he has in a great measure withdrawn the light of his countenance . . .[68]

It was perhaps because of this criticism that at Whitsun she made an effort to show friendliness to Mlle Haussé, the part prototype of Hortense Moore in *Shirley,* going for a long walk through the Belgian countryside with her and three of the pupils.[69]

In July she wrote another essay, 'La Mort de Moïse'.[70] It was one of those seen by Mrs Gaskell (who was mistaken in thinking that it was written during the first part of Charlotte's time at the pensionnat). M. Heger told her that Charlotte chose the subject after he had read her 'De La Vigne's poem on Joan of Arc'.[71] It must be admitted that the link between the two themes is tenuous in the extreme. There is little similarity between Casimir Delavigne's *La Mort de Jeanne d'Arc,* one of his patriotic elegies in *Les Messéniennes,*[72] and Charlotte's prose account of the death of the aged Moses, except for the fact that in both cases the central figure is a patriot who is doomed to die. In her choice of an Old Testament theme, Charlotte turned to a source which was familiar to her from childhood. Mrs Gaskell quotes M. Heger's remark: 'Elle était nourrie de la Bible.' She had not drawn on this source to any noticeable extent in the Angrian writings, where the occasional biblical allusions tend to be satirical — the context as a rule made any other use of them difficult. But in Brussels, according to Mrs Gaskell, whose informant must have been M. Heger, 'in the choice of subjects left to her selection, she frequently took characters and scenes from the Old Testament', though 'La Mort de Moïse' is the only surviving example. The influence of the Brussels milieu probably helped to explain her increased use of biblical sources. She was, as her letters show, uneasily as well as defiantly conscious of the separating influence of her Protestantism, and no doubt particularly regretted this with reference to M. Heger, a convinced and practising Catholic. But biblical subjects concerned Protestant and Catholic alike. Perhaps also she was not averse to showing her knowledge of the Bible, for she was convinced that here the Protestant was demonstrably superior.

In 'La Mort de Moïse' Charlotte Brontë reaches a higher level of art than in any previous essay. The only real artistic flaw, and criticised as such by M. Heger, is the digression on the miraculous element in the Old Testament which temporarily interrupts the initial description, but this is forgotten in the movement and colour of the scenes that follow. As in 'Le Palais de la Mort', the composition is essentially pictorial, but here it is a triptych that is presented. The firm, concise introduction gives just as much information as is necessary for the understanding of the situation. The first picture shows Moses climbing Mount Nebo, while the Israelites wait at its base; in the second, he has reached the summit and looks down over the long vista of the Promised Land. Both the natural scenes are a preparation for the culminating one where sight grows into vision as Moses gazes into the future. Finally, he sees in the sky above him the star that announces the Nativity; he has a vision of the infant Messiah, held in the arms of his mother, and in that supreme moment of revelation he dies.

The descriptive power shown by this pictorial method of composition was inborn in Charlotte Brontë, but in 'La Mort de Moïse' she gives proof of her growing mastery of her medium. Nothing shows this more than the way in which she combines breadth of vision with vivid foreground details. She owes something here to the 'echo of a style' she had caught from French masters of landscape painting, above all Chateaubriand. There are reminiscences of the frescoes of *Atala* in her description of the fertile plain at the foot of the mountain.[73] It may be only the closeness with which both follow the text of Deuteronomy[74] that accounts for the similarity between her picture of the panorama Moses sees from Mount Nebo and Vigny's treatment of the same theme in his *Moïse* but the fact that it is possible to mention her *devoir* in such a context shows what stylistic progress she has made.

Her Moïse is not, however, like Vigny's, a purely symbolic figure, taken out of the biblical context to serve as an illustration of the sufferings of the modern man of genius. Her intention is to show the Hebrew leader, at the end of his career, as the Bible shows him. Before, when her subject had been a great man, she had seized the opportunity for expressing her own ideas on greatness. Peter the Hermit was very much her own idea of the man of genius and, like Vigny's Moïse, 'plus moderne qu'antique'. The exile of St Helena provided her with a pretext for speaking of exile as it affected herself, before being pushed aside to make way for Wellington, her hero and her own ideal of greatness, still not without Angrian overtones. Moïse belongs to another dimension. It seems as if, in drawing the biblical figure familiar to her since childhood, her main concern is to preserve the majesty of the Old Testament original. *La Mort de Moïse* is the least subjective of her *devoirs,* though written at a time of mounting unhappiness. Perhaps the very finality as well as the majesty of the theme appealed to her at a time of tension. It is on the visionary plane that the essay ends, not with a return to the lower stage of reality but with the final release from it.

Only a few days after she had reached this level of sustained excellence in her art, she expressed her personal unhappiness in the most desponding letter she had yet written from Brussels. The *grandes vacances* were imminent, and she dreaded the loneliness she foresaw for herself in the deserted pensionnat: '. . . it is the first time in my life that I have really dreaded the vacation.'[75] The 15th of August saw the end of the school year. It was a date of special significance for M. Heger, for it was one of the two occasions when he gave the annual speech-day address at the Athénée Royal.[76] He gave Charlotte a copy of this speech which, like the previous one in 1834, was still remembered in Brussels many years later.[77] He also gave her, on the actual speech-day, a copy of the works of Bernardin de Saint-Pierre.

The solitude of the pensionnat in the following days must have been all the more oppressive by contrast with the preceding stir and animation. In the deserted building only one servant remained, and, unfortunately, of the few friends Charlotte had made in Brussels, Mary Dixon was away and the Wheelwrights were preparing to leave shortly.[78] The weather, at least, was fine, without being as 'Asiatically hot' as it had been the previous summer, and she took advantage of this to walk as far as possible and try to get 'a clearer acquaintance with the streets of Brussels'. But she was suffering from considerable nervous strain in her solitude. One evening at the beginning of September, she wandered into the cathedral of Ste Gudule, with no other motive than to postpone the inevitable return to the lonely pensionnat. She stayed till vespers were over, and then, seeing a few people kneeling by the confessionals, an 'odd whim' came into her head and she decided to follow their example. The letter to Emily in which she recounts the incident, afterwards transposed in *Villette,* shows her consciousness of the need to offer some kind of explanation of an episode so out of character: 'I felt as if I did not care what I did, provided it was not absolutely wrong, and that it served to vary my life and yield a moment's interest. I took a fancy to change myself into a Catholic and go and make a real confession to see what it was like. Knowing me as you do, you will think this odd, but when people are by themselves they have singular fancies.'[79] Her conscience and her ignorance of the formula of confession made her reveal her Protestantism to the priest, but he consented to listen to her: 'I actually did confess — a real confession.' But the act of confiding in a sympathetic listener gave her the relief she needed, and the incident ended there, in spite of his offers of further help. She did not tell Emily what was the matter of her 'real confession', but her letters of that summer suggest that what she probably revealed was her total dissatisfaction with her life as it was, and as it promised to be, rather than any consciousness of being in love with M. Heger.

September must have been a long and dreary month for Charlotte. The return of the French teacher, Mlle Blanche, to the pensionnat during the holidays did little to mitigate her solitude, since she found her completely antipathetic. The only incident that she found worth mentioning during the month, and that only in answer to a question from Emily, was the fact of her having seen Queen Victoria 'flashing through the Rue Royale in a carriage and six' during her visit to her uncle King Leopold.

At the beginning of October the new school year began. Although the pensionnat was no longer empty, Charlotte was more than ever conscious of inner loneliness. Writing to Emily, she has nothing good to say of the Belgian milieu. On the contrary, thoughts of Haworth fill her with acute longing for home: 'How divine are these recollections to me at this moment!'[80] But in the next sentence she affirms her intention of remaining in Brussels for the present: 'Yet I have no thought of coming home just now. I lack a real pretext for doing so . . .'

It was at this period of acute discontent with the present and uncertainty as to the future that she wrote her last *devoir* for M. Heger, 'Athènes sauvée par la Poésie'.[81] This time her subject was not the death of a great man but an incident, probably of legendary origin, connected with the history of Greece. Whether she chose it herself or whether, as seems more probable, it was suggested to her by M. Heger, there is no doubt as to the source from which it was taken. The incident is mentioned by Plutarch in his *Life of Lysander* (chapter 15) and is supposed to have taken place after the surrender of Athens to the Spartans at the end of the War of the Peleponnessus. Athenian resentment at the terms imposed by Lysander made the Spartans and their allies consider even harsher measures, and it was said a proposal was made to raze the city to the ground. According to the story, however, when the principal delegates met for a banquet, a musician from Phocis sang the opening chorus from the *Electra* of Euripides, which so moved its hearers that they felt it would be an outrage to destroy a city which had produced such great men.[82]

Charlotte's treatment of her theme is this time essentially dramatic. The incident as she tells it falls naturally into a sequence of vividly imagined scenes. The first is in the tent where Lysander is feasting his generals after the fall of Athens. An Athenian poet, who has been taken prisoner by the Spartans, is brought in to amuse them and invited to celebrate in advance, on his lyre, the sack of Athens, planned for the next day. At first he calmly refuses. Lysander in anger hurls a lance at the poet, but it misses him and accidentally severs the cord by which a flap of the tent is held in place. It falls back, to reveal the moonlit landscape outside. This brilliant coup de théâtre was the invention of Charlotte Brontë and is praised by M. Heger in a marginal comment as 'détail remarquablement! heureux'. The classic landscape thus revealed serves both as backcloth and inspiration for the next scene. The Athenian sees Mount Hymettus and the city of Athens rising from the moonlit plain watered by the Ilissus; the columns of the Parthenon gleam in the distance like pearls in a diadem. Moved by love for the doomed city, he takes up the lyre he had laid down, in the hope of touching the hearts of his enemies. The sufferings of Electra, the daughter of Agamemnon, serve as the inspiration for his song, which is listened to in a silence which encourages him to continue. When he pauses for breath, after reaching the climax, he looks round to assure himself of the effect of his verses. At this point Charlotte Brontë introduces a second coup de théâtre, but one which is in complete contradiction with the story as told by Plutarch. Instead of being greeted with sympathy and applause, the poet discovers that his audience were silent not out of consideration but because they were fast asleep. His first reaction is one of anger, but this soon changes to bitter amusement at the expense both of himself and the Spartans, and he makes good his escape. The short concluding scene is written in a deliberately flat tone. Next day Lysander wakes up with a headache, cursing the wine of Samos and having apparently forgotten both the poet and his own plan of revenge on the Athenians. Athens thus escapes the complete ruin which threatened her. In the concluding sentence Charlotte Brontë, intervening personally as narrator, attributes this result partly to the effect of the wine of Samos on Lysander and his generals, but still more to the lyre and Electra, whose narcotic effect is thus shown to have been sufficiently powerful to justify the title 'Athènes sauvée par la Poésie'.

Not the least remarkable thing about this essay is the authenticity with which, until the deliberately ironical conclusion, the classical atmosphere is maintained. For Charlotte Brontë knew far less about classical antiquity than about biblical antiquity. She was not completely ignorant on the subject, for she had gleaned what knowledge she could at second-hand from Branwell. In the crucial year 1830, when their imaginary kingdom first acquired the Greco-French name Verreopolis, she wrote a poem showing her awareness of the greatness of the Greek poets,[83] and Homer at least was accessible to her in translation.[84] But her most direct contact with Greece, both then and later, was through the poetry of Byron, which brought to life for her the beauty of the Mediterranean landscapes, the past glory of Hellas and the unhappy plight of modern Greece. From these sources she had acquired a certain amount of knowledge, enough perhaps to make M. Heger suspect, like M. Paul in *Villette*, that his pupil knew more about the classics than she would admit.

But when faced with a classical theme, she probably found herself obliged to do a good deal of preliminary reading. Lucy Snowe found herself in a similar predicament:

> The subject was classical. When M. Paul dictated the trait on which the essay was to turn, I heard it for the first time; the matter was new to me, and I had no material for its treatment. But I got books, read up the facts, laboriously constructed a skeleton out of the dry bones of the real, and then clothed them, and tried to breathe into them life, and in this last aim I had pleasure . . . but the knowledge was not there in my head, ready and mellow . . .[85]

In Lucy's case, the result was so successful that her critics mistook her work for the 'work of a ripe scholar'. It would not be unreasonable to make a similar claim for 'Athènes sauvée par la Poésie.' Until the ironic conclusion, it is in all seriousness that Charlotte Brontë aims at reconstructing the atmosphere of ancient Greece. The primitive nature of the feast in the tent of Lysander is modelled on a scene in the *Iliad,* to which direct reference is made, where Achilles receives Odysseus and the other envoys who have come with overtures of peace.[86] The character of the Spartan leader seems in line with Plutarch's portrait of him. Cold, crafty and ambitious, Lysander, when he has drunk enough, begins to show his underlying arrogance and malice. In contrast, the captive Athenian has all the dignity of the truly civilised man in the presence of barbarians. Physically their inferior, he is infinitely their superior in grace and culture, 'nourri de la philosophie de Platon et de Socrate, de la poésie de Sophocle et d'Euripide.' When he improvises, to the accompaniment of his lyre, he is inspired, like his prototype in Plutarch's tale, by the remembrance of the sorrows of Electra, though there is no direct mention of the chorus from the *Electra* of Euripides.

But Charlotte Brontë has done more than simply show a general fidelity to classical sources. The imagined improvisation of the Athenian poet is her own creation, and is yet completely in tune with the classical background. The most remarkable part of the essay is, in fact, this recitative which centres round the two memories that obsess the daughter of Agamemnon: her father's departure when she was a child and his fatal return to Argos, accompanied by Cassandra, the captive princess of Troy. In her treatment of Greek mythology, Charlotte Brontë was helped by the response it woke in her own temperament. It is the deeply felt sense of nearness to nature which inspires her Athenian poet in the prelude to Electra's song, which earned M. Heger's special praise. When she speaks of the horses of the Sun, of Night descending on Argos, of the satyrs and fauns, the Dryads and Oreads that people the forest where Electra has taken refuge, she is not constructing an unconvincing pastiche but describing forces of whose action she had been conscious since childhood. In the early poem 'The Violet', written in 1830, she had recognised that, if she was ever to emulate the Greek poets in any degree, it could only be seeking her inspiration in Nature. But in the same poem she had also recognised how much English poets owed to having drunk deeply of 'the sacred fount of Helicon'. Greek mythology had for her the charm of nature enhanced by the warmth of meridional landscapes and the prestige of art. How strongly she reacted to the Greek norm of beauty may well have astonished M. Heger when he read her essay and he, like M. Paul, may have found it hard to believe that she had not enjoyed the privileges of a 'classical education'.

But he was evidently still more surprised by the bitter irony of the conclusion of 'Athènes sauvée par la Poésie', where the atmosphere which had been so carefully built up is deliberately shattered and Lysander, tyrant and materialist, replaces the poet as the central figure. As once before, he judged it necessary to supplement the essay by a criticism of what he considered mistaken in Charlotte's attitude. It is noticeable that this time he uses the third person, and refers to her as 'l'auteur'. On the previous occasion, it had been her incomplete understanding of the importance of form in the work of art which had prompted his criticism. This time he criticises first a formal weakness and then what he considers an error of judgment. He points out the discrepancy between the satirical tone of the ending and the rest of the essay, and he affirms that this satirical attitude is unfair to the reader:

'On ne doit pas se moquer de son lecteur.'

The aesthetic objection is certainly justified. Emotion and irony are not incompatible in a work of art, but they should be combined, not simply juxtaposed. Charlotte had had ample illustration of the effectiveness of such a combination in the work of Byron. Her conclusion has indeed a surface resemblance with that of Byron's *Mazeppa*, where the veteran narrator of the tale receives no thanks from his principal hearer, because

> The king had been an hour asleep.

But in *Mazeppa* the final irony is thoroughly in harmony with the grim humour of the narrator and had been prepared from the start.

It is ethics, however, not aesthetics that motivate the main part of M. Heger's criticism. He held the classic belief that literature should please, stimulate, and, in the widest sense, educate the reader, and he was not mistaken in thinking that the disconcerting conclusion of her essay gave a final impression of intense disillusionment. Her Athenian poet tells himself it would be ridiculous to be annoyed by the stupidity of a few barbarians. But his sense of superiority is grounded on disillusion; he is the exceptional being, capable of appreciating beauty; on others it acts only as a soporific. Athens is saved not because her barbarian conquerors appreciate her but because they forget her. This combination of disenchantment and irony reminded M. Heger of Alfred de Musset, whom he quotes in illustration, though he obviously considered the analogy rather in the light of a warning than as matter for congratulation. And it is true that characters like Fantasio and Lorenzaccio do illustrate, in varying degrees, a disillusionment not unlike that of Charlotte's Athenian faced with the incomprehension of the barbarians, and that they have the same disquieting capacity for laughing both at others and at themselves. *Athènes sauvée par la Poésie,* with its magnificent evocation of Greece, is the finest of Charlotte's *devoirs.* But it betrays her growing sense of frustration in an uncongenial milieu and M. Heger's criticism shows, if not his awareness of the fact, at least the recognition that some want of equilibrium is threatening the full development of her abilities.

The three essays written in the summer and autumn of 1843, 'La Mort de Napoléon', 'La Mort de Moïse' and 'Athènes sauvée par la Poésie' mark the highest level of achievement reached by Charlotte Brontë during her stay in Brussels. At the same time the subjects represent some of the main sources from which the French Romantics drew their inspiration. The Napoleonic legend had epic repercussions in the French literature of the first half of the nineteenth century. When she crossed the Channel, Charlotte, though always faithful to her cult of Wellington, came to realise more of the power and prestige of the name of Napoleon than she had ever done before, and also to reflect, like so many of the Romantics, on the problem of the relationship between Bonaparte, the heir of the Revolution, and Napoleon, the founder of the Empire. She did not need to cross the Channel to appreciate the Bible as a source of poetry. But the emphasis put by Chateaubriand on the immense poetic resources of Christianity, the ways in which the French Romantics used biblical sources, even her consciousness of the differences in outlook between Catholic and Protestant, opened her eyes to fresh possibilities in the use of religious themes. Greece she had learnt to know through Byron and what she could glean from her brother's classical studies. But the philhellenism of Byron and his admiration of Greek landscapes and art she found again among the French Romantics. Casimir Delavigne in his *Messéniennes* aimed at a combination of atticism and modernity. And André Chenier — one of the French poets most congenial to Charlotte Brontë, though he does not feature in her transcriptions, and one who was much admired by the Romantics — had already shown how to unite modern attitudes with a passionate love of Greece. Chateaubriand himself possessed to perfection the art of evoking Greek landscapes and Greek mythology. But it is probable that Charlotte owed most here to the direct example of M. Heger, himself a classical scholar, and that it was through him that she first fully understood the fundamental rôle of the classical tradition in European literature and not least in European Romanticism.

In addition to the *devoirs* read and commented on by M. Heger, Charlotte, at some stage of her second year at the pensionnat, wrote the draft of a letter in French which may have been intended as a *devoir* but never received the finishing touches.[87] As far as literary value is concerned, it cannot compare with the finished compositions. As evidence of her personal unhappiness, it is still more revealing, for it shows that on this occasion she was unable to find an anodyne, even in an attempt at creative writing. Both the tone and the material suggest that it was written some time during the final months at the pensionnat. It is addressed to an imaginary correspondent called Jane, who is reproached with idleness and self-indulgence. However, by an unexpected *volte-face,* the writer suddenly admits that she is guilty of comparable faults: she, too, can be lazy but her kind of idleness is more lethal than Jane's, for it springs from intense depression. In an attempt to react, she imagines the relief of escaping from the classroom where she is evidently writing, and from the drabness of an urban setting, and of climbing among the hills. And she makes a comparison between the inhabitants of low-lying country and hill country very un-flattering to the former, who are said to have acquired a frog-like nature, while the latter have an affinity with the eagle, king of the air. But by another sudden *volte-face,* she recognises that she is being unfair, since all mountaineers are not angels and sometimes a man is found in the lowlands worthy by his talents to have been born on the summit of Ben Nevis. After this qualified concession she remarks: 'J'ai fait l'amende honorable et je continue . . .'

The *devoir,* if such it was intended to be, breaks off at this point. It is more formless than anything else she wrote in Brussels, more so by far than her real letters of the same period, which remain incisive and vigorous. But her artistic faculty was only dormant and even now, though she aban-doned her unfinished attempt at a written composition, she continued her praise of the highlander in another medium. Inserted in this draft of a letter is a pencil sketch of a man in Highland dress which has all the vitality so noticeably lacking in the written text.[88] While she was drawing this sketch at least, she must have shaken off the depression that was weighing on her so heavily when she tried to write to her imaginary correspondent.

But such attempts to react against her unhappiness at the pensionnat could not be more than passing interludes, and a week after she had finished the most remarkable of her *devoirs,* 'Athènes sauvée par la Poésie', she gave notice to Madame Heger. When M. Heger heard of it, he evidently thought she had acted on impulse and persuaded her to reverse her decision. She wrote her account of the situation to Ellen Nussey:

> . . . Brussels is indeed desolate to me now . . . I am completely alone . . . I cannot count the Belgians as anything — Madame Heger is a polite — plausible and interested person — I no longer trust her . . . sometimes the solitude oppresses me to an excess — One day lately I felt as if I could bear it no longer — and I went to Mme. Heger and gave her notice — If it had depended on her I should certainly have soon been at liberty but Monsieur Heger — having heard of what was in agitation — sent for me the day after — and pronounced with vehemence his decision that I should not leave — I could not at that time have persevered in my intention without exciting him to passion — so I promised to stay a while longer — how long that while will be I do not know — I should not like to return to England to do nothing . . .[89]

The day after she wrote on the fly-leaf of her school atlas: '. . . I am very cold — there is no fire . . . I am tired of being among foreigners — it is a dreary life — especially as there is only one person in this house worthy of being liked — also another, who seems a rosy sugar-plum but I know her to be coloured chalk.'[90]

A month later, when she wrote again to Ellen, the situation had not improved. Speaking of her loneliness, particularly when there is a holiday and the pupils and teachers are all out visiting friends, she says:

> You will hardly believe that Madame Heger (good and kind as I have described her) never comes near me on these occasions . . . Yet, I understand, she praises me very much to everybody, and says what excellent lessons I give . . . You remember the letter she wrote me, when I

was in England? How kind and affectionate that was? Is
that not odd? I fancy I begin to perceive the reason of this
mighty distance and reserve; it sometimes make me laugh,
and at other times nearly cry. When I am sure of it, I will
tell it you. In the meantime the complaints I make at
present are for your ears only . . .'[91]

It must have been a mutual relief to Charlotte and to
Madame Heger, in these circumstances, that they now saw
even less of each other than before, since Madame Heger's
fifth child, her daughter Victorine, was born in mid-
November, on the very day this letter was written. One event
at least occurred to break the monotony of Charlotte's
existence at this period. Winifred Gérin has shown that she
must have been present at the concert in the Salle de la
Grande Harmonie on December 10th, attended by the King
and Queen of the Belgians, which was later to provide the
source of a crucial episode of *Villette*.[92] But a few days later
her final decision to leave Brussels was announced in a letter
to Emily: 'I have taken my determination. I hope to be at
home the day after New Year's Day. I have told Mme.
Heger . . . Low spirits have afflicted me much lately, but I
hope all will be well when I get home . . .'[93]

In coming to this decision, Charlotte was influenced by a
letter from Mary Taylor, whose forthright advice was thus
instrumental in spurring her on both to go to Brussels and to
leave it when the purpose of her stay had been achieved.[94]
She had also received reports from home of her father's
increasing blindness, and this was a reason for her leaving
which the Hegers understood and accepted.[95] They recognised that she had perfected her French so that she was now
in a position to pass on her knowledge of it to pupils of her
own, and M. Heger gave her a diploma sealed with the official
seal of the Athénée Royal, certifying that she was thoroughly
proficient in the language and well qualified to teach it.

During her final weeks at the pensionnat Charlotte found
that, in spite of her conviction of Belgian stolidity, her pupils
had felt more friendly to her than she had imagined. 'I was
surprised at the degree of regret expressed by my Belgian
pupils, when they knew I was going to leave,' she wrote, after

her return, to Ellen Nussey, 'I did not think it had been in their phlegmatic nature.'[96] Charlotte's relationship with the Hegers themselves seems to have improved during this brief final period. The possibility of their sending one of their own daughters as a pupil, when she had a school, was discussed, and such a project would certainly not have been mentioned if Madame Heger had not been prepared to consider Charlotte as a friend in spite of the previous coolness between them. With M. Heger there had never been any real misunderstanding, and he gave her on the morning she left the gift of a recent anthology of French poetry.[97] It was thanks to his teaching and friendship that the stay at the pensionnat had been epoch-making for her and, in spite of the intense homesickness to which she had latterly admitted, she could not part with him without feeling it a painful ordeal: 'I suffered much before I left Brussels. I think, however long I live, I shall not forget what the parting with M. Heger cost me; It grieved me so much to grieve him, who has been so true, kind and disinterested a friend.'[98]

The emotional overtones in these sentences, written after the return to Haworth, show clearly enough that most of the cost of the parting still remained to be paid. But to describe M. Heger's friendship as true, kind and disinterested was to pay him a tribute to which he had every right. For him teaching and friendship were inseparable. For he was a born teacher, to whom the first was the natural way of showing the second. His teaching method, as he later told the Abbé Richardson, had as its first condition complete self-giving, 'un dévou absolu,' and as its second a tireless and sympathetic study of the character of each individual pupil.[99] In the case of Charlotte Brontë, this method very soon led him to discover her unusual skill in composition. He concentrated chiefly on developing this gift of hers and he was eminently fitted to do so, since he himself combined a wide culture and discriminating taste with an ardent love of literature. There was nothing narrowly pedantic about his correction of her *devoirs;* he gave more attention to choice of words than to slips of grammar, still more to style and expression and most of all to the total impression made on the reader.[100]

His ultimate aim was to equip a teacher of French, but he

helped to form an author. He gave her what she needed, a critic whose encouragement was as generous as his standards were exacting. He made her aware of the dangers of her style, especially the tendency to redundancy and digression, all the more obvious in a language with the natural clarity and concision of French. He saw that she sometimes over-indulged her love of imagery. It was probably of his criticism she was thinking when she confessed, in her unfinished draft of the letter to 'Jane', to the 'bad habit' of seeing everything through 'the coloured glass' of simile. His own view of imagery was that it should illuminate and interpret, and that 'any image that does not serve both these purposes is a fault in style.'[101] But he knew that the flaws in her style came not from any intrinsic weakness but from the richness of the inspiration she had not yet entirely learnt to master. He realised its natural qualities and increasingly showed his admiration of them. He gave Charlotte the ideal reader she had never had, and in response to his critical standards she began to use her genius less exclusively to satisfy her own imaginative needs and with more attention to the exacting and impersonal demands of art. Unconsciously, M. Heger paid her the highest compliment in his power when he wrote at the end of her 'Athènes sauvée par la Poésie', disconcerted by the unexpectedly satirical conclusion: 'Il ne faut pas se moquer de son lecteur'. It meant that instinctively he had given his pupil the rôle of author and himself that of her reader, and a reader who was not accustomed to be disappointed.

# 3 After Brussels

To read in uninterrupted sequence the four letters from Charlotte Brontë to Constantin Heger after her return from Brussels is to receive an impression of almost unrelieved despondency deepening into despair. But to think of the period between her return to Haworth in January 1844 and November 1845, when the last of the letters was written, as one of complete inaction and melancholy would be as untrue as it would be unjust. As recent biographers, especially Winifred Gérin, have shown and as her own correspondence indicates, it was only gradually that she came to realise the extent of her dependence on memories of Brussels and the impossibility of maintaining the kind of contact she desired.

It was at once evident that the return to Haworth did not cure her of depression, in spite of the homesickness of which she had so often complained during the last months in Brussels. She was conscious of a change in herself: '. . . something in me, which used to be enthusiasm, is tamed down and broken.'[1] It seemed to her now that the most desirable course would be to leave home again and set up a private school, as she had originally planned: '. . . what I wish for now is active exertion, a stake in life. Haworth seems such a lonely quiet spot, buried away from the world.'[2] But this course was impracticable because of the family circumstances; Mr Brontë's eyesight was failing and her presence at home was necessary. There was, however, the possibility of taking a limited number of pupils at the parsonage. Circulars were printed and for several months Charlotte did her best, loyally seconded by Ellen Nussey, to contact any of her acquaintances who might be likely to send their children to her. The school project was of long standing and had been the avowed cause of her going to Brussels. But if she pursued it now with renewed vigour, it was undoubtedly because it was closely associated in her mind with M. Heger who, she knew, would thoroughly approve of it. Consciously or not, to maintain unbroken her friendship with him had become at this period the chief motive of her life.

The only way of doing so was by correspondence and consequently this became her dominant preoccupation. M. Heger had authorised her to write to him from time to time. It was probably not long before she availed herself of this permission. Though the first of her letters to him which has been preserved is dated July 24, she had written at least one and probably more before then. M. Heger replied at intervals, and the fact that he did so showed his interest in her, since letter-writing was something he found far from congenial.[3] His share of the correspondence has not survived, but its nature can be surmised from his telling Mrs Gaskell that his letters contained advice about Charlotte's 'character, studies, mode of life'.[4]

Unfortunately they came at too long intervals to satisfy Charlotte who, in the letter of July 24, admits that the suspense of waiting for them was already making her unreasonable. 'Ah Monsieur! je vous ai écrit une fois une lettre peu raisonnable, parce que le chagrin me serrait le coeur . . .'[5] She promises to be more patient in future, but it was soon evident that patience in these conditions was beyond her power.

A good deal of the letter of July 24 is taken up with an account of her present circumstances. She explains the impossibility of accepting a teaching post away from home and then refers to the project of taking a few pupils at the parsonage, recognising at the same time the difficulty of finding any willing to come to such a remote spot as Haworth. When writing this she may well have had in mind the suggestion made in Brussels of sending one of the Heger children which, if acted on, would have provided a natural way of remaining in close and friendly contact. But, whatever hope she might have had of such an arrangement taking place in the future, she knew that the decision to take up a teaching career would have M. Heger's full sanction and approval.

The situation, however, was complicated by another factor, and one which was ultimately to prove decisive — teaching was not and never had been the career she would herself have chosen, and in the same letter where she has just referred to the school project, she cannot resist making this abundantly clear. After speaking of the lethargy due to enforced inaction at present weighing on her, she goes on to say that the natural cure for this would have been to write: 'Je ne connaîtrais pas cette léthargie si je pouvais écrire . . .' And she complains of the weak state of her eyesight which prevents her from doing so. The decision to enter on a teaching career thus proves to be one forced on her by circumstances rather than made voluntarily, a poor second best for the author's life she would herself have chosen: '. . . la carrière de lettres m'est fermée — celle de l'instruction seule m'est ouverte — elle n'offre pas les mêmes attraits — c'est égal, j'y entrerai . . .'

It is evident that she is by no means confident of M. Heger's entering into her feelings over this disappointment with the sympathy she knew he would feel for the school project. She finds it necessary to assure him that she had formerly passed days, weeks and whole months in writing and not without result, since Southey and Coleridge, 'deux de nos meilleurs auteurs', had expressed their approval of the manuscripts she sent them. That she should feel this need to defend her ability as a writer to the very man who had done so much to foster it shows her awareness of the possibility of disagreement between them on what was, for her, an all-important issue.

There is no doubt that M. Heger had been keenly interested by the signs he soon discovered in Charlotte's *devoirs* of her outstanding literary gifts. But the *devoirs* were a recognised part of her training as an intending teacher of French. When in the course of time these compositions began to suggest that she felt a personal involvement in artistic creation, his comments showed his sympathy with her love of art, but he made no definite allusion to the desirability of a literary career for his brilliant pupil, even though it is highly probable that he was also shown the selection from the Angrian manuscripts which was found much later in a bound copy in Brussels.[6] What he thought of these works, if he did in fact see them, and, what is more important, what he thought of Charlotte's literary ambitions in general, has to be deduced from absence of comment, rather than from definite statements. Years later, when an English pupil at the pensionnat ingenuously asked him why he had kept the Brontës' *devoirs,* he replied: 'Comment? Mais, parce que j'y ai vu le génie.'[7] But the first time he used the word in connection with them seems to have been in conversation with Mrs Gaskell, after the appearance of their novels. It would have been much easier to gauge his real views on this crucial question if his side of the correspondence with Charlotte had survived. It is not likely that an issue so vital to her as her literary ambitions would have been neglected. But it was hardly to be expected that, after devoting so much care to preparing her for a teaching career, he should have encouraged her to abandon it for that of a writer. The practical reasons for her need to earn an assured living were, in view of her father's age and health, as urgent as before. But, for M. Heger, there were far higher advantages than purely practical ones in the choice of teaching as a profession. He had once, as Charlotte reminds him in her letter, wanted to be a barrister. But when she writes: '. . . le sort ou la Providence vous a fait professeur — vous êtes heureux malgré cela', she shows how widely different were their views of the same career. For him teaching was a vocation. He was a true lover of literature but, for him, to communicate his love of art to his pupils was to enhance his own enjoyment of it. He may have thought Charlotte would ultimately find more real satisfaction in introducing her pupils to literature than in writing. He may also have thought she lacked the maturity and experience necessary to form a writer, unaware that she was in the process of painfully acquiring them.

His advice to her on the subject, had his letters survived, might have been not unlike that of Southey in 1837:

> . . . The day dreams in which you habitually indulge are likely to induce a distempered state of mind . . . Literature cannot be the business of a woman's life, and it ought not to be . . . But do not suppose that I disparage the gift you possess nor that I would discourage you from exercising

it . . . Write poetry for its own sake; not in a spirit of emulation, and not with a view to celebrity; the less you aim at that the more likely you will be to deserve and finally to obtain it . . .[8]

But the only writing that had any attraction for her at this time was in reality the correspondence with M. Heger. Had she felt able to write a book it would have been primarily, as she says, to show her gratitude for his teaching by dedicating it 'à mon maître de littérature — au seul maître que j'ai jamais eu . . .' Even the knowledge of French she had acquired was valued by her principally as a means of communication with him. It was her command of spoken French that she was most anxious not to lose, for she could not give up the hope of one day seeing him again. It was for this reason that, as she tells him, she memorised every day half a page of French: '. . . quand je prononce les mots français il me semble que je cause avec vous.' In a postscript she repeats her hope of seeing M. Heger again and even dreams of making it a reality: 'Oh c'est certain que je vous reverrai un jour — il le faut bien — puisque aussitôt que j'aurai gagné assez d'argent pour aller à Bruxelles j'y irai — et je vous reverrai si ce n'est que pour un instant.'

No reply came to this letter. In October the fact that Mary Taylor's brother Joe was going to Brussels on business gave her the opportunity to send the next one by his hand, instead of by post. From her note — it is hardly more — of 24 October, it is clear she suspects that the reason for M. Heger's silence, now of six months' duration, may be that the two previous letters never reached him. The hope of renewed communication gives this one a more cheerful tone. She reiterates her gratitude for his past kindness and, in a postscript, enumerates the books he has given her, which she has just had bound: the complete works of Bernardin de Saint-Pierre, the *Pensées* of Pascal, an anthology of French poetry, two German books and, finally, copies of his two speeches at the prize-giving of the Athénée Royal, 'ce qui vaut tout le reste'.

Joe Taylor had promised that any letter written in reply would be brought back to her without fail, either by himself or by Mary, then again in Belgium, teaching and studying music. But his return was delayed by a visit to Switzerland. In the meantime Charlotte was indebted to the Taylors for another contact with France, since Joe began to send French newspapers to Haworth, a source of interest and pleasure to her which was to continue for years, 'I am very glad of them',[9] she wrote to Ellen Nussey. As the days went on, the suspense of waiting increased, and she could no longer find occupation in the school project, for by now it was clear there were no pupils to be had. Joe Taylor finally returned, bringing no letter. But there was still the possibility that Mary, when she came, would have one for her. Mary arrived in England and came to stay at the parsonage at the beginning of January; she brought no word from M. Heger.

The disappointment was intense. Under its impact Charlotte wrote, on 8 January, a letter which shows the sense of injustice which now enters into her feelings. M. Heger's failure to reply is considered a 'malheur' she has not deserved. She refers to the strain under which she is living and the cost at which she maintains an outward calm. That she did impose such control on her feelings and continue to play her part in the family life is beyond doubt, but the constant effort only increased the tension — 'une lutte intérieure presque insupportable' — which at last finds an outlet in this letter.

She deliberately refrained from re-reading it, but she could hardly have stated more clearly the basic reason for her misery, however unreasonable it might appear in the light of common sense. M. Heger's friendship had become, in her eyes, the corner-stone of her existence; the fear of losing it was intolerable. 'Si mon maitre me retire entièrement son amitié je serai tout à fait sans espoir . . .'[10] The poignancy of the situation lies, as Margaret Lane says, in the fact that she asks so little:[11] ' . . . je n'ai pas besoin de beaucoup d'affection de la part de ceux que j'aime je ne saurais que faire d'une amitié entière et complète — je n'y suis pas habituée . . .' But she reminds him that he did show a *little* interest in her when she was his pupil in Brussels; all she asks is the maintenance of that *little* interest. ' . . . je tiens à conserver ce *peu* d'interet — j'y tiens comme je tiendrais à la vie.'

The feeling expressed here is evidently far more than

ordinary friendship but, as M. H. Spielmann said in his introduction to the letters, there can be no question of 'unrequited love' in the ordinary sense of the word.[12] M. Heger was a married man, in whose family life and affections she could expect no part. It was precisely because he was a married man that she felt she could justifiably express her desire for the continuance of an entirely different relationship, that of his devoted pupil, without danger of being misunderstood.[13] Aware herself of how little she asked, and of how much that little would mean to her, she did not scruple to express herself with a passionate intensity which, in her judgment, was fully justified. She had already suspected in Brussels, and she was now convinced, that her feelings were misinterpreted by Madame Heger, to whom there is a transparent allusion when she refers to the reasonable and cool-headed people who would accuse her, on reading this letter, of talking nonsense. What is far harder to bear is the awareness that her master himself now blames her for being morbidly emotional: 'Vous direz encore que je suis exaltée — que j'ai des pensées noires, etc.' Rather than sever their friendship, however, she declares herself ready to submit to reproaches of every kind — a tacit admission that it was already irretrievably impaired.

In these conditions life became a continual struggle to control a sorrow which no one but herself was likely to understand. During this difficult period Mary Taylor's decision to emigrate to New Zealand, taken some time before, and carried out in March, deprived her of the companionship of one of her two closest friends. Fortunately Ellen Nussey remained and in June they spent three weeks together at Hathersage in Derbyshire. During the journey back she had a few minutes' conversation with a fellow passenger whom she rightly judged to be French. The incident was still vividly remembered by her when she wrote her last letter to M. Heger four months later.

But when she returned to the parsonage it was to find the family in the grip of a calamity grave enough in its nature to compare with her own personal sorrow. Her brother Branwell had suddenly been notified of his dismissal from his post by his employer, Mr Robinson, who had discovered that the tutor was in love with his wife. In his desperation he thought only of 'stunning or drowning his distress of mind'. The situation was all the harder for Charlotte to bear because she had been from childhood the sister closest to him, his collaborator in the Angrian saga and the confidante of his ambitions. His unexpected success as a tutor must have to some extent reassured her in recent months, in spite of his evident instability. Her disappointment was all the keener and her letters show how little hope she felt of his ever recovering from the catastrophe in which both his feelings and his material prospects were involved, and which he seemed unable to fight except with drink and drugs.

It is not surprising that in these circumstances the correspondence with M. Heger became, if possible, even more important to Charlotte Brontë than before. The tone of her last letter to him in November shows this but it also shows, from the start, that the continuance of communication between them was becoming increasingly precarious. Previously she had not appeared too concerned because she was writing out of turn. Now she begins by pointing out that she has been careful to let the promised interval of six months pass, and is therefore entitled to send another letter.[14] But she does not conceal what it cost her to keep silence, and herself receive no letter, during these six monthly periods. On the contrary she asks M. Heger to imagine what would be his reactions if he himself were separated for the same length of time from one of his children and obliged to remain without any news of his child's welfare. The use of this comparison makes it clear that she herself rates her feeling for her 'master' far beyond friendship in the ordinary sense. Love is the only adequate word for devotion of this calibre, but the comparison with paternal love at its finest suggests a devotion which is passionate without sensuality and completely unselfish. The image is a poignant one, all the more so because one suspects that it might be as true in reverse.

It is in harmony with the heightened emotional tone of the whole letter. In her solitude, M. Heger's image had inevitably become more obsessive, and she herself acknowledges that she is a slave to memories and regrets against which she has vainly tried to react: '. . . c'est humiliant cela — de ne pas

savoir maîtriser ses propres pensées, être esclave à un regret,
un souvenir, esclave à une idée dominante et fixe qui
tyrannise son esprit.'[15] One can sense in such lines the
possibility of the transposition of experience into art which
will ultimately liberate her from what she feels as a mental as
well as an emotional servitude. But at present she is too close
to the intractable reality of facts for any such escape to be
possible. On the contrary, it is in this letter that she forces
herself to face their full implications for the first time. At the
start of the correspondence she had proudly said that, if she
thought he only answered her out of pity, she would be
deeply hurt. Now she recognises without illusion that, when
he did eventually reply to her last appeal for a letter; it must
have been out of compassion, and that if he sends her
another, it will be principally for the same reason. Far from
not recognising the onesidedness of their relationship, she
now empasises it with all the force at her command:
'. . . écrire à une ancienne élève ne peut-être (sic) une occupation fort intéressante pour vous — je le sais — mais pour
moi c'est la vie . . .'

There is probably some unconscious self-dramatisation in
this letter, there are touches of bitterness and there is a
recognisable challenge in the statement that she will never
voluntarily give up the correspondence which is 'la seule joie
que j'ai au monde . . . mon dernier privilège.' But for the first
time she adds a postscript in English, in which there is no
more protest, no more bitterness, only the resigned fore-
knowledge that she will never see him or Brussels again and
the instinctive desire to retain enough knowledge of French
to give substance and enduring freshness to her memories:

> I must say one word to you in English . . . do not be
> irritated at my sadness . . . truly I find it difficult to be
> cheerful so long as I think that I shall never see you more.
> You will perceive by the defects in this letter that I am
> forgetting the French language — yet I read all the French
> books I can get, and learn daily a portion by heart — but I
> have never heard French spoken but once since I left
> Brussels — and then it sounded like music in my ears —
> every word was most precious to me because it reminded

me of you — I love French for your sake with all my heart and soul . . .

The valedictory tone of the postscript was justified, for by November 1845 the correspondence was virtually over. Only Charlotte's four letters survive. They were shown by M. Heger to Mrs Gaskell when she visited Brussels in 1856. If, sooner or later, he tore them up, it was not because he thought them of no importance. It is much more likely to have been for the reason he gave later to Ellen Nussey, when she consulted him about the publication of the letters of Charlotte in her possession and their eventual translation into French. He asked her to put to herself the question a friend must consider first in such circumstances, whether to do so would not be the betrayal of a confidence: 'Pourrais-je, sans l'assentiment de mon ami, publier ses lettres intimes, c'est à dire ses confidences? Ne m'a-t-il pas laissé voir de lui-même plus qu'il ne voulait montrer au premier venu? . . .'[16] The letters eventually survived only because Madame Heger re-assembled the torn up pieces in case they should ever be needed as proof of the complete integrity of her husband's conduct in a difficult situation.

It is impossible not to feel sympathy with M. Heger, even though his dilemma was far less tragic than Charlotte's. He was neither insensible nor insensitive to her misery. He had admired her intellectual gifts, pitied her loneliness, appreciated her courage. That he could speak of her with sympathy to Mrs Gaskell only a few years after the publication of *Villette* says much both for his magnanimity and for his understanding of her emotional sufferings. When he saw from her letters that, while asking only friendship, she idolised him to an extent that he had never guessed, the discovery must have been as distressing as it was unexpected. It was no fault of his that his character presented a rare combination of the qualities she valued most: integrity, intellect and imagination, as well as possessing the imperiousness and dynamism which were, for her, essential masculine attributes.

Had the tragic situation not arisen, he would no doubt have continued to write to her at intervals in the same tone, half teasing, never uncritical, but eloquent of frank and warm-hearted friendship which characterised his infrequent but charming letters to others of his former English pupils.[17] As it was, he had little alternative but coolness and eventual silence, and there is small doubt that any written attempt by him at an *éclaircissement* would have been found by Charlotte to be more wounding still.

But his position was very different from hers, not only because he was far less emotionally involved but because of the incessant claims on his time, as a devoted husband and father, and as a tireless teacher, which made it impossible for him to concentrate on one problem to the exclusion of all others. Charlotte, on the other hand, found herself in a situation which offered no apparent outlet for her emotions: she felt herself immured with her misery. When long afterwards Dr Paul Heger referred to the situation while writing to Marion H. Spielmann about his decision to present the Brontë letters to the British Museum, he pointed out this crucial difference: 'Doubtless my parents played an important part in the life of Charlotte Brontë, but she did not enter into theirs as one would imagine from what passes current to-day. That is evident enough by the very circumstances of life, so different for her and for them.'[18]

But in her solitude she still had one resource which was never to fail her: her creative genius. There was no one to whom she could talk of her sufferings, for she had deliberately ceased to speak of M. Heger, even to Emily. But it was possible ultimately to transpose them into art. Any complete transposition was as yet impracticable, for the traumatic experience was still too recent. But she took the first steps towards it in a number of poems inspired by memories of Brussels which, with others of an earlier date, were shortly to form her contribution to the first published work of the Brontë sisters, *Poems by Currer, Ellis and Acton Bell.*

Of her part in the collection she wrote afterwards to Mrs Gaskell in terms which showed how unflattering was her final opinion of it, ranking her own poems below those of Emily and of Anne and pointing her criticism, as she often did, by a metaphor: 'I do not like my own share of the work . . . Mine are chiefly juvenile productions; the restless effervescence of a mind that would not be still. In those days, the sea too often "wrought and was tempestuous", and sea, sand and shingle — all turned up in the tumult. This image is much too magniloquent for the subject, but you will pardon it.'[19] The image was, in fact, brilliantly accurate. There is elemental force in some of these poems; they do not, except in isolated verses, constitute successful poetry, though they show the same inborn talent for versification as the Angrian poems of her early youth, but they hold the promise of what she might achieve when the chaos of the emotions had subsided and the formative work of the imagination had begun.

A number of them were written when the Brussels experience was still fresh in her mind and heart, and, among those of an earlier date, some have acquired during revision overtones of the same crucial period. It also inspired *Master and Pupil,* first published in *The Professor,* and *Reason* and *He saw my heart's woe . . .,* published only after her death. Together such poems constitute a series of significant variations on the same tragic theme.

That theme is unrequited love. The cessation of all communication with M. Heger meant that Charlotte Brontë was free to transpose the Brussels experience imaginatively in the interests of her art. She had been obliged to restrict herself, in her letters to M. Heger, to what she intended to be only the expression of a despairing friendship, but the heroines of her poems, like those of her novels, were free to express all the anguish of unrequited love. In the novels, and supremely in *Villette*, this expression, however intense, is given form and cohesion through the artist's controlling hand. In the poems such control has not yet been attained, and the situation is seen in retrospect rather than in perspective. The frequent shifts in emphasis and mood are motivated by resentment as well as love. The passionate devotion of Jane Eyre to her 'master', the slowly maturing and never uncritical but profound love of Lucy Snowe for M. Paul belong to a different and, in spite of storms, a serener climate.

The most tragic of the verses are those where the speaker recognises that she has been the victim of self-delusion. This is most starkly stated in *Reason:*

> . . . Devoid of charm, how could I hope
> My unasked love would e'er return?

What fate, what influence lit the flame
I still feel inly, deeply burn?[20]

In *Frances* there is a similar recognition that the speaker's
love has never been returned:

. . . Oh! Love was all a thin illusion;
Joy but the desert's flying stream;
And glancing back on long delusion
My memory grasps a hollow dream.[21]

But there is also resentment at the inexplicable change of
attitude on the part of the man who apparently loved her,
and it is noticeable that he alone is held responsible for this
change; there is no suggestion of a rival who intervenes, as in
*The Professor* and *Villette,* to separate the lovers:

Yet whence that wondrous change of feeling,
I never knew, and cannot learn;
Nor why my lover's eye, congealing,
Grew cold and clouded, proud and stern . . .[22]

The indictment is far more vehement in the poem *He saw
my heart's woe,* written later[23] but in which the memory of
what she had endured when her last letters to Brussels
remained unanswered revives the bitterness of the actual
experience:

. . . He saw my heart's woe, discovered my soul's anguish,
How in fever, in thirst, in atrophy it pined;
Knew he could heal, yet looked and let it languish, —
To its moans spirit-deaf, to its pangs spirit-blind . . .[24]

But such bitterness does not characterise all the poems.
Very different is the tone of *Master and Pupil,* where the
'Master's' apparent calm when parting with his favourite
pupil proves to have been only a mask to conceal his
emotions.[25] The rôle of the lover seems in fact in these poems
to oscillate between the poles of callous indifference and
protective tenderness. But whatever the variations, it is clear
that the Don Juan-like qualities of Zamorna are no
longer among the attributes of Charlotte Brontë's ideal hero.
*Preference,* though not particularly successful as a poem, is

interesting for this reason. Of two rival suitors, it is the man of integrity and high ideals who is preferred:

> Man of conscience — man of reason:
> Stern perchance, but ever just . . .[26]

But the chief accent throughout is on the anguish caused by unrequited love rather than on the lover. It is considered as something that must not only be endured but ultimately conquered. The poem *Frances* is particularly revealing in its fluctuations of despair and hope. To the girl in her state of awakened sensibility the only cure seems to lie in action of some kind:

> . . . 'The very wildness of my sorrow
>     Tells me I yet have innate force;
> My track of life has been too narrow,
>     Effort shall trace a broader course . . .
>
> New scenes, new language, skies less clouded,
>     May once more wake the wish to live;
> Strange foreign towns, astir and crowded,
>     New pictures to the mind can give.
>
> New forms and faces, passing ever,
>     May hide the one I still retain,
> Defined and fixed, and fading never,
>     Stamped deep on vision, heart and brain . . .'[27]

The wish to travel again and visit other foreign cities was also Charlotte Brontë's at the same period. Unlike Emily, for whom nearness to the moors was all the outlet she wished, she dreamed of returning to the Continent. Her sister Anne wrote in her 'Diary Paper' of July 1845: 'Charlotte is thinking about getting another situation. She wishes to go to Paris. Will she go?'[28]

But, as is clear from the poems, life at this period was still desolate, in spite of her determination not to be over-whelmed by her sorrow. Love had had for her the intensity of a religion. It was inevitable that in this crisis she should feel acutely in need of the support her religious faith could give. *Pilate's Wife's Dream*, the opening poem of the collection, has no direct connection with the Brussels experience.

But it shows, by its position, the place she wished religious themes to have in her art, and by its content how she saw in Christianity the means of attaining what she had always desired — truth. In *Frances* the forsaken girl tries at one stage to comfort herself with the thought of freedom from sorrow in the world to come, but she is still too absorbed by her passionate grief to be able to content herself with any solace which does not offer immediate action as a diversion. It is in *He saw my heart's woe*, where she equates her unhappy love with idolatry and condemns it as such, that Christianity is recognised as the only adequate source of consolation. There is far more conviction of lasting solace here than in the reluctant appeal to 'Reason', though it is eloquent of the depth of Charlotte Brontë's suffering that she feels it can only be truly healed in another dimension than that of Time, when the soul can at last

. . . feel the peril past of Death's immortal birth.

The depth of feeling that speaks in poems like this gives them an eloquence that cannot be ignored, but it was not through the medium of verse that Charlotte Brontë was to express herself most successfully as an artist. Her verse is least effective when it is most purely lyrical, but it shows her inborn narrative and dramatic gifts and her sure instinct for finding the images best calculated to suggest her emotions. Some of the archetypal imagery of her novels is already apparent, her preoccupation with effects of light and shade that harmonise with emotional states, the association between sea imagery and disaster that emerges with almost hallucinatory power in the poem *Gilbert*. But most of all her verses mirror with fidelity the shock of her contact with a reality so much less tractable than the world of Angria, but with infinitely greater possibilities both for joy and pain. It was an experience that made a fresh escape into her art essential and at the same time made nonsense of an art based only on escapism.

To all appearance the dark period through which she was passing held singularly little promise of a brighter future. Yet the time had at length come when the career of authorship which had been the cherished dream of all the Brontës was to become a reality, not only for Charlotte but for her sisters also. For all three sisters were reunited at last at Haworth, and in Emily and Anne, Charlotte found what she imperatively needed, the companionship of kindred minds with aspirations like her own. Long ago şhe had found a similar stimulus in her collaboration with Branwell, now so tragically incapable of participating in any artistic achievement. But the sisters to whom she was united in bonds of closest sympathy were amply qualified to do so. It was the discovery of a manuscript volume of Emily's poems, in the autumn of 1845, that fired Charlotte with renewed purpose and enthusiasm. 'They stirred my heart like the sound of a trumpet when I read them alone and in secret.'[29] The discovery aroused Emily's indignation, but it re-established the sisters' habit of showing each other what they had written, which had been broken by absence. Anne, too, had been writing poems, which she now showed to Charlotte. It was already Charlotte's conviction that Emily's merited publication and, once her reluctant consent had been won, they decided to compile a volume made up of selections from the work of all three. A publishing firm was found, Messrs Aylott and Jones, who agreed in January 1846 to publish the collection, on condition the authors contributed towards the costs. They decided to use the pseudonyms they were also to use in publishing their novels, and in May 1846 the *Poems by Currer, Ellis and Acton Bell* appeared.

The book attracted no attention, but the fact of having been engaged in the work that was their true vocation had acted as such a powerful stimulus that their determination to pursue a literary career remained unshaken. Referring later to the failure of the poems, Charlotte wrote: 'Ill-success failed to crush us: the mere effort to succeed had given a wonderful zest to existence; it must be pursued . . .'[30] She adds: 'We each set to work on a prose tale . . .' They must in fact have begun to do so considerably before the actual publication of the poems, since in April Charlotte was in a position to write to Aylott and Jones: 'C., E. and A. Bell are now preparing for the press a work of fiction, consisting of three distinct and unconnected tales . . .'[31] The tales were *The Professor, Wuthering Heights* and *Agnes Grey*.

Although the manuscripts were completed by July 1846, and subsequently offered to a number of publishers, it was not till July 1847 that *Wuthering Heights* and *Agnes Grey* were finally accepted by T. C. Newby. But *The Professor* was again rejected. Charlotte, however, was not shaken in her belief in the merits of the work. Later, while recognising its weak points, she was still convinced that 'all that relates to Brussels, the Belgian school etc., is as good as I can write . . .'[32]

It is now recognised that this novel, the first and still incomplete transposition of her Brussels experience, is an integral part of her total achievement. The essential datum of the situation is contained in the poem *Master and Pupil,* included in the text, but in all probability written before the novel itself. Its tone suggests that it was composed very shortly after the return to Haworth, when Charlotte still felt confident of M. Heger's continuing friendship, but the writing of the novel is more likely to have been begun during the last painful stages of the one-sided correspondence. It does not introduce, like *Villette,* a character offering close affinities with M. Heger, but the Belgian setting is a vital part of the whole. It is evident that, as Winifred Gérin says, 'she could not have written a novel at that time which excluded Brussels.'[33]

Even though it failed to find a publisher in her lifetime, *The Professor* was a factor of importance in her life and art. In writing it she assuaged much bitterness and gained a new confidence in her own powers. Finding herself, at the moment when the manuscript was returned to her for the first time, in August 1846, in need of comfort at an anxious period — she had taken her father to Manchester for a cataract operation — she at once set to work on a second novel. But while *Jane Eyre* was being written, *The Professor* was still going the rounds of the publishers. In the July of 1847, as a 'forlorn hope', the firm of Smith, Elder was approached. They, too, refused *The Professor* but were so much impressed by its quality that, when returning it, they enclosed a letter to the author discussing it and saying that 'a work in three volumes would meet with careful attention'.[34] *Jane Eyre,* already almost finished, was sent to them in August 1847, accepted immediately and published by October. It was the book that first brought her fame as an author, but it was *The Professor,* first-fruits of the Brussels experience, that in fact inaugurated the great creative period of her maturity.

The same crucial experience is reflected in varying ways, and at different levels, in each of the three novels that followed. *Jane Eyre,* in which an astringent realism is tempered by imagination and passion, does not offer, at surface level, the same affinities with it as *The Professor.* The continental setting has receded to the background; the action takes place in the 'healthy heart of England' and the hero and heroine are English by birth. Jane Eyre is 'amazed at hearing the French language' on her introduction to her pupil at Thornfield Hall. But the appearance of Adèle has an emotional logic of its own, for it is the natural prelude to the love of Jane and Rochester. And the master of Thornfield is a Romantic with a Romantic's love of European culture and is as much at home in the capitals of Europe as in his native shire. The affinities with the Brussels experience are still more evident in *Shirley,* in spite of the fact that *Shirley* is the most Yorkshire of the novels. *Shirley* has a firmly localised setting and yet, once one enters Hollow's Cottage, one is almost on Belgian soil. Both heroes are half Belgian, and French has an important, and — in the case of Shirley, at least — a formative rôle in the education of the heroines.

After *Shirley,* it was at last possible for Charlotte Brontë to choose Brussels again for the stage of a novel. The miracle of artistic transposition was now complete, and Brussels had become 'Villette'. In *Villette* memories of Brussels are blended with themes that had haunted her since childhood, as well as with more recent memories, to form a perfect symphony. *Villette* is not perhaps her best-loved work, but it is her masterpiece, in which Angria and Brussels are fused in a poetic realism that attains the serenity of truth.

# 4 Foreign settings in the novels

When Charlotte Brontë began to write *The Professor,* it was with the conscious intention of eschewing romance and restraining imagination: '. . . In many a crude effort, destroyed almost as soon as composed, I had got over any such taste as I might once have had for ornamented and redundant composition, and come to prefer what was plain and homely.'[1] It is evident that M. Heger's criticism must have strengthened her resolve to guard against the over-indulgence of the imagination, but it was no part of his aim to inculcate an extreme or arid form of realism; it was not in an endeavour to make her prefer 'what was plain and homely' that he offered her Chateaubriand and the French Romantics as working models. Her insistence on the need for truth to life in the Preface to *The Professor* derives both from her renunciation of Angria and from the lessons of Brussels, but her emphasis on its essentially prosaic quality comes from neither of these; it is the result of the bleak period which followed, with its bitter self-accusation succeeding self-delusion.

While still in Brussels she had jotted down, in May 1843, a 'scheme of a magazine tale', giving details for the actual plot of a novel.[2] In this the 'country' is given as 'England', but the 'occurrences' include 'going abroad and returning', though only in the closing stages of the action. Back in Haworth, Charlotte Brontë felt impelled to stage the principal part of the action of her novel in Belgium, though it begins and ends in England.

The setting is seen entirely through the eyes of the Englishman William Crimsworth, for the story is a first person narration. Crimsworth is a keen observer, with a strong visual memory, for whom the past crystallises in pictorial form: 'Three — nay, four — pictures line the four-walled cell where are stored for me the records of the past.' The first is Eton, the second the manufacturing town of X—, the third Belgium and the fourth a scene which he does not name with the others, but which proves to be his final home in England.

The reference to the four pictures as though they were of equal importance is misleading, for it is the Belgian scene which is described most frequently. The fact that Crimsworth can allude to them in this way betrays the chief structural weakness of the novel, for the space given to the initial period in England is out of proportion to its real significance. Not much description is included in this part of the narration. But from the moment when he sets foot on Belgian soil, Crimsworth's descriptions acquire a more emotive tone:

> . . . Belgium . . . I will pause before this landscape . . . Belgium! name unromantic and unpoetic, yet name that whenever uttered has in my ear a sound, in my heart an echo, such as no other assemblage of syllables, however sweet or classic, can produce. Belgium! I repeat the word, now as I sit alone near midnight. It stirs my world of the past like a summons to resurrection . . . (ch. 7)

The first sight of the Flanders plain is evoked with a fidelity to fact which is similarly tempered with feeling. Flat and dull as it might appear to some, it was neither to the young traveller whose 'sense of enjoyment possessed an edge whetted to the finest, untouched, keen, exquisite'. Perhaps Charlotte Brontë even found a challenge in the absence of conventional romantic attributes. She had looked at Flemish painting in the museums of Brussels and she knew what charm an artist's eye could find in the Low Country scene. Above all, this landscape was 'different', was 'foreign' and therefore stimulating. She paints it in phrases as deliberately lacking in colour and subdued in movement as the features she describes:

> . . . what did I see? I will tell you faithfully. Green, reedy swamps; fields fertile but flat, cultivated in patches that made them look like magnified kitchen-gardens; belts of cut trees, formal as pollard willows, skirting the horizon;

narrow canals, gliding slow by the road-side; painted Flemish farm-houses; some very dirty hovels; a grey, dead sky; wet roads, wet fields, wet house-tops; not a beautiful, scarcely a picturesque object met my eye along the whole route; yet to me, all was beautiful, all was more than picturesque . . . (ch.7)

Crimsworth's arrival in Brussels is less dramatic than Lucy Snowe's in Villette. He spends the night at an hotel and next morning surveys his surroundings with the same enjoyment of their novelty he had felt when looking at the countryside. Charlotte Brontë's first description of a Belgian interior rivals her first Belgian landscape. The painting of the Low Country masters was consciously in her mind as she evoked the sense of space, the reflection of the light in mirrors and polished floors, the strong, clear colours:

> . . . such a fine mirror glittered over the mantelpiece — the painted floor looked so clean and glossy; when I had dressed and was descending the stairs, the broad marble steps almost awed me . . . On the first landing I met a Flemish housemaid: she had wooden shoes, a short red petticoat, a printed cotton bedgown . . . if she was not pretty or polite, she was, I conceived, very picturesque; she reminded me of the female figures in certain Dutch paintings I had seen in other years at Seacombe Hall. (ch.7)

Crimsworth's first impressions of Brussels itself are equally favourable. It is the aristocratic quarter of the 'Haute-Ville' with which he first makes acquaintance: 'I saw what a fine street was the Rue Royale . . .' As he approaches the entrance to the park, he pauses to look at the statue of General Belliard and is drawn instinctively to gaze down the steps beyond at what was to be the focal point of Brussels for him, as it had been for Charlotte Brontë:

> . . . I looked down into a narrow back street, which I afterwards learnt was called the Rue d'Isabelle. I well recollect that my eye rested on the green door of a rather large house opposite, where, on a brass plate, was inscribed 'Pensionnat de Demoiselles.' (ch.7)

The fact that the actual name of the street is given, and the exact location of the pensionnat, shows that the writer is not attempting to transpose the scene but to describe it. Had Charlotte Brontë wished to make it more romantic, the material was at hand. Mrs Gaskell later evoked the historic past of the Rue d'Isabelle,[3] and there still remained traces of former days, such as the gateway to the pensionnat garden, built by the Infanta Isabella to give entrance from the new road to the archery ground. But no such colourful associations soften the austerity of Crimsworth's description. On the contrary, its actual situation is located with precision. The 'narrow back street' was only a short distance from the most fashionable part of Brussels. The contrast between the animation of the higher quarter of the city and the almost provincial quietness of the street was felt more keenly by Lucy Snowe in *Villette* than by Crimsworth, but his description of the pensionnat brings out this contrast sharply because of the visual angle from which the building is first seen.

Charlotte Brontë shows equal precision in describing the complex of classrooms, playground and garden that lie behind the still facade. The description is not as detailed as in *Villette,* but in both cases is modelled on the pensionnat Heger.[4] Behind the frontage on the street was a considerable area, once part of the archery ground. To the right a quadrangular playground was enclosed on three sides by the school buildings, the fourth side — at right angles to the street — being formed by a glass-covered 'galerie' which divided the playground from the garden on the left. The classrooms were on the side of the quadrangle furthest from the street. The Hegers' own house fronted the Rue d'Isabelle and was connected with the school buildings by a corridor and a large square hall, the 'carré'. At the back their house overlooked the long rectangle of the garden, bounded on the opposite side by a parapet wall separating it from the playground and buildings of the adjacent boys' Athénée, and at the far end by the back of a boarding-house of the Athénée in the adjacent Rue Terarken.

When Crimsworth becomes visiting English master at the 'pensionnat de demoiselles' adjoining the school owned by M.

Pelet where he has secured a post, he is particularly attracted
by the garden, which forms a pleasant contrast to the 'bare
gravelled court' of the boys' school. He is introduced to it by
slow degrees, and each successive picture adds further authentic touches to this evocation of the old garden in the Rue
d'Isabelle. The first sketch fixes its essential features:

> It was a long, not very broad strip of cultured ground, with
> an alley bordered by enormous old fruit trees down the
> middle; there was a sort of lawn, a parterre of rose-trees,
> some flower-borders, and on the far side, a thickly-planted
> copse of lilacs, laburnums, and acacias. (ch.9)

On a bright May afternoon it is an even pleasanter place, for
then the fruit trees that border the central alley — those
famous pear trees whose fame spread beyond the borders of
Belgium[5] — are in flower. But the same night, when
Crimsworth looks down on it from his window in the
adjacent building,[6] it has a more subtle charm:

> . . . Splendid moonlight subdued the tremulous sparkle of
> the stars — below lay the garden, varied with silvery lustre
> and deep shade, and all fresh with dew — a grateful
> perfume exhaled from the closed blossoms of the fruit-
> trees — not a leaf stirred, the night was breeze-
> less . . . (ch.12)

Distant music contributes to the harmony of the whole, the
notes of 'a bulge very skilfully played, in the neighbourhood
of the park . . . or on the Place Royale'. The chief attraction
of the garden, however, lies in its situation, so near the
teeming life of the city, yet sheltered and tranquil between
its walls. The most sheltered part of all is the 'allée défendue',
the walk beneath the parapet wall, forbidden to the pupils on
account of its proximity to the adjacent boys' school, where
the lilacs and laburnums grow thickest.

There is no question of the accuracy of these descriptions.
Even a detail so perfectly in keeping with the context as the
distant music heard in the moonlit garden had its source in a
remembered incident.[7] Such realism is not photographic, it is
consciously selective and not incompatible with a certain

poetic quality, as in the sensitive nocturne. But Charlotte Brontë deliberately shatters this latent poetry by associating the garden in *The Professor* with treachery and disillusion. It belongs to the young directress of the pensionnat, Mlle Reuter, and it is in his dawning attraction to her which is the real secret of its charm for Crimsworth. It is of her he is thinking as he sits at his window in the moonlight — and overhears her conservation with Pelet which shows him that his romance was founded on illusion. The garden proves to be the setting not of first love but of youth's first disillusionment.

It is in the more prosaic milieu of the schoolroom that Crimsworth's real and durable love has its inception. But this monochrome décor, uninteresting in itself, has considerable possibilities as a stage. The great folding-doors which lead to the classrooms give prominence to the entrances and exits of the principal actors. The teacher's chair and desk are set on an 'estrade' of one step high, and from this vantage point he commands the scene. He observes the first timid entry of Frances Henri and the embarrassment with which she sits down in a vacant seat at the desk nearest the door.[8] Later it is from the eminence of the estrade that he reads in public one of Frances' *devoirs,* and in doing so puts the finishing touch to the jealousy with which the directress now regards her.

There is evidently no possibility of Crimsworth's dawning love for Frances finding fulfilment in the Rue d'Isabelle. Mlle Reuter soon finds a pretext stopping her from giving sewing lessons at the school and disclaims any knowledge of her address. As a result he resigns his post at the pensionnat, determined to find his 'best pupil' again and prepared to seek her through Brussels.

His search takes him beyond the confines of the Rue d'Isabelle and his enumeration of the places he visited shows his increased acquaintance with the topography of Brussels:

> I sought her . . . on the Boulevards, in the Allée Verte, in the Park; I sought her in Ste Gudule and St Jacques; I sought her in the two Protestant chapels . . . (ch.19)

The list of places obviously corresponds to those Charlotte Brontë herself visited in her free time in Brussels, on

Thursday half-holidays or on Sundays. The boulevards which marked the boundary line of old Brussels were then of relatively recent construction.[9] To follow them constituted in fact a tour of the city. But, within this circumference, the area of Crimsworth's search rapidly narrows to the upper part of Brussels, not far from the pensionnat itself. The towers of Ste Gudule, whose deep bell he had often heard tolling the hours, could be seen from the Rue d'Isabelle, and the neo-classic church of St Jacques sur Coudenberg was on the nearby Place Royale. Neither of these was, of course, attended by Charlotte Brontë, but she was certainly well acquainted with 'the two Protestant chapels', St George's Chapel and the Chapel Royal in the Rue du Musée, not far from the Pensionnat, to which she often went.[10] It is therefore only a circumscribed part of Brussels that concerns Crimsworth, even now, and he merely lists the places he visited, without attempting to describe them. The limitations of this view of Brussels are symptomatic of the limitations of the novel itself. They contrast with the far wider view of the city in *Villette*, where Lucy Snowe visits theatre, art gallery and concert hall, sees the park in carnival guise and even penetrates on occasion into the 'old and grim Basse-Ville'.

On the fourth Sunday of his apparently fruitless quest Crimsworth is at last impelled to wander further afield. Having passed the city boundary at the Porte de Louvain, he climbs the hill beyond and finds himself, as once before, surveying the fertile Low Country landscape. But what before seemed picturesque now appears desolate: '. . . No inhabitant of Brussels need wander far to seek for solitude . . . he will find her brooding still and blank over the wide fields, so drear though so fertile, spread out treeless and trackless round the capital of Brabant . . .' (ch.19). The sky is livid with the colours of an approaching thunderstorm which harmonises with his own sombre mood. Leaving the high road, he follows a path which leads to a white wall enclosing what he first takes for a plantation of trees. But these are not the pollarded trees of the earlier landscape but yew and cypress, for the heart of this landscape is a graveyard: there could hardly be a clearer indication of the limitations of the reality which Charlotte Brontë evokes in *The Professor*.

It is significant that the graveyard itself is described in terms more poetic than any yet used: '. . . Under the trees of this cemetery nestled a warm breathless gloom, out of which the cypresses stood up straight and mute, above which the willows hung low and still . . .' But his funereal setting proves to be the place where Crimsworth at last finds Frances, come to visit a newly made grave. Charlotte Brontë had melancholy cause to know 'the Protestant Cemetery outside the gate of Louvain,' for it was here that Martha Taylor was buried. She and Emily had come with Mary Taylor to visit the grave a few weeks after Martha's death, and in the dreary August of the following year her solitary walks had included 'a pilgrimage to the cemetery'.[11] Even if nothing remains of the scene she described, the brooding landscape and the stillness of the graveyard live on, as surely as on any painter's canvas, in the central scene of *The Professor*.

The most sombre landscape painting in the novel is followed by the most delicate genre painting: the interior of Frances' home in the Rue Notre Dame aux Neiges. Charlotte Brontë showed her usual topographical precision in lodging her heroine in this old street, 'not far from the Rue de Louvain' and near enough for Frances and Crimsworth to reach it on their hurried return to the city, before the thunderstorm breaks at last.[12] On a miniature scale Frances' modest rooms have the same qualities which characterised the earlier Belgian interiors: brightness, cleanliness, meticulous order. The sense of comfort is completed by the fire she lights on the hearth, whose glow is reflected, once the storm is over, by the reviving brilliance of the summer sky outside.

The clearing away of the thunder-clouds is symbolic of the beginning of a happier era for Crimsworth. From this stage on the Brussels scene becomes simply a backcloth to the happiness of the lovers who, after their marriage, settle in a small house in a faubourg which is a pale copy of the charming little apartment in the Rue Notre Dame aux Neiges. Ten years of teaching on the part of both — for Frances soon starts a pensionnat of her own — make them financially independent (not the least of the indications that romanticism still survives in *The Professor*), and they then decide to leave the Belgian capital and settle in England. Crimsworth has begun to long for his native country and for Frances this is the realisation of the 'dream of her lifetime'. The story ends where it began, in Crimsworth's native shire.

The weaknesses of *The Professor* spring from the same source as its strength; Charlotte Brontë had found the right material for her genius to work on, but at great cost. She was still too emotionally involved to transmute the whole of the Brussels experience into art. When she said she wanted to avoid 'over-bright colouring' and produce something which should be 'soft, grave and true',[13] she defined the sort of subdued colouring which is characteristic of the work in general. She put into *The Professor* all of Brussels which she could, at that time, endure to resuscitate. In choosing the scene of her next novel she returned, like Crimsworth, to the surroundings of her childhood and youth. It is only in imagination that Jane Eyre, like the young Brontës, can travel to foreign countries. But when the master of Thornfield speaks to her of his stormy past, the unknown world beyond her limited horizon comes momentarily to life. The disaster of his youth had an exotic background and he gives her a graphic description of the hurricane during which his decision to leave the West Indies was taken. His allusions to the Parisian background of his intrigue with Céline Varens are less convincing. After the authenticity of the Belgian descriptions, their artificiality is only too obvious. Something more was needed than references to the Parisian Opera house or a duel in the Bois de Boulogne to give them substance. Had Charlotte Brontë realised her wish to go to Paris, these passing references would have had a more authentic ring.

The action of her following novel *Shirley* takes place entirely in Yorkshire but its two heroes, the mill-owner Robert Moore and his brother, are Belgian on their mother's side, and their sister Hortense does her best to perpetuate the atmosphere of their native country in the cottage beside the mill. 'She did not choose to adopt English fashions because she was obliged to live in England; she adhered to her old Belgian modes, quite satisfied that there was a merit in so doing.' Belgian costume, housekeeping and cooking all combine to give a foreign air to Hollow's Cottage, which seems almost like a minute enclave of Belgium on English soil, just as later in *Villette* the manor house of La Terrasse recalls to Lucy Snowe her childhood in Bretton.

It was not till 1851 that Charlotte Brontë finally decided on the subject of her next work. Ever since the publication of *Jane Eyre* she had been attracted by the idea of recasting the still unpublished *Professor*, but her publishers were not in favour of this project and she finally decided to make Brussels the scene of a new novel. *Villette* was begun in 1851 and finished in 1853. The novel marks 'the end of the road back from Brussels'.[14] As the title implies, the foreign setting is necessary to the development of the theme, but the transposition from actuality to art is total. *Villette* is situated on another plane from Brussels. Charlotte Brontë can now allow her creative imagination freer play with the material supplied by memory, without fear of its being overwhelmed by the emotions thus released, and the result is something at once more original and more profoundly true than the muted realism of *The Professor*.

As in *The Professor,* the action begins in England, but instead of constituting as before an over-long introduction this section is the necessary prelude to Lucy Snowe's experience in *Villette*. The 'clean and ancient town of Bretton' where she stays as a child seems the epitome of a pleasant English provincial town and emphasises her English background. It is with no fixed intention of leaving England that she later decides to grant herself the brief respite of a holiday in London. Yet in little more than twenty-four hours after her arrival, the decision to try her fortune on the Continent has been taken. The nearer view of the capital acts in fact like a catalyst on her nature, and the decision to go to the continent is taken in the state of heightened vitality induced by the excitement of the London scene.

The account of Lucy's visit to London is immediately followed by that of the Channel crossing. No mention was made of this in *The Professor*. By making it a major episode in *Villette*, Charlotte Brontë accentuates the significance of this venture into the unknown. For the description of Lucy's midnight arrival on the Ostend packet she utilised the memory of her own experience on her second journey to Brussels. As the waterman rows Lucy out from the wharf to the ship, she thinks of 'the Styx, and of Charon rowing some solitary soul to the Land of Shades'. The sombre image is consonant with the impression given by the whole episode of some mysterious destiny that carries the heroine along, almost without her own volition.

It is during the crossing that she first hears, in casual conversation with an English schoolgirl returning to her foreign school, the name of the city to which her destiny is guiding her. Ginevra simply says at first that she is going to 'chose', this being a convenient substitute for any French word she does not consider worth remembering. It has been suggested that Charlotte Brontë first intended to use 'Choseville' as her principal place name, and that the one surviving mention of it in a later chapter betrays her original intention.[15] 'Chose', however, is shortly found to stand for 'Villette — the great capital of the great kingdom of Labassecour'. 'Labassecour' is the reverse of flattering: it pinpoints the satire implicit in previous references in *The Professor* to landscapes with fields 'like magnified kitchen-gardens', and the use of the diminutive for the capital city is ironical.[16] Yet the use of the diminutive in itself can imply a degree of affection, and irony and affection are not always incompatible. The substitution of fictional for real place names is consistently carried out henceforward. Lucy lands at Boue Marine, spends the night at an hotel and travels next morning to Villette, acting on Ginevra Fanshawe's casual suggestion that she might find employment at the school where she is a boarder.

The route is the same as that followed by Crimsworth, the time of year is the same — early Spring — and she, too, sees, under the same grey skies, pollarded trees, fields tilled like kitchen-garden beds and sluggish canals. In her case, too, the novelty of the experience makes it enjoyable, but her enjoyment is of a more precarious nature, for the dangers of her situation are more menacing and the prospect of being homeless and destitute more imminent. The anxiety she tries to suppress betrays itself when she involuntarily compares the slow-flowing canals to 'half-torpid green snakes'.

Like Crimsworth, she arrives at the unknown capital in darkness and rain. Not possessing any 'speaking French' she is at first completely at a loss, but a young Englishman speaking fluent French sees her dilemma, tells her of a quiet inn where she can stay and himself acts as her guide for the first part of the way. But, when left alone, she misses the turning she should have taken and wanders on until finally destiny guides her steps to 'a rather large house' in a quiet street, which proves to be not the inn she was looking for but the school where Ginevra Fanshawe is a pupil and has advised her to seek a post.

The whole account of Lucy's bewildered progress through nocturnal Villette is as convincing as such accounts can only be when they are based on a known reality. M. H. Spielmann has claimed that her itinerary could be followed by anyone who knew Brussels at the time, including the more complicated latter portion of it when, after leaving the Place Royale, she must have come eventually to one of the two flights of steps which descended from the higher level to the Rue Terarken, which in turn would bring her into the Rue d'Isabelle.[17] But it is not the accuracy of the topography in itself that matters; it is the effect it achieves. Lucy's wanderings cover a considerable area and, by the time she halts outside the pensionnat, the long line of the boulevards, the trees of the park, the brilliance of the Rue Royale and the towering buildings of the adjacent square have become part of the total setting of *Villette* and form a counterpoise to the quiet of the secluded street. Lucy's arrival in Villette sets the pattern for the future action of the novel, which makes periodical and widening incursions into the world beyond the walls of the school, while always returning, until the closing pages, to the pensionnat as its centre.

The pensionnat itself is a far more varied and colourful milieu than in *The Professor*. Like Crimsworth, Lucy first makes acquaintance with the clean and glittering but chilly salon, but, as nursery governess to the children of the directress, she becomes, unlike him, an inmate of the dwelling-house and, as a result, there is from the first a certain warmth and colour at the heart of the foreign scene. From the 'watch-tower of the nursery' Lucy soon forms a general idea of the 'little world of the Rue Fossette'. The choice of name contains an oblique reference to the historic site of the actual Rue d'Isabelle, since in the Middle Ages the ground had been occupied by the kennels for the ducal hounds and called the 'Fossé aux Chiens'.[18] As in the case of Villette itself, the use of the diminutive implies familiarity and can be equally expressive of disparagement or affection, or possibly of both at once.

It is not long before Lucy finds herself summoned from her nursery observation post and 'compelled into closer intercourse' with this little world, for Madame Beck, who needs a new English teacher, is determined to test her suitability for the post. The schoolroom thus becomes an essential part of her life in the Rue Fossette. Unlike Crimsworth who, once he entered the unknown Eden, found it singularly drab, she is impressed by the colour and animation of the new milieu: 'here . . . was a foreign school; of which the life, movement and variety made it a complete and most charming contrast to many English institutions of the same kind.' (ch. 8)

But in the first six months of her stay at the pensionnat — which, as in the case of Crimsworth and of the Brontës themselves, extend from early spring to high summer — the action takes place almost as much in the garden as under a roof. The different rôle the garden will have in this novel can be foreseen from the outset, for the first full description of it is prefaced by an allusion to the nun who is said to haunt it. No such legend seems to have actually attached to the Heger house in the Rue d'Isabelle, though the site, before it became an archery ground, was occupied by a hospital belonging to a monastic order,[19] and the pensionnat itself was the direct continuance of a school founded in much more recent times by an authentic nun. Probably these associations were in Charlotte's mind when she invented the legend of the nun of the Rue Fossette.[20] She made it a sombre story of medieval fanaticism: the ghost is that of a girl 'buried alive for some sin against her vow' in a vault whose position is said to be indicated by the stone slab at the foot of one of the ancient pear trees.[21]

Such an introduction of the supernatural would have been impossible in *The Professor*. Lucy herself is careful to equate the legend with 'romantic rubbish' in the same sentence in which she begins to describe the garden itself, and its remembered charms. As in *The Professor* a particular interest attaches to the shadowed 'allée defendue' on the further side of the garden. In *Villette,* however, this alley is important not only because of its strategic situation, which makes it indispensable to the working out of the plot, but because of its attraction for Lucy, who feels at home in its shelter. There is a secret harmony between the seclusion and gloom of the walk and the passivity which she deliberately cultivates, convinced that her fate is to be a 'mere looker-on at life'.

The initial period at the pensionnat culminates in the 'fête of Madame', the first of a series of set-pieces which punctuate the narrative. In it can be seen, in their full development, the assurance and the artistry with which Charlotte Brontë uses the setting of school and garden for her own purposes, contriving her effects with all the skill of the metteur en scène. As usual, the basic material is furnished by her memories of the Rue d'Isabelle. Madame Heger's fête was on the 12 August, the day of Ste Claire, and was celebrated by a school party, supper and a ball.[22] Charlotte Brontë transforms the occasion into a drama in which the whole pensionnat becomes the stage on which Lucy Snowe for the first time plays a leading rôle. She is sitting absorbed in a dream world of her own when she is dragged back to reality by M. Paul, the professor of literature, who persuades her to take a part, at a few hours' notice, in the school play, in place of a pupil who is ill. He rushes her up to the third floor attic to learn her part, then down to the kitchen for a hasty meal and finally across 'carré', court and garden, back to the classroom transformed for the occasion into a stage. Seen through the prism of the artist's imagination, the little world of the Rue Fossette offers, on this occasion, the excitement of a transformation scene: 'In the carré he stopped a moment: it was lit with large lamps; the wide doors of the classes were open, and so were the equally wide garden-doors . . . Within the long vista of the schoolrooms presented a thronging, undulating, murmuring, waving, streaming multitude, all rose, and blue, and half translucent white . . ..' (ch. 14)

The fact that the first major scene in *Villette* is concerned with a play is no accident. Though it is only 'an amateur

affair . . . a *vaudeville de pensionnat'*, it introduces a recur-
rent theme. Henceforward the concert hall, the theatre and
ultimately the carnival will intrude at intervals into Lucy's
quiet life.

The bright lights of the fête temporarily transform the
pensionnat. It is a very different place in the long vacation.
When writing of this Charlotte Brontë drew on her memories
of the second and solitary vacation she spent in Brussels. The
remembrance of it was still vivid when she wrote her last
novel: 'That vacation! Shall I ever forget it? I think not.'
When emotional depression finally produces physical col-
lapse, Lucy Snowe's feverish imaginings transform the long
deserted dormitory where she lies into a place of spectral
visions. When relief of some kind becomes imperative, she
finds herself drawn to the confessional in 'an old solemn
church' in the vicinity, as Charlotte Brontë had done during
her visit to Ste Gudule. The action, though made almost
without her conscious volition, marks another stage in her
deepening knowledge of Villette.

It is immediately followed by her first penetration into the
old 'Basse-Ville', 'full of narrow streets of picturesque,
ancient and mouldering houses'. She does not make this
incursion voluntarily but in the weakness of semi-delirium.
There is a parallel between this crisis and the evening of her
arrival in Villette; once again she is driven out of her course
into unknown surroundings, but now the tension is heightened, for the elements themselves combine against her. In
her exhausted state she cannot resist the gale that is blowing
and falls in a faint while attempting to reach the porch of 'a
great building near', later identified as 'an old church belonging to a community of Béguines' and probably suggested
by the great church of St Jean Baptiste au Béguinage.[23] This
introduction to the medieval quarter of Villette sets the tone
for its subsequent treatment: it is always to be associated, for
Lucy Snowe, with the dark and non-rational side of existence.

On recovering from her faint, Lucy is astonished to find
herself apparently back in England, for she is surrounded by
the furniture familiar to her from her godmother's house in
Bretton. The Brettons are in fact now living in Belgium and

Graham Bretton — the 'Dr John' of the pensionnat, whom Lucy had recognised some time ago — has brought her to his home after his attention had been called to her plight, when he was riding through the Basse-Ville, by the priest who had heard her confession. The Brettons have rented a small château outside Villette, 'about half a league without the Porte de Crécy'. It is probable that, like most other places in the novel, it was suggested in part by a remembered model. It has been thought that the location of the original must have been near the Chaussée de Waterloo.[24] More recently, however, the manor farm of Carefeld, beyond the Porte de Flandre, has been suggested as the original of La Terrasse.[25] But Charlotte Brontë is as usual concerned not with topographical details in themselves but with the use she can make of them. The situation of 'La Terrasse' exactly suits her purpose, for it recalls an English country house with its turfed walk in front and its avenue of beeches. Inside, no detail is neglected which can suggest the English ideal of comfort. Carpeted floors replace polished ones; there are damask curtains and worked covers; above all, there is a 'wood fire on a clear-shining hearth' instead of a porcelain stove.

In describing Lucy's stay at La Terrasse, Charlotte Brontë did not draw entirely on her memories of Belgium. It is well known that the prototypes of the Brettons were her London publisher Geroge Smith and his mother. It was thanks to their genial hospitality that she had been able to make some contact with the social and artistic life of the capital. The relationship between Dr Bretton and Lucy is that between physician and convalescent, not between publisher and author, but his rôle in introducing her to the sights and intellectual riches of a capital city are reminiscent of George Smith's entertainment of his guest: 'Under his guidance I saw, in that one happy fortnight, more of Villette, its environs, and its inhabitants, than I had seen in the whole eight months of my previous residence.'

It is the artistic treasures of the city that make the greatest appeal to Lucy Snowe. When she finds the door of 'every hall sacred to art or science' unexpectedly open to her, the picture galleries draw her like a magnet. She is happy 'not always in admiring, but in examining, questioning, and forming conclusions'. The material offered for her eager scrutiny is the same that Charlotte Brontë had found in the Brussels Salon of 1842, visited during her first long vacation in Belgium. The picture which 'seemed to consider itself the queen of the collection' and forced itself on Lucy's attention by its 'portentous size' is known to have been suggested by the painting 'Une Almée' by the artist De Biefve.[26] In Lucy Snowe's account the Egyptian dancing girl is metamorphosed into 'Cleopatra', but her increased status only emphasises the defects her critic sees in the picture. Contemporary critics had found in it more of the indolence of the harem than of the grace of the dancing girl.[27] Lucy emphasises the lethargy of the 'gipsy-queen' and does her best to disparage the opulent beauty by dwelling on her size and estimated weight. Her irony at the expense of 'The Cleopatra' is at the same time a protest against the sensuality which she recognises in Flemish painting and instinctively resists. She was equally critical of the same quality in the work of the masters, as a later reference to Rubens and 'all the army of his fat women' shows. At the opposite extreme to the voluptuous beauty of the Cleopatra is the series of four paintings called 'La Vie d'une Femme'. The Brussels Salon of 1842 included a canvas of the same name, divided into three compartments, by Mme Fanny Geefs.[28] Lucy dislikes the 'flat, dead, pale and formal style' of these paintings and stigmatises the central figures of the series as bloodless, brainless nonentities 'as bad in their way as the indolent gipsy-giantess, the Cleopatra, in hers'. Taken in conjunction, the Cleopatra and 'La Vie d'une Femme' represent two extremes which she finds equally uncongenial in the milieu of *Villette*.

But placed unobtrusively underneath the 'coarse and preposterous canvas' which is supposed to be 'the queen of the collection', are other, smaller paintings of a kind which was also represented in the Salon of 1842.[29] These are little pictures of still life, a genre which Charlotte Brontë had admired as a child through the medium of some of Bewick's vignettes. Lucy Snowe recognised with delight how Flemish realism could produce in the same genre small masterpieces of truth and beauty:

I . . . betook myself for refreshment to the contemplation
of some exquisite little pictures of still life: wild-flowers,
wild-fruit, mossy woodnests, casketing eggs that looked
like pearls seen through clear green sea-water . . . (ch. 19)

The visit to the picture gallery is a solitary pleasure, but
the period at La Terrasse includes an evening at the concert
hall, which brings Lucy into contact with an as yet unknown
Villette. As she drives with the Brettons along the brightly lit
streets, their lively conversation adds to the pleasure of the
occasion. Charlotte Brontë herself had visited opera and
theatre with George Smith and his mother, during her visits
to them in London, and the memory of their congenial
company has overflowed into the account of Lucy's drive
from La Terrasse into Villette. But her description of the
concert itself was suggested by one she attended while in
Belgium. On 10 December 1843 a concert, followed by a
lottery in benefit of a charity, was given in Brussels by the
Société de la Grande Harmonie, in the presence of the King
and Queen of the Belgians and their eldest child, the Duke of
Brabant. That it was the only such concert exactly corresponding to the main features of Charlotte Brontë's description, during her two sojourns in Brussels, was shown by
Professor Charlier,[30] and the researches of Winifred Gérin
have established the identity of the performance of the 10
December 1843 with Lucy Snowe's account, not only in
outline but often in detail.[31] As usual in *Villette,* there is no
question of photographic realism: out of her memories of a
Brussels concert hall the artist has constructed a scene which
transfuses reality with the remembered magic of her childhood dreams.

The concert hall itself is a dazzling sight. The actual Salle
de la Grande Harmonie, built by the architect Cluysenaar and
only opened a few months before,[32] helped no doubt to
suggest the description which is unusually rich in structural
details. The general effect of the 'sweeping circular walls and
domed hollow ceiling' and of their prevalent dead gold
colouring, relieved by cornicing, fluting and garlandry of
mingled gold and white, is to recall the blend of architectural
realism and exotic beauty in the palaces of Angria. The great
chandelier 'sparkling with facets, streaming with drops,

ablaze with stars . . .' reminds Lucy Snowe irresistibly of the supernatural creations of 'eastern genii'.

The resplendent building is filled with an audience as vast as those which filled the theatres of Angria. As in Angria, there are handsome women in the assembly. The character of their beauty, however, makes it clear that this is, after all, no Angrian dream world. Charlotte Brontë, who had shown how successfully she could paint Low Country landscapes and interiors, is equally successful in her portraiture of a physical type made familiar by Flemish and Dutch painters:

> Some fine forms there were here and there, models of a peculiar style of beauty; a style, I think, never seen in England; a solid firm-set, sculptural style. These shapes have no angles: a caryatid in marble is almost as flexible; a Phidian goddess is not more perfect in a certain still and stately sort. They have such features as the Dutch painters give to their madonnas: Low-country classic features, regular but round, straight but stolid; and for their depth of expressionless calm, of passionless peace, a polar snow-field could alone offer a type. Women of this order need no ornament, and they seldom wear any; the smooth hair, closely braided, supplies a sufficient contrast to the smoother cheek and brow; the dress cannot be too simple; the rounded arm and perfect neck require neither bracelet nor chain. (ch. 20).

The focal point of the hall is the compartment waiting to be occupied by the royal party. Lucy experiences a vague sense of surprise on her first sight of the royal couple: 'Looking out for a king and queen, and seeing only a midle-aged soldier and a rather young lady, I felt half cheated, half pleased.' It is in keeping with the homeliness implied in the name of Labassecour that its royal family should not seem unduly majestic, but the melancholy king and his 'mild, thoughtful, graceful' queen certainly show no trace of the stolidity Lucy so persistently associated with their subjects. In this brief sketch for which the models were Leopold, formerly Prince of Saxe Coburg and husband of the Princess Charlotte, and Louise d'Orléans, his second wife, Charlotte Brontë conveys an impression of latent tragedy out

of tune with the festive evening but all too readily compre-
hensible to Lucy Snowe.

An interval of only a few weeks separates the evening at
the concert from the next major set piece in *Villette,* Lucy's
visit to the theatre in company with Graham Bretton. In
Angrian days Charlotte Brontë had imagined Mrs Siddons on
the stage of the Theatre Royal in Verdopolis.[33] The theatre
episode in *Villette* is based on memories of great acting she
had herself witnessed. The prototype of the actress Vashti
was Rachel. She had played at the Théâtre de la Monnaie in
Brussels in the summer of 1842, and it has been suggested
that Charlotte was present at one of these performances,[34]
but it was not till her London visit to the Smiths in 1851 that
she actually saw Rachel act.[35] The playing of Rachel in the
name part in Scribe's *Adrienne Lecouvreur* and, above all, as
Camille in Corneille's *Les Horaces* was one of the great
experiences of her visit. As usual, she had used the material
supplied by memory for her own artistic purposes. It is the
rôle of Vashti alone on which she concentrates, for it is a
manifestation of the quality which, as an artist, she so deeply
revered; she wrote of Rachel 'the great gift of genius, she
undoubtedly has',[36] and Lucy says of Vashti 'the strong
magnetism of genius drew my heart out of its wonted
orbit . . .' Her genial inspiration is, however, terrifying in its
intensity. Charlotte said that Rachel's acting 'transfixed me
with wonder, enchained me with interest, and thrilled me
with horror'.[37] Lucy is conscious of the demonic character of
Vashti's acting, which she does not hesitate to qualify as
demoniac. The actress seems to her passion incarnate, and
passion at its most destructive. Yet her genius impresses also
by an inherent dignity: '. . . she stood locked in struggle, rigid
in resistance. She stood, not dressed, but draped in pale
antique folds, long and regular like sculpture.' (ch. 25). The
description fits not only Vashti but the type of rôle she is
playing; it is a rôle in a classical tragedy. On the stage of a
continental capital there could be no more fitting choice, but
it is significant of her growing adaptation to her new
environment that Lucy Snowe can appreciate it as she does.
When as a child Charlotte Brontë had imagined a play on a
Parisian stage, she had visualised a melodrama. Vashti's acting

belongs to another dimension: '. . . Even in the uttermost frenzy of energy is each mænad movement royally, imperially, incedingly upborne.'

The theatrical performance is abruptly terminated by what turns out to be an unnecessary alarm: a spark falling on some drapery causes a blaze which is extinguished at once. The momentary conflagration, followed by extinction, marks the end of Lucy's brief period of happiness in the society of Graham Bretton, and the beginning of his interest in Paulina de Bassompierre, to whose help he is called in the panic following the false alarm. The Bassompierres live in the aristocratic Haute-Ville. The model for their flat in the Rue Crécy is thought to have been the apartment of Charlotte Brontë's friends the Wheelwrights in the Hotel Cluysenaar in the Rue Royale.[38] Henceforward Lucy Snowe is a welcome visitor in the Hotel Crécy as well as at the little château of La Terrasse. But from this time on her true life centres in the Rue Fossette, though she is no longer ignorant of the wider world beyond its boundaries.

With her dawning love for M. Paul, the emotional tempo of her reaction to her environment is heightened. Lights become brighter, and shadows blacker, in her painting of the pensionnat. The change had already begun with her frustrated love for Graham Bretton, and it was at this stage that the suggestion of a supernatural element had first been introduced. It had been while reading his letters in the gloom of the third storey attic that she had first seen the figure of the nun supposed to haunt the Rue Fossette. It is when burying his letters in the garden, in the pale moonlight of a frosty evening, that she sees the nun again. The nun next appears in the garden on a wet and windy Spring evening, but this time Lucy has a companion in M. Paul and, sure of his sympathy, no longer feels the same dread of the supernatural. The garden is becoming, as it never did in *The Professor,* a favoured spot where happiness is possible.

It is when Lucy makes an excursion to 'the old and grim Basse-Ville' that the scene again darkens. She does so not on her own initiative but at the instigation of Madame Beck. It is in keeping with the character of this episode that the situation of the 'Rue des Mages' cannot be located like that of the Rue Fossette, though it may no doubt be considered, in a general way, as being in the same locality as the church of the Béguinage.[39] It is primarily an atmosphere Charlotte Brontë wishes to suggest — an atmosphere of superstitious fear: 'Well might this old square be named the quarter of the Magi — well might the three towers, overlooking it, own for godfathers three mystic sages of a dead and dark art.' (ch. 34) There is an affinity between the atmosphere of 'numéro 3, Rue des Mages' and the apparitions of the nun in the Rue Fossette. Lucy has been brought to the old house to hear from Père Silas, whose home it is, that his former pupil M. Paul can never marry because he is for ever committed to the worship of his lost love, who became a nun, and to the support of her aged grandmother. The setting of the Basse-Ville becomes a symbol of superstitious bondage to the past, made all the more sinister because the scene is accompanied by the busting of a thunderstorm.

On Lucy's return to the Rue Fossette, the pensionnat becomes the battle-field on which she fights against the continued strategems of Madame Beck and Père Silas. But for the great climactic scene of the novel a wider stage is necessary. As on the night of her arrival in Villette, Lucy seems to be swept by an irresistible force to the place appointed for her next and strangest encounter with fate. But this time the force is one within herself; the opiate given her by Madame Beck to make her sleep has the contrary effect of releasing the deepest instinct of her nature, her imaginative power. Looking out at the splendour of the summer night, she has a longing to see the park, only a short distance away, and above all to see the moon mirrored in a stone basin, 'deep-set in the tree-shadows', beside which she had often stood. Stealing out of the Rue Fossette, she makes her way to the 'palatial and royal Haute-Ville' and finds herself suddenly in the midst of an excited crowd. The gateway to the park is spanned by an arch 'built of massed stars' and leads not to the solitude she had anticipated but to a 'land of enchantment'.

But this apparently unreal world is once again linked with Charlotte Brontë's memories of Brussels. She knew how the park could be transformed by pageantry and illumination on fête days. Prominent among these were the annual festivities to commemorate the Belgian Revolution of 1830. Lucy Snowe, when she recovers from her initial stupor at the sight of the crowds, remembers that this is the day when the patriots who died in the Revolution are honoured. It is possible that Charlotte Brontë herself was present at the September celebrations of 1843.[40] Winifred Gérin has shown the evidence for her presence in her park on August 15 of the same year, the feast of the Assumption.[41] From such memories she has drawn the material for her version of the fête in which Lucy becomes an involuntary participator. It takes place, however, in *Villette*, not in August or September but in July, the change of month being made necessary by the fact that the school year at the pensionnat had not yet ended at the time.[42]

The last great set-piece in *Villette* is thus based, like the previous ones, on a foundation of observed and factual reality; but like them it is also a festival of the imagination, and to an even greater degree than before. There is a strange charm in the decorations that have transformed the park into:

> ... a land of enchantment ... a plain sprinkled with coloured meteors ... a region, not of trees and shadow but of strangest architectural wealth — of altar and temple, of pyramid, obelisk and sphinx; incredible to say, the wonders and symbols of Egypt teemed throughout the park of Villette.(ch. 38)

Even if the material fabric of these constructions may only have been, as a few minutes later Lucy realises, the timber, paint and pasteboard of a popular display, her imagination has made of them something very different: they suggest solemn rites, entombed splendours and a wisdom revealed only to the initiate. What her own function is to be in this mysterious festival is suggested by her position on first entering the park, 'fathoming the deep, torch-lit perspective of an avenue, at the close of which was couched a sphinx'.

The first discovery she makes is of Villette itself, seen as she has never seen it before. All classes are represented: 'Half the peasantry had come in from the out-lying environs of

Villette, and the decent burghers were all abroad and around, dressed in their best.' It is the real Villette, but the whole effect is of a masquerade of which the masks are the least important part.

'. . . every shape was wavering, every movement floating, every voice echo-like — half-mocking, half-uncertain.' Here at last is the 'kermesse' scene which the setting of the novel demanded. The music, faintly heard in the distance, swells to a crescendo as she moves in the direction of the pool. All the joy in living, the natural sunlight, the gaiety which she had resisted in the painting of Rubens and disdained in the riotous games of the young Labassecouriennes bursts upon her with overwhelming force as she listens to the singing of a 'wild Jäger chorus' and its orchestral accompaniment:

> . . . The song, the sweet music rose afar, but rushing swiftly on fast strengthening pinions — there swept through these shades so full a storm of harmonies that, had no tree been near against which to lean, I think I must have dropped. Voices were there, it seemed to me, un-numbered; instruments varied and countless — bugle, horn and trumpet I knew. The effect was as a sea breaking into song with all its waves. (ch. 38)

But the festival which yields so much illumination denies her what she most wished, the truth about her personal drama, though the leading figures in her life are at the masquerade. Misled by jealousy, she leaves the park con-vinced that M. Paul is in love with his ward. As she moves away from 'the well-lit Haute-Ville', she notices once more the beauty of the moonlight, no longer obscured by the artificial brilliance of the fête,and sees in it the type of a higher truth than any the masquerade could yield:

> . . . The music and the mirth of the fête,the fire and bright hues of those lamps had out-done and out-shone her for an hour, but now, again, her glory and her silence triumphed. The rival lamps were dying; she held her course like a white fate . . . (ch. 39)

In the dormitory of the Rue Fossette, place of melancholy and sinister dreams, Lucy has a final encounter with illusion.

The figure of the nun is found there, apparently asleep, but proves to be no more than the costume. The frenetical violence with which Lucy shakes the puppet, and tears the habit and veil, is her reaction against all she has suffered through superstitious fears and illusory hopes. Next morning the mystery is explained in a note from Ginevra Fanshawe, who has just eloped with Count Alfred de Hamal. It was he who, hearing of the legend of the Rue Fossette, had masqueraded as a nun in order to have stolen interviews with Ginevra. The explanation effectively strips all false romance from the appearances of the nun, but it does not remove the aura of mystery which made the 'allée défendue' a place of strange apprehensions in misty moonlight or wind-swept darkness. The Gothic legend has been used by Charlotte Brontë to show that the human mind has its haunted places and that an out-dated literary convention can be transformed into a new avenue of approach to reality.[43]

In the final stage of the novel the pensionnat ceases to be the theatre of the action. M. Paul knows there will be no happiness for Lucy if she remains there, and finds a home for her in a small house in a faubourg. 'Faubourg Clotilde' has no obvious counterpart in the topography of Brussels, but its general locality is significant: on the outskirts of the city, it shares in the peace and freedom of the country. The interior of the small house has the qualities Charlotte Brontë admired in Flemish interiors: meticulous neatness, cleanliness, brightness. M. Paul's own taste speaks in the vines trained about the windows and the flower-pots each filled with 'a fine plant glowing in bloom'. The finishing touch is given to the friendly character of the little house by the pleasant intimacy of a shared meal. As often in Flemish painting, the homely realities of food and drink are part of the charm of the scene: 'Our meal was simple: the chocolate, the rolls, the plate of fresh summer fruit, cherries and strawberries bedded in green leaves formed the whole; but it was what we both liked better than a feast . . .' (ch. 41)

The house in the faubourg is, however, not only a home but a school. One of the rooms is furnished as a classroom with benches, desks, estrade. M. Paul intends that Lucy should be the directress of this miniature school during the three years of his enforced absence abroad, and hands her the prospectus in which her future residence is firmly established as 'Numéro 7, Faubourg Clotilde'. It is evident that there are general similarities between numéro 7, Faubourg Clotilde, and the house in a faubourg of Brussels where Crimsworth and Frances established themselves after their marriage. But they only remained in Belgium long enough to achieve the financial security which enabled them to give up teaching and return to England. Lucy Snowe remains in the continental capital and is content to spend her time within the four walls of the schoolroom, since this is the occupation M. Paul had chosen for her. But she lives for his return: 'The spring which moved my energies lay far away beyond seas, in an Indian isle.'

The dénouement of *Villette* does not take place within the schoolroom walls, nor even within the wider boundaries of the capital. A vaster stage is reserved for it. Whether in England or in Villette, Lucy Snowe had never lost the sense of being in communication with cosmic forces. The turning points of her life came when she was alone with a mysterious universe. It was under a sky made strange by the presence of the aurora borealis that she had taken the decision to leave the familiar scenes where her youth was stagnating. In Villette it was 'certain accidents of the weather' which proved most potent in stiring into action the latent forces of her nature. On the night when she buried her letters in the pensionnat garden, she was conscious of a quality in the misty moonlight similar to that she had sensed in the aurora borealis. It was a storm that carried her to La Terrasse, and a storm that held her prisoner in the Rue des Mages, while the dark rush of rain swept the streets of the capital, transforming 'a Villette into a Tadmor'. It is the equinoctial gales that preside at the dénouement of the novel. The storms blow round the little house in the faubourg and across the vast spaces of an unseen Atlantic. Their destructive yet triumphal course has been foretold, for eyes that can read the signs, in the purple and flame of the morning skies, and in clouds that 'cast themselves into strange forms — arches and broad radiations.'

# 5 Foreign life and characters in the novels

Charlotte Brontë's reactions to the foreign way of life and the people she met abroad were more variable than her reactions to the places and things she saw, and more complex in origin. What she actually saw she transmuted into art, thanks to the strength of her memories, with such freshness and often such precision of detail that the school and garden in the Rue d'Isabelle and certain aspects of the Brussels scene live on in her novels with all the truth of remembered reality. But when she is concerned with a culture other than her own, and people with a different racial background, her vision, though equally vivid, is more variable. The dichotomy which was evident from the start in her attitude to France is reflected in her alternations between satire and sympathy. But the subject never leaves her indifferent. Whether her interpretation is satirical to the point of caricature or charged with sympathy, it is always vibrant with life. And it was in drawing the portrait of a foreigner that she achieved her most finished masterpiece.

In considering Charlotte Brontë's sometimes conflicting responses to life on the Continent, it should be remembered that she was nearly twenty-six when she crossed the Channel for the first time. She brought with her the opinions she had imbibed, from childhood onwards, in the Tory atmosphere of Haworth parsonage. Prominent among these was the conviction of British superiority, raised to the intensity of a passion by her pride in the triumph of her hero Wellington in the Peninsula and at Waterloo. Such a conviction was not likely to go unchallenged in a continental environment. It involved her in disputes with her Belgian associates, such as the one recalled by Louise de Bassompierre, and it was with the intention of achieving a balanced political judgment that she wrote the *devoir* 'La Mort de Napoléon'. In her novels the Wellington-Napoleon conflict is a touchstone by which the political reactions of characters of differing nationalities can be judged. Frances Henri admires Wellington as much as she admires Tell, her country's hero, but in *Shirley,* where the action takes place in 1812, the success of Wellington in the Peninsula is no cause of satisfaction to the half-Belgian Robert Moore. From Moore's clash of opinion with the Tory Helstone, the two antithetical views of the European conflict emerge with uncompromising bluntness:

'Does your Peninsular news please you still?' he asked.

'What do you mean?' was the surly demand of the Rector.

'I mean have you still faith in that Baal of a Lord Wellington?' . . .

'I believe Wellington will flog Bonaparte's marshals into the sea the day it pleases him to lift his arm.'

'But, my dear sir, you can't be serious in what you say. Bonaparte's marshals are great men, who act under the guidance of an omnipotent master-spirit; your Wellington is the most humdrum of common-place martinets, whose slow mechanical movements are further cramped by an ignorant home-government.'

'Wellington is the soul of England. Wellington is the right champion of a good cause; the fit representative of a powerful, a resolute, a sensible, and an honest nation.'

'Your good cause, as far as I understand it, is simply the restoration of that filthy, feeble Ferdinand, to a throne which he disgraced; your fit representative of an honest people is a dull-witted drover, acting for a duller-witted farmer; and against these are arrayed victorious supremacy and invincible genius.'

'Against legitimacy is arrayed usurpation; against modest, single-minded, righteous and brave resistance to encroachment, is arrayed boastful, double-tongued, selfish and treacherous ambition to possess. God defend the right!' (ch. 3).

The vigour with which this verbal duel is fought is in tune with the general tone of *Shirley,* the novel where Charlotte

Brontë makes the most conscious effort to deal with political issues as well as personal ones. The fact that it is also the only novel of hers to be written in the third person ensures that both sides of the question are presented with far more cogency than is possible in a first person narration. But although Moore is eloquent in the cause of Bonaparte, his attitude is disingenuous, for it is principally as a manufacturer whose trade is threatened by the Orders in Council that he is so violently opposed to the war-party. It is for the same motive that he continues to oppose it till the repeal of the Orders in Council, but by that time he has come to admit at heart that the British troops, with such a leader, are certain to triumph in the end. In the concluding pages of *Shirley*, Napoleonic disaster and Peninsular triumph are celebrated with an epic grandeur of tone. In her youth Charlotte Brontë had wished that she had lived 'in the troubled times of the late war'[1] and she does so vicariously in these pages where Wellington is not the veteran attacked by contemporary politicians but the victorious general:

> ... we are now in the heart of summer ... the June of 1812. It is burning weather: the air is deep azure and red gold; it fits the time; it fits the age; it fits the present spirit of the nations. The nineteenth century wantons in its giant adolescence ... This summer, Bonaparte is in the saddle: he and his host scour Russian deserts ... In this year Lord Wellington assumed the reins in Spain; they made him Generalissimo, for their own salvation's sake. In this year, he took Badajos, he fought the field of Vittoria, he captured Pampeluna, he stormed St. Sebastian; in this year, he won Salamanca. (ch. 37).

The bells that ring throughout England for the victory of Salamanca seem to drown, with their authentic jubilation, the wedding bells that ring for the conventional 'happy ending' of the novel. In *Villette* the use of fictitious place names precludes direct reference to Waterloo, though the scene of the novel is so near the battlefield. But the 'Rue Crécy' recalls by its name a famous victory in an earlier epic struggle with France.

But there was another side to the struggle with France

beside the military conflict. Its origin had been the great social upheaval of the French Revolution. Napoleon began his career as Bonaparte, the general of the Republic, and had he remained a republican leader, he would have inspired a much more whole-hearted admiration in the half-Belgian Robert Moore, who qualifies his praise of him by expressing the involuntary regret that he should have forsaken the republican ideal for the imperial adventure:

> 'Oh, in Italy he was as great as any Moses! He was the right thing there; fit to head and organise measures for the regeneration of nations. It puzzles me to this day how the conqueror of Lodi should have condescended to become an emperor — a vulgar, a stupid humbug; and still more how a people, who had once called themselves republicans, should have sunk again to the grade of mere slaves. I despise France! If England had gone as far on the march of civilisation as France did, she would hardly have retreated so shamelessly.' (ch. 3).

The claim that republican France was superior to imperial France infuriates Helstone and does in fact reveal a deeper and more irreconcilable difference between the two men than their respective allegiance to Napoleon and Wellington.

Moore is not the only character in the novel with republican sympathies. The manufacturer Hiram Yorke, one of Moore's few friends, who has travelled on the Continent in his youth, before the French Revolution, has, in theory at least, a hatred of all established authority. 'Kings and nobles and priests, dynasties and parliaments and establishments . . . were to him an abomination — all rubbish.' A similar outlook and a similar acquaintance with the Continent had already been shown by the mill-owner Yorke Hunsden in *The Professor*. Hunsden describes the English as a 'lord-and-king cursed nation' and himself as a 'universal patriot'. At his home in Yorkshire he entertains guests, foreign as well as English, whose chief concern is politics. At the time of the action of *The Professor* the Napoleonic Wars belong to the past, and the focus of radical thought has shifted, in England, from anti-war propaganda to economic doctrines and abroad from Jacobinism to the liberalism and the new belief in progress which were rapidly gaining ground on the Continent. On his return to Yorkshire Crimsworth is often present at these discussions and says of the foreign visitors: '. . . they take a wider theme — European progress — the spread of liberal sentiments over the Continent; on their mental tablets, the names of Russia, Austria and the Pope, are inscribed in red ink.' In the last of the novels, *Villette*, the Belgian Revolution is referred to with scant respect as 'an awful crisis in the fate of Labassecour'. But the patriotic feeling expressed by M. Paul in his speech at the Athénée is none the less appreciated by Lucy Snowe. 'Who would have thought that the flat and fat soil of Labassecour could yield political convictions and national feelings such as were now strongly expressed?'

There can be no doubt that Charlotte Brontë herself shared the conviction of the injustice of Napoleonic aggression and the pride in Wellington's triumph felt by Helstone and by Lucy Snowe. She had shown this attitude since the early days of the Angrian cycle. The capacity to present with a degree of objectivity and even with a certain sympathy the liberal views which were in direct opposition with her own Tory principles was of more recent growth. Yet during her adolescence her friendship with Mary Taylor — whose father Joshua Taylor was the prototype of Yorke Hunsden and of Hiram Yorke — had begun to broaden her outlook by bringing her into contact with a household where radicalism and Dissent were held as sacred as Church and monarchy at Haworth Parsonage. In spite of her liking for the Taylors, Charlotte Brontë retained her Tory principles, but she was too independent in thought and speech herself not to value the same qualities in others, and she went to Belgium better prepared than appeared on the surface to broaden her political outlook, especially as she was also a reader of Byron, the most cosmopolitan of the English Romantic poets.

In Belgium she encountered the Napoleonic legend as a living force, and she also came to realise that it was possible to make a vital distinction between the general of the Republic and the emperor.[2] In the writings of the politically orientated French Romantics she found expressed the liberal ideas of contemporary France, some of them no doubt known to her already through the medium of the modern French novels, including in all probability works by George Sand, sent to her at Haworth by the Taylors.[3] On her return to England she continued in contact with ideas and events across the Channel through the intermediary of the French newspapers sent to her by Joe Taylor, which were to be a source of interest to her for the rest of her life and which, as her correspondence shows, she read with special avidity in the years immediately following her return from Brussels. The broadening influence of these contacts with European political thought is evident in the place given in the novels to the presentation of liberal and republican views. Though she distrusted theorising, and the use of violent action to remedy social evils, Charlotte Brontë could not be indifferent to aspirations for freedom or hatred of tyranny. Her own attitude is perhaps mirrored in the mingled approval and mistrust with which Crimsworth listens to the political discussions of Hunsden's foreign guests:

> I have heard some of them talk vigorous sense — yea, I have been present at polyglot discussions . . . where a singular insight was given of the sentiments entertained by resolute minds respecting old northern despotisms, and old southern superstitions; also, I have heard much twaddle, enounced chiefly in French and Deutsch, but let that pass . . . (ch. 25)

The year 1848, during which the first part of *Shirley* was written, saw a resurgence of Chartism in England and risings and revolution in Europe. The mixed feelings with which Charlotte Brontë followed the course of the February Revolution in France are clearly reflected in her correspondence. She has a condescending pity for Louis Philippe, whom she views with the notable lack of enthusiasm she shows for royal personages in general. But she is prepared to recognise that 'every struggle any nation makes in the cause of Freedom and Truth has something noble in it . . .'[4] She admires the humane legislation of the Provisional Government: 'The abolition of slavery and of the punishment of death for political offences are two glorious deeds . . .'[5] But she distrusts the theoretical bias of the government and with strong practical sense foresees what the result of this will be: '. . . how will they get over the question of the organisation of labour! Such theories will be the sandbank on which their vessel will run aground if they don't mind. Lamartine, there is not (sic) doubt, would make an excellent legislator for a nation of Lamartines — but where is that nation?'[6] Her fear of future violence is basically stronger than her hope in the new régime, and she dreads the possibility of its having an adverse effect on her own country: 'That England may be spared the spasms, cramps, and frenzy-fits now contorting the Continent and threatening Ireland, I earnestly pray!'[7] Her fear as to the consequences of revolution is closely connected with her persistent scepticism with regard to the French: 'Has Paris the materials within her for thorough reform?'[8] By the time she had begun her next novel *Villette,* the Second Republic was already doomed. There is no reference in her correspondence to the coup d'état of 2 December 1851, but she makes an unflattering reference to Louis Napoleon a few weeks later: 'As to the French President — it seems to me hard to say what a man with so little scruple and so much ambition will *not* attempt.'[9]

But politics only enter into Charlotte Brontë's novels in the proportion in which they entered into her own experience. Her chief concern as a novelist is not with wars and revolutions — which she increasingly distrusted — but with the world in which her characters live their everyday lives, a world which has been shaped by historical events but which is normally an uneventful one. The chief interest of her picture of life in Belgium lies not in its political implications but in the impact made on Crimsworth and Lucy Snowe by another culture. Their experience was necessarily restricted by the fact that their chief contacts with foreigners were limited to one milieu. Crimsworth points out to Frances Henri the limitations of what can be seen from 'the interior of a school, or at most of one or two private dwellings'. But she replies that one can learn something by analogy — 'a sample often serves to give an idea of the whole' — and Charlotte Brontë shared the same belief.

The school community indeed offered from the start an example of one salient quality of Brussels life: its cosmopolitanism. Belgium has always been a crossroads of Europe. When Crimsworth glances over the long range of desks, he sees 'French, English, Belgians, Austrians and Prussians'. Lucy Snowe realises that a possibility of increased experience is offered her by the variety of nationality among her pupils: 'Experience of a certain kind lay before me, on no narrow scale. Villette is a cosmopolitan city, and in this school were girls of every European nation...' (ch. 9).

In another respect also the school community was a microcosm of the society of Belgium as a whole. Crimsworth noticed that though the majority of his pupils belonged to the 'class bourgeois', girls of a very different social rank were to be found sitting side by side in the same classroom. Lucy Snowe observes this also, and makes a deduction of general significance: 'Equality is much practised in Labassecour; though not republican in form, it is nearly so in substance...'

The general picture of Belgian life given by Charlotte Brontë is not a flattering one. Her insular sense of superiority helps to account for the condescending tone in which she most often speaks of 'Labassecour'. It has been pointed out that she is not alone in this, and that Thackeray, writing of Brussels at the time of her visit there, thought the capital city had 'an absurd kind of Lilliput look with it.'[10] Her personal unhappiness during much of her stay at the pensionnat Heger also had a strong influence on her painting of life in Belgium. The colours are noticeably darker and the outlines harsher in the earlier novel. Lucy Snowe is clearly not intended to be considered always as a reliable narrator, and the fact contributes to soften the edge of some of her indictments. By this time Charlotte Brontë was not unaware of the dangers of insularity. She had written in the year in which *The Professor* was completed: 'I suspect...that there are not unfrequently substantial reasons underlaid for customs that appear to us absurd — and if I were ever again to find myself among strangers — I should be solicitous to examine before I condemned.'[11] Her prejudices were sometimes too strong for her, and her judgment could be emotively biased, but there is truth as well as caricature in her portrayal of Belgian life.

For one aspect of it at least she has nothing but praise. When he wishes to marry Frances, Crimsworth reflects that he could afford to do so in Brussels on his modest teacher's salary, because of the simple standard of living, untroubled by the need to 'keep up a certain appearance' which would make the same income inadequate in England:

> Two persons whose desires are moderate may live well enough in Brussels on an income which would scarcely afford a respectable maintenance for one in London . . . I have seen a degree of sense in the modest arrangement of one homely Belgian household, that might put to shame the elegance, the superfluities, the luxuries, the strained refinements of a hundred genteel English mansions. In Belgium, provided you can make money, you may save it; this is scarcely possible in England; ostentation there lavishes in a month what industry has earned in a year . . . (ch. 21)

Simple standards of living would not have satisfied Charlotte Brontë if they had not been combined with high standards of cleanliness, neatness and order. These too she found in the Belgian interior. She introduces these qualities into her descriptions with success, but perhaps she did not value them enough as evidences of industry, discipline and even of a taste for formal perfection not dissimilar in origin from the skill that created the 'scores of marvellously-finished little Flemish pictures' seen by Lucy Snowe in the picture gallery.

There is one accomplishment in which Charlotte Brontë considers that the Belgians, and foreigners in general, excel: the art of dress. Crimsworth notices the contrast in this respect between the English colony in Brussels and the 'freshly and trimly attired foreign figures'. Lucy Snowe, observing the cut of the dresses worn by the pupils on gala evenings, realises its perfection: '. . . though simple, it must be allowed the array was perfect — perfect in fashion, fit and freshness.' The perfection of the dresses is increased by the air with which they are worn. '. . . foreigners . . . seem to possess the art of appearing graceful in public . . .'

The externals of life are pleasant enough. And the character of the people, as Charlotte Brontë sees it, is well equipped for material enjoyment. Her observations are naturally based chiefly on the school community she knows. An excellent physique is the rule: 'neither pale nor puny faces were anywhere to be seen in the Rue Fossette'. Its concomitants are a healthy appetite, and, in leisure moments, a boisterousness which finds its fullest expression in carnival or kermesse. These manifestations of physical vitality had no natural appeal for Charlotte Brontë. 'A strange, frolicsome, noisy little world was this school,' is the unenthusiastic comment of Lucy Snowe, who remembers that when she first came, a 'riotous Labassecourienne' would sometimes seize her by the arm and drag her towards the playground, and is thankful she has been able to discourage all such attempts to invade her solitude. She does justice to Flemish gaiety only when she can transpose it through her art till the quintessence alone remains, as in the climactic scene of the fête in the park.

She is more interested in mental processes and psychological reactions. Crimsworth analyses the character of his pupils, beginning with the boys in M. Pelet's school, and finds them slow in mentality and opposed to any sustained intellectual effort. Lucy Snowe credits her pupils with rather more capacity, but an equal dislike of mental exertion. But they both find that their classes would not be slow to mutiny in face of any arbitrary attempt to extort more effort than they are prepared to make. This blend of lethargy and resistance seems to Crimsworth typical of the nation as a whole: ' "The boy is father to the man" . . . so I often thought when I looked at my boys and remembered the political history of their ancestors. Pelet's school was merely an epitome of the Belgian nation.' (ch. 7) The judgement is based on too superficial a knowledge of the Belgians, and probably of their history too, to be convincing. Their tenacity Crimsworth correctly sensed, and their power of coalescing in the face of aggression. But as the native of an island whose soil had not been invaded since the Norman Conquest, he could not appreciate at its true moral value the capacity for stubborn resistance generated in a people who had had for centuries to wage successive revolutions against foreign occupation.

Charlotte Brontë's insular sense of superiority prevented her from fully understanding either the boisterousness or the taciturnity which were part of the Belgian character. She is equally prejudiced when their capacity for feeling is in question. Her instinctive appreciation of the type of beauty often seen in her pupils, which recalled the Madonnas of Low Country painters, is in striking contradiction with her conviction that such placidity is synonymous with insensibility. One of Crimsworth's pupils in Mlle Reuter's school looks like a 'figure de Vierge' in a Dutch painting, but has the complete passivity of 'some large handsome figure moulded in wax'. In the concert hall in Villette are women of the same sculptural type, whose 'grand insensibility' causes ironic amusement to Lucy Snowe and the Brettons, who are convinced that there is a fundamental incompatibility between such external calm and the slightest depth of thought or feeling.

By far the most serious barrier to Charlotte Brontë's complete understanding of the continental milieu was undoubtedly her prejudice and suspicion where religious beliefs and practices different from her own were concerned. It must be remembered that she never hesitated to criticise what she disliked in forthright terms. Their Protestantism did not exempt the curates in *Shirley,* still less the Dissenters, from vigorous attack. It was not likely she would be any more tolerant of a form of religious belief she had been brought up to dislike and distrust. But she was unprepared for the strength of the hostility she felt towards Catholicism from the start of her stay in Brussels, and which grew with her growing unhappiness and her growing sense of isolation. Its bitterness was accentuated by the fact that she found herself in a community where religious beliefs and practice were of primary importance. Catholicism commanded deep loyalties in Belgium, as it had done in the southern Netherlands. For Belgian Catholics the acceptance of their religion was the foundation of the social order, and there was no sphere in which its importance was more fully recognised than in education. The description in the prospectus of the pensionnat Heger of the 'cours d'instruction' as 'basé sur la Religion' was no mere conventional statement but a fact, and one which had its origin in religious views as sincerely held as those of the Brontës themselves.

The fundamental importance of the religious issue is

evident in *The Professor.* Crimsworth sees a direct correlation between the overt adolescent sensuality of his girl pupils and their upbringing on the restrictive lines he thinks characteristic of a Romanist milieu. Lucy Snowe, who lives in a pensionnat and falls in love with a foreigner, is more personally involved with Catholicism because of its effects on her own life. '. . . a subtle essence of Romanism pervaded every arrangement' is her verdict at an early stage of her stay in the Rue Fossette. Passionately independent by nature, she sees in the authority of the spiritual director and the confessional a threat to the freedom of conscience of the individual. This is the root cause of her objection to the daily 'lecture pieuse' which seems to her to afford frequent examples, in the lives of Saints, of 'moral martyrdom inflicted by Rome'.

In a period of crisis, Lucy Snowe herself seeks — and finds — relief in the confessional. But Charlotte Brontë's own comment on this action of her heroine's is: 'It was no impetus of healthy feeling which urged her to the confessional . . . it was the semi-delirium of solitary grief and sickness.'[12] In the closing stages of *Villette,* there is a determined effort, on the part of the priest Père Silas, to remove Lucy's hostility to Romanism. It is not doctrinal differences that primarily concern her, and she only glances at the theological works he lends her. He is on surer ground when he tries to shake her aversion by pointing to the works of philanthropy due to the Roman Church, but in Lucy Snowe's eyes these, too, are vitiated by the same authoritarian principle. Among its most to be pitied victims, in her eyes, were women who become nuns, unless indeed they were of the stamp of Eliza Reed in *Jane Eyre,* 'in matters of religion a rigid formalist'. The nun of the Rue Fossette is not only an admirable example of Charlotte Brontë's 'new Gothic', a crystallisation of her heroine's neurotic and psychic disturbances; she is also the epitome of the fanaticism of the 'drear Middle Ages', of what Lucy Snowe considers to be the totally mistaken self-sacrifice of women like the pale Justine Marie who have immolated themselves on the altar of a misunderstood ideal.

Charlotte Brontë's general view of the Belgian character, as shown in her novels, is one in which much criticism, some of it intolerant, is mixed with a certain amount of approbation. It has been said with some truth that she never forgave Belgium for not being Angria. It would be truer to say that she never entirely forgave it for not being France. It was the French language which had introduced her to continental culture at first hand. In Brussels she found herself in what was predominantly a French-speaking community, but one with a mixed racial background, in which Flemish were in the majority. In the novels the fullest studies of foreigners are naturally those of the Belgians and 'Labassecouriens' among whom Crimsworth and Lucy Snowe lived. But there are also characters of other nationalities reflecting the cosmopolitan nature of a continental capital, and these include French of Parisian origin. French remains the language which is for most the natural medium of expression. And France, which had been the chief adversary of Britain in the Napoleonic Wars, still seems to stand, in Charlotte Brontë's mind, as a synonym for both the best and the worst in continental culture.

The observation of a foreign milieu, and of the salient characteristics of its inhabitants, would not in itself afford a sufficient basis for a novelist to create living characters, without the power to see them as individuals. Differences of sex, age, temperament, family background and circumstance have also to be considered in the understanding of any individual character. Charlotte Brontë, who had the Romantic's interest in personality, was not likely to forget this. She was to show in *Villette* how even a small school community in Labassecour could provide startling contrasts. The garden of the school in the Rue Fossette was, to an acute observer, an open book where human nature in its diversity could be studied 'for hours together'.

But such knowledge cannot be acquired all at once by a resident in a foreign country. This is explicitly recognised by Lucy Snowe in *Villette*. But in *The Professor,* first-fruits of the Brussels experience, the narrator Crimsworth seems to combine the knowledge gained by integrated observation during his whole period abroad with memories of more cursory, though vivid, early impressions. His first description of his girl pupils in Mlle Reuter's pensionnat consists largely of a catalogue of their racial characteristics, chiefly physical, with the result that the reader gains only a superficial impression, though from the visual point of view there is much to admire in the triple portrait of the 'queens of the school' who grace the front row in the schoolroom: Eulalie, Hortense and Caroline. Together they form a striking example of contrasing types of beauty to be found in the Brussels milieu. Eulalie is fair and placid like a Dutch painter's Madonna, the laughing Hortense resembles a study by Rubens, Caroline's beauty suggests an admixture of French blood, for it is of the Latin type characterised by dark hair and eyes, classic features and a colourless olive complexion. Their juxtaposition is effective, and that it was not accidental may be inferred by the remark made later by the Frenchman Pelet to Cromsworth; 'Lovely creatures all of them — heads for artists; what a group they would make, taken together!' But Eulalie is lethargic, Hortense frivolous and Caroline remarkable chiefly for her precocious sensuality. None of them plays any part in the future action of the novel, but their efforts to disrupt the lesson give a practical demonstration of the difficulties to be encountered by a foreign teacher in Mlle Reuter's school.

The three women teachers resident in the pensionnat provide another trio for the artist's sardonic delineation. They are all French in nationality. Mlles Pélagie and Suzette are summed up by the colourless epithet 'ordinary'. The third, Mlle Zéphyrine, is not dismissed quite so summarily, but the terms in which she is described are far from flattering to her Parisian origin: 'Zéphyrine was somewhat more distinguished in appearance and deportment . . . but in character a genuine Parisian coquette, perfidious, mercenary, and dry-hearted.'

Later on in the novel occurs another description of a foreigner which is hardly more than a sketch. M. Vandenhuten's very minor role is a necessity for the plot, since he helps Crimsworth to obtain the teaching post he urgently needs. Crimsworth evidently thinks his Dutch origin helps to account for the reliability and benevolence that characterise him: 'The Dutchman (he was not Flamand but pure Hollandais) was slow, cool, of rather dense intelligence, though sound and accurate judgment . . . I thought the benevolence of his truthful face was better than the intelligence of my own.' (ch. 22)

None of these sketches, though it is made clear — except in the case of the Dutchman Vandenhuten — that they were 'pencilled after nature', really comes to life in any vivid sense, though the 'queens of the school' have visual charm. But their inclusion shows how consciously Charlotte Brontë aimed at utilising her observation of a cosmopolitan milieu as a means of giving variety to a work necessarily restricted in scope.

There is more functional importance in the rather more developed sketch of Sylvie, the pale little 'model pupil' of Mlle Reuter's establishment. Sylvie is docile and intelligent, but in Crimsworth's eyes an object of compassion rather than admiration; her future destiny is the cloister, and he is convinced she has already given up her freedom of thought and action 'into the hands of some despotic confessor'.

Midway between these sketches and the more finished studies of the two proprietors of schools who have leading roles — M. Pelet and Mlle Reuter — come the vignettes of the two mothers, Mme Pelet and Mme Reuter. Both are French speaking, but the first is French and the second Flemish, and the contrast between them is one of race as well as of temperament. They are on excellent terms and have in common a liking for gossip and good food. Physically they are very different, 'Madam Reuter being as fat and rubicund as Mme Pelet was meagre and yellow'. Though both are fluent speakers, the old Frenchwoman is the more punctilious and her Flemish counterpart more relaxed in speech and manner; 'Madame Reuter looked more like a joyous, free-living old Flemish fermière, or even a maîtresse d'auberge, than a staid, grave, rigid directrice de pensionnat.' Crimsworth's awkward attempts at compliments, which are politely received by Mme Pelet, only amuse her:

> 'Quel charmant jeune homme!' murmured Madame Pelet in a low voice. Madame Reuter being less sentimental, as she was Flamand and not French, only laughed again.

'You are a dangerous person, I fear,' said she; 'if you can forge compliments at that rate, Zoraïde will positively be afraid of you . . .' (ch. 8)

M. Pelet has the distinction of providing the only full--length portrait of a Frenchman attempted by Charlotte Brontë. In physical appearance and ease of manner he seems to have had a prototype in François Lebel, the director of the boarding-house of the Athénée Royal which provides in the novel the location for the boys' school where Crimsworth taught. M. Lebel was a Frenchman who had emigrated to Belgium at the time of the July Revolution in Paris, a contemporary of M. Heger, and a colleague of his on the staff of the Athénée.[13] Those who knew him in Brussels remembered him as 'the French refugee schoolmaster, the man distinguished in air, quiet in method, Parisian in characteristics, suave and silky in manner. Parisian indeed, to the finger tips . . .'[14] Crimsworth's first impressions of M. Pelet give a very similar impression:

> He was a man of about forty years of age, of middle size, and rather emaciated figure . . . his features were pleasing and regular, they had a French turn (for M. Pelet was no Fleming, but a Frenchman both by birth and parentage), yet the degree of harshness inseparable from Gallic lineaments was, in his case, softened by a mild blue eye, and a melancholy, almost suffering expression of countenance; his physiognomy was 'fine et spirituelle'. I use two French words because they define better than any English terms the species of intelligence with which his features were imbued. He was altogether an interesting and prepossessing personage. (ch. 7)

Pelet's character is revealed gradually as Crimsworth comes to know him — a realistic approach. His apparently effortless way of keeping order among his unruly pupils soon causes Crimsworth to realise that his mildness is not weakness. Closer acquaintance shows he is an intelligent and cheerful companion. These pleasant characteristics Pelet no doubt shared with his prototype. But, as the portrait is developed, it evidently becomes the expression of Charlotte Brontë's own estimate of the virtues and vices of the French character.

Intelligent, witty, reasonably kind and wise in his relations with his pupils, he is motivated largely by self-interest. Crimsworth is most repelled by his libertinism. 'He was not married, and I soon perceived he had all a Frenchman's, all a Parisian's notions about matrimony and women.' Pelet, on his side, is not slow to discover that beneath the austere young Englishman's reserve is 'a fathomless spring of sensibility', and to exercise his wit on the subject. He foresees that Crimsworth will fall in love with Mlle Reuter, but treacherously conceals the fact that he is himself shortly to marry the young directress of the school next door to his own, an arrangement founded largely on mutual self-interest. The discovery of the truth effectually disgusts Crimsworth with both of them, but the result of his subsequent coldness is paradoxically that Mlle Reuter becomes temporarily infatuated with him, and Pelet violently jealous. The crisis lasts long enough for all Pelet's concealed hostility to the foreigner to reveal itself during an uncharacteristic bout of drunkenness. The fierceness of his hatred for the Englishman seems out of character, but it shows how the belief in French ferocity, heritage of the Napoleonic Wars and evident in episodes of the Angrian cycle, still lingered in the imagination of Charlotte Brontë. 'A thorough Frenchman, the national characteristic of ferocity had not been omitted by nature in compounding the ingredients of his character . . .' (ch. 20). The crisis, however, is not of long duration. Mlle Reuter and Pelet are reconciled and, once reassured as to her indifference to Crimsworth, the astute director does all he can to conciliate the competent young English teacher. But he prefers to resign his post, foreseeing no peace under the same roof with the Pelet ménage. And M. Pelet ceases to play an active part in the action of the novel.

This character study was described by Mrs Humphry Ward as 'an extremely clever sketch'; it hardly achieves the status of a finished portrait. The reason for this is to be found partly in the structural imperfection of the novel, where the main theme, the love of Crimsworth and Frances, is not introduced till halfway through. Pelet ceases to be important to the plot once he has been the agent of Crimsworth's disillusionment with Mlle Reuter, and he is not on the stage long enough to be appreciated as he deserves. But the chief reason for the partial failure of this study is the overstress on national characteristics. In the case of her Belgian characters, Charlotte Brontë had lived long enough in the country to know how very different they could be as individuals in spite of the racial traits they had in common. But Pelet is presented as a Frenchman first and foremost, and an individual only in the second place. Yet he is far from being a complete failure. He comes into his own in the dialogue, where his alert mind and lively wit — untouched by the sentimentality which Charlotte Brontë considers in theory as invariably part of the French character — find direct expression. One of the most effective conversation pieces in the novel is the one where he effortlessly elicits from Crimsworth his first impressions of Mlle Reuter; and equally effective is the nonchalant grace of his exit at the end of the scene:

> Just then the bell rang; the play-hour was over; it was an evening on which M. Pelet was accustomed to read passages from the drama and the belles lettres to his pupils. He did not wait for my answer, but rising, left the room, humming as he went some gay strain of Béranger's. (ch. 11)

Mlle Reuter shares with her lover the disadvantage of disappearing from the stage before the end of the novel. But she appears at more frequent intervals than he does, and a stronger light is focused on her. As in the case of Pelet, her external appearance is described first. Crimsworth notices the Belgian character of her looks, though she is not a statuesque beauty like some of her pupils. Without being beautiful, however, she is attractive because of her fresh colouring, grace of movement and the calm good sense expressed in her face. She has 'a certain serenity of eye, and freshness of complexion, most pleasing to behold. The colour on her cheek was like the bloom on a good apple, which is as sound at the core as it is red on the rind.' (ch. 9)

The physical portrait of Mlle Reuter owes something to Mme Heger. And there is perhaps a reminiscence of Mme Heger's name, Zöe, in her name, Zoraïde. But it is still closer to that of the heroine Zorayde in one of the Angrian romances.[15] The juxtaposition between the exotic 'Zoraïde' and the unromantic 'Reuter' is obviously satirical. Crimsworth gives a rather disingenuous explanation of it: 'I remember that I was very much amused when I first heard her Christian name . . . But the continental nations do allow themselves vagaries in the choice of names, such as we sober English never run into . . .' This unlikely juxtaposition of the romantic and the prosaic sets the tone for the predominantly satirical study of Mlle Reuter's character.

Crimsworth is attracted from the start, not only by her good looks but by her air of poise and serenity — 'a tranquillity which soothed and suited me singularly . . .' Serenity was also one of the qualities of Mme Heger. So, too, was the quiet efficiency with which she ran her school, another quality shared by Mlle Reuter, the 'sensible, saga-cious, affable directress' who holds her turbulent pupils in check without apparent effort. But a satirical turn is given to the portrait from the start and, as it develops, it becomes, like that of M. Pelet, the novelist's own creation.

It is at once evident to Crimsworth that Mlle Reuter is a finished diplomat, and he soon sees that her success in managing the school is due primarily to constant watchful-ness and skilful manoeuvring. But he cannot help admiring her intelligence and aplomb, even while he suspects her of craftiness. Before long he is sufficiently in love to argue with himself that her failings, like those of her pupils, may be due to the disadvantages of her Catholic education. 'Even if she be truly deficient in sound principle, is it not rather her misfortune than her fault? She has been brought up a Catholic: had she been born an Englishwoman, and reared a Protestant, might she not have added straight integrity to all her other excellences?' (ch. 12). The obvious cure would be for her to marry 'an English and Protestant husband'. But before he can make this suggestion, he overhears her conver-sation with Pelet, and her power over him is practically at an end. That it does not disappear completely is due to the cool courage with which she faces the revelation that he has heard their talk. 'Looking at her, I was forced . . . to offer her good sense, her wondrous self-control, the tribute of involuntary admiration.'

Up to this point Zoraïde Reuter, if not a wholly admirable character, is in no sense a ridiculous one. When Crimsworth transfers his affections to Frances Henri, she becomes infatuated with him herself, and the reasonableness that had always characterised her gives way to a sensuality whose existence he had not suspected. Once she has separated him from Frances by devious means, she becomes almost servile in her attempts to conciliate him. Her subservient attitude is described in a metaphor which is both a satirical echo of the Byronic climate of Angria and an ironic comment on her oriental first name: 'When she stole about me with the soft step of a slave, I felt at once barbarous and sensual as a pasha.' He is not completely indifferent to this 'slavish homage', though it irritates him. But when she persists in denying all knowledge of Frances' address, though he is sure she is well aware of it, he resigns his post in her school, and the act seems to restore her to her senses. She is reconciled with Pelet, and succeeds in convincing him that he has never had a rival in the English master. But Crimsworth is sure that her real feeling for him is unchanged and that, if he remains as an inmate of Pelet's house after their marriage, it will not be long before she tries to initiate an intrigue reminiscent of 'a modern French novel'. After his departure from Pelet's school, he sees no more of her, though he hears of her marriage soon after.

Zoraïde Reuter is a vigorously drawn character, though she is more convincing as the competent Belgian schoolmistress than as the infatuated admirer of a young man she had previously belittled as 'an unknown foreigner'. Her rôle, like Pelet's, is necessary to the plot, but her part in the novel is more important than his, for her character serves to throw into relief the totally different temperament and qualities of Frances Henri.

The 'little lace-mender' is the most finely realised character in the book, 'a drawing in pale, pure colour, all delicate animation and soft life'.[16] The choice of a French-speaking heroine was a functional necessity in a novel based on the master-pupil relationship, where the master himself is a teacher of English, but in giving her Swiss nationality, Charlotte Brontë ensures that she is differentiated from the

Belgians around her. Crimsworth's first clear impression of her underlines the racial difference:

> I felt assured, at first sight, that she was not a Belgian; her complexion, her countenance, her lineaments, her figure, were all distinct from theirs, and evidently the type of another race — of a race less gifted with fulness of flesh and plenitude of blood; less jocund, material, unthinking. When I first cast my eyes on her, she sat looking fixedly down, her chin resting on her hand, and she did not change her attitude till I commenced the lesson. None of the Belgian girls would have retained one position, and that a reflective one, for the same length of time. (ch. 14).

Her Swiss origin has another consequence, for, as a pastor's daughter from Geneva, she is doubly an alien in the Catholic milieu and admits to Crimsworth that she longs to live once more among Protestants. She is proud of her Swiss nationality, and in conversation with Yorke Hunsden, who persistently denigrates all nationalism, defends her country with energy, speaking of the 'natural glories' of its mountains and the heroic resistance to tyranny of heroes like Tell.

But, as the percipient Hunsden points out, Frances is more English than Swiss in features and figure. She is, in fact, only half Swiss, having had an English mother. She feels herself that she belongs to both countries. 'I am English, too . . . I have a right to a double power of patriotism, possessing an interest in two noble, free, and fortunate countries.' Her chief ambition, at the time when Crimsworth first sees her, is ultimately to obtain a post in England, her mother's country which she has never seen.

The character study of Frances Henri is the most interesting in the novel. The fact that there is a masculine narrator makes it possible for her to be seen through the eyes of her lover, and the portrait comes as near to idealisation as the deliberately restrained style permits. At first an almost insignificant figure, she gradually reveals her true personality as she becomes conscious of the genuine sympathy beneath his brusque and dictatorial manner. Her development in personality is matched by the improvement in her physical appearance; from a colourless shadow she becomes a figure whose delicate grace of line and colour is more congenial to her lover than all the opulent beauty of 'Rubens' painted women'.

Frances Henri is, of all Charlotte Brontë's characters, the one who most clearly reflects what had been her own reactions during the Brussels period; the determination to do what she can to increase her narrow experience by teaching in a foreign country, her rapid increase in self-confidence as her talent is revealed in the *devoirs,* her exclusive and unswerving devotion to the man who has seen and fostered her gift, her despair at being separated from him. All the tragedy of Brussels is contained in four lines of the poem which Crimsworth overhears her reciting to herself:[17]

> The strong pulse of Ambition struck
> In every vein I owned;
> At the same instant, bleeding broke
> A secret, inward wound.

Frances is none the less an autonomous artistic creation. The master pupil relationship she shares with Charlotte Brontë, but Crimsworth says of the poem he overhears that it is, for the most part, 'not exactly the writer's own experience, but a composition by portions of that experience suggested'. Frances never has to endure more than a moderate share of adversity, and she has the resilience of youth to help her and the knowledge that she has no rival in her master's affections. Their period of separation, though agonising, is brief and she is married to the man of her choice within a year of their first meeting. She comes to life most vividly in the charming scenes in the Rue Notre Dame des Neiges, where she is still 'the little lace mender' and has not yet developed into the capable wife, and unexpectedly successful headmistress, of the concluding section. Her capacity for still but intense happiness is as evident as her capacity for endurance had formerly been. But she is not all 'monotonous mildness'; the latent fire in her nature sometimes finds expression and she delights Crimsworth by showing in her conversation flashes of the originality formerly shown only in her *devoirs.* It must be admitted that this side of her nature is best illustrated in the scene where

Yorke Hunsden is her guest. It is in keeping with the conscious avoidance of overt romanticism in *The Professor* that the heroine should have a lover as quiet and unemotional in appearance and manner as she usually is herself, but the eccentric Hunsden, by provoking her to retort and argument, brings out her native wit and intelligence much more effectively than the authoritarian but taciturn Crimsworth.

It is because of her unusual personality that Frances is interesting. The foreign strain in her is an integral part of it, not an artificial addition made necessary by the plot. Simple as she has to be in her way of living, there is a continental neatness and taste almost amounting to elegance in her perfectly kept little home and her well-fitting dress. Crimsworth notices that she curtsies 'with foreign grace'. Her strongly expressed wish to continue teaching after their marriage reflects her continental background as well as her independent spirit, and would certainly not have been understood in a middle-class milieu in Victorian England: 'Think of my marrying you to be kept by you, Monsieur! I could not do it; and how dull my days would be!' More significantly still, French is and remains her natural medium of expression, although she has had an English mother and marries an Englishman. Even after marriage she remains the 'young Genevese' who sometimes teases her husband about his 'bizarreries anglaises', his 'caprices insulaires', making the most of her linguistic advantage in the war of words: 'her tongue did ample justice to the pitch, the point, the delicacy of her native French, in which language she always attacked me.'

It is impossible not to accept Frances' foreign origin and background as belonging to the essence of the character. Whether her Swiss nationality is as successfully suggested is another matter. Hunsden finds her mentality more French than Swiss, saying that the 'pale-faced, excitable little Helvetian' has 'infinitely more of the nervous, mobile Parisienne in her than of the robust "jungfrau"'. It may have been partly, as Frances' argument with Hunsden suggests, the association between Switzerland and the idea of resistance to tyranny that caused Charlotte Brontë to make her heroine a countrywoman of Tell and Hofer, but Hunsden's criticism shows her consciousness that it might be more accurate to qualify as 'Parisian' those qualities of intellectuality, vitality and grace — unmixed, in her case, with the alloy of sensuality — which characterise Frances Henri.

The concluding chapter of *The Professor,* though unconvincing in itself, anticipates in some ways the Thornfield section of *Jane Eyre.* When the Crimsworths finally settle in what is obviously Yorkshire, their nearest neighbour is Yorke Hunsden, whose complex personality anticipates Rochester as well as the Hiram Yorke of *Shirley.* He does not spend more than a few months at a time in the Elizabethan mansion he has inherited from his father, and, when he has visitors, they are often foreigners. He would have liked to marry a foreign bride, though the mysterious Italian 'Lucia', whose portrait he once shows to the Crimsworths, is very different from the Creole Bertha Mason, and seems indeed, to judge from Frances' deductions after close study of the miniature, strikingly similar to Madame de Staël's Corinne.[18]

*Jane Eyre* is a work predominantly English in atmosphere, but with overtones of Angria. Rochester is the most Byronic of Charlotte Brontë's heroes, and travel is a part of his way of life. In the rich motivation of the novel his Creole wife, who becomes a maniac, stands, among other things, for the voluptuous exoticism which had attracted him in his youth and which he now repudiates, even when he encounters a paler version of it in Blanche Ingram. Before meeting Jane Eyre, he had spent ten years living first in one European capital, then in another, and had sought for his ideal woman among 'English ladies, French countesses, Italian signoras and German gräfinnen.' Although, after their meeting, her presence reconciles him to some extent to Thornfield Hall, he plans, after their marriage, to introduce her in turn to the beauty and culture of Europe, its scenery and its cities: 'You shall sojourn at Paris, Rome, and Naples: at Florence, Venice and Vienna: all the ground I have wandered over shall be retrodden by you: wherever I stamped my hoof, your sylph's foot shall step also.' (ch. 24)[19]

Jane Eyre's continental travels remain in the realm of fantasy. But life at Thornfield, when she first arrives there, centres round Adèle Varens, child of a Parisian opera dancer for whom Rochester had once entertained a 'grande passion', and rescued by him from poverty when abandoned by her mother. It is as governess to Adèle that Jane comes to his house. The governess-pupil relationship is ancillary and subordinate to Jane's relationship with Rochester, who dominates her life, once he enters it. But, without the continued presence of Adèle, an essential theme would be missing from the symphony into which the central part of the novel develops.

Her function in the novel is more important than at first appears. Neither Rochester nor Jane have any deep feeling for the child. Rochester, though he has taken pity on her plight, does not believe she is his daughter and shows her at best a patronising kindness. Jane feels at most a 'conscientious solicitude' for her pupil's progress, and a 'quiet liking to her little self'. She is in herself unremarkable, though not unattractive. Yet without Adèle the development of the novel would lack a vital constituent. When she appears in the dining-room of Thornfield, dressed like a miniature edition of her mother, the French opera dancer, she provides unconsciously the prelude to the account Rochester gives soon afterwards to Jane of the perfidy of Céline Varens. He anticipates its main theme in his ironic analysis of Adèle: '. . . coquetry runs in her blood, blends with her brains, and seasons the marrow of her bones.' Whether she is his daughter or not, she certainly embodies the qualities that charmed him in her mother: grace, vivacity, the ability to please and flatter, and he sees in her delight in her *cadeau* proof that she will be as frivolous and as mercenary. The houseparty scenes give a practical demonstration that society is Adèle's natural element. Jane Eyre notices with a mixture of amusement and regret her intense preoccupation with her 'toilette': '. . . there was something ludicrous as well as painful in the little Parisienne's earnest and innate devotion to matters of dress.'

But the impression made by Adèle is not simply one of superficiality and frivolity. Thornfield would be a more sombre place without her. She expresses herself chiefly in her own language and the phrases of conversational French bring lively overtones into the dialogue, just as her satin frock and her dancer's steps introduce something of the lightness of

ballet into an atmosphere of boding tension. Although she
has 'no great talents', she can declaim a fable of La Fontaine
'with an attention to punctuation and emphasis, a flexibility
of voice and an appropriateness of gesture, very unusual
indeed at her age and which proved she had been carefully
trained.' The dichotomy evident in Charlotte Brontë's attitude to France is illustrated once more in the portrait of this
child who is called a 'genuine daughter of Paris', whose
mother was an actress and who would herself be in her
element on the stage. She is depreciated as almost the 'little
puppet' Blanche Ingram scornfully calls her, but she is at the
same time the undeniably charming 'French floweret' of
Rochester's careless phrase, the 'love of a child' whom his
other guests admire and spoil.

Adèle Varens is the only foreigner of any importance in
*Jane Eyre* apart from the Creole, whose violent temper and
unbridled sensuality have developed into insanity and who is
no longer an integrated character but a malevolent force.
Madame Pierrot, who has the doubtful honour of teaching
French at Lowood, is mentioned briefly as 'a strange foreign-
looking elderly lady' who comes from 'Lisle, in France'. She
is responsible for Jane's proficiency in speaking French,
which at once wins the approval and confidence of Adèle.
Sophie, Adèle's nurse, appears and remains a completely
colourless figure.

When Rochester begs Jane not to leave him, after the
interrupted wedding, it is to France that he proposes to take
her, to a 'white-washed villa on the shores of the Mediterranean'. The situation recalls that of Zamorna and his
mistress Mina Laury, who take refuge in 'France' during his
exile. Here, as in the previous history of Céline, France is
associated with the idea of sexual licence. After Jane Eyre's
rejection of Rochester's proposal, the French element dis-
appears. In the Moor House section of the novel, the
preference for German shown by Diana and Mary Rivers,
who are both absorbed in reading Schiller when Jane first
sees them, helps to establish the completely different atmosphere of the new environment.[20] For her it is an unknown
tongue, though she begins to study it under Diana's guidance

with more enthusiasm than she later shows for the study of Hindustani imposed on her by their brother. When Jane is finally reunited to Rochester, all extraneous influences have been removed from a setting reduced to its bare essentials, fitting framework for a love which has at last emancipated itself from all illusion. Adèle, who has been sent to school, is not even mentioned at first, but the final account of her shows an unexpected transformation: 'As she grew up a sound English education corrected in a great measure her French defects . . .'

The atmosphere of *Jane Eyre* is far removed from the muted tones of *The Professor*. There is more poetry than prose at Thornfield, and there is little in common between the corrosive analysis of the pupils in the Rue d'Isabelle and the light touch with which Adèle is drawn. By the alchemy of the creative imagination, Charlotte Brontë has recaptured the vision of Europe, seen through the medium of *Childe Harold* and *Don Juan* and coloured with the after-glow of Angria, which had once been her own, and has made it the background for the figure of Rochester, as he first appears to the eighteen year old Jane Eyre. It is disturbed by no hint of the monotony of the level plains of Brabant, or the solid comfort of Flemish interiors. But there is a link none the less between Brussels and Thornfield. It is in the language spoken by Adèle, of which for seven years Jane has learnt a portion by heart daily, whose accents are a constant reminder of the intrusion of the Continent into the seclusion of Thornfield Hall.

*Shirley* is the most Yorkshire of the novels. It is also the most socially conscious, giving a cross-section of Yorkshire society at the time of the Luddite riots. Its characters are drawn from mill-owners, landed gentry, the middle class and the workers. Such a scheme seems to offer little justification for the introduction of a foreign element. But Shirley herself and her friend Caroline marry men who are half Belgian in origin and whose sister manages to maintain, in the heart of Yorkshire, the customs and traditions of her Belgian background. Hollow's Cottage, in its sheltered lane close to the mill, is one of the focal points of the story, as vital to its development as the mill itself, as Briarfield Rectory or

Fieldhead. Its threshold is the frontier over which Caroline crosses temporarily into another country, and in doing so becomes more conscious of her own.

But it is an organic link and not a mere fictional necessity that accounts for the presence of this half-Belgian family in Yorkshire. It was the recommendation of the manufacturer Yorke Hunsden that had been Crimsworth's passport to Belgium. And commercial interests have provided the background to the mixed marriage of which Robert Moore, owner of Hollow's Mill, his brother Louis and his sister Hortense are the children. His father, partner in a Yorkshire firm, had married Hortense Gérard, daughter of an Antwerp mercantile house closely connected with the English one. He was a resident of Antwerp, where his children were born. But the consequences of the French Revolution have involved the house of Gérard and Moore in disaster. His son has returned to Yorkshire with only capital enough to rent a cloth-mill in 'an out-of-the-way district', and the adjoining cottage, where his sister Hortense keeps house for him.

Hortense Moore is a minor character, as far as the action of the novel is concerned, but she it is who is mainly responsible for the Belgian atmosphere of Hollow's Cottage. She is known to have had a part prototype in Mlle Haussé, one of the women teachers at the pensionnat Heger. The resemblance was so evident that the Wheelwright family, who had known Charlotte Brontë in Brussels, claimed they could have deduced from this portrait alone that *Shirley* was by a former pupil of the pensionnat.[21] But the Brussels material has been used as the basis for a new creation; Hortense Moore is a character in her own right, militantly Belgian in a foreign environment, devoted to the interests of the brother whom she reveres as the present head of their once influential but now impoverished family, and glad to find an outlet for her self-importance, as well as for some natural kindness, in instructing her young cousin, Caroline Helstone, in the skills and disciplines sadly lacking in an English education.

Her physical appearance is described in a way that sets the tone for the serio-comic nature of the portrait as a whole:

... perhaps she was thirty-five, tall, and proportionately stout; she had very black hair, for the present twisted up in curl-papers; a high colour in her cheeks, a small nose, a pair of little black eyes. The lower part of her face was large in proportion to the upper; her forehead was small, and rather corrugated; she had a fretful, though not an ill-natured expression of countenance; there was something in her whole appearance one felt inclined to be half provoked with, and half amused at. (ch. 5)

Her morning dress, consisting of 'jupon and camisole', is reminiscent of Mme Pelet's, and she never at any time achieves the elegance seen to characterise most foreigners in *The Professor,* because of her exaggerated economy. She wears sabots on Sundays, to the amusement of her neighbours — it is true they are 'not common sabots' but 'sabots noirs, très propres, très convenables' — considering them as suitable for English country roads as for the mud of the Flemish chaussées. It is in the kitchen above all that she insists on remaining faithful to the domestic traditions of her Belgian background, for there she finds them challenged by the Yorkshire servant Sarah. Sarah is as convinced of the superiority of sugar to treacle in preserving black cherries as Caroline is of the superiority of Shakespeare to Racine, and her convictions find unconscious expression in her carelessness in watching the preserving pan, whose contents are inevitably reduced to 'dark and cindery ruin', to the intense indignation of her mistress.

Intellectually Hortense prides herself on possessing an 'esprit positif'. Caroline's French lessons with her consist chiefly in interminable grammatical analysis. Her over-insistence on method and detail are as evident here as in her over-careful housekeeping. But she has some sterling qualities: honesty, family affection and good nature as long as her opinions are accepted without criticism. Her most obvious foible is her self-importance, which is understandably exaggerated by the sense that she does not receive, in her new environment, the attention that is her due. 'Of what an excellent family are the Gérards . . . and the Moores also! They have a right to claim a certain respect, and to feel wounded when it is withheld from them. In Antwerp I was always treated with distinction . . .'

The character of Hortense Moore is indispensable to the

novel. She gives a Belgian quality to the domesticity of Hollow's Cottage, and her presence there provides both an occasion and a semi-foreign background for the meetings of Caroline and her brother. But she remains a serio-comic figure. Her complacent hope that the fortunes of her family will be restored by a marriage between her elder brother and the heiress of Fieldhead is perfectly in character. And there is much obtuseness, though no malevolence, in her refusal to consider Caroline except as more or less a child, in spite of the cruel innuendoes of Mrs Yorke on the subject of her attitude to Robert.

The complexities of *Shirley,* the widest in scope of Charlotte Bronte's novels, are well illustrated in the character of the simple Hortense's far from simple brother. Robert Moore is an extraordinary though very human mixture of opposing qualities. From the outset his mixed nationality is emphasised as largely responsible for his position and outlook as a partial 'outsider'. In drawing his character Charlotte Brontë is known to have had as part model William Cartwright who, at the time of the Luddite riots, held on lease the cloth finishing mill of Rawfolds at Liversedge, near Roe Head.[22] It was during her school days at Roe Head that she first heard the story of his defence of his mill from Miss Wooler, though she documented herself on the subject with the care she showed in general over the economic background of *Shirley,* consulting the files of the *Leeds Mercury* for 1812-14.[23] In Mrs Gaskell's account of the tales told by Miss Wooler to her pupils of the Luddite riots, allusion is made to a foreign strain in Cartwright, which made him unpopular even before he dared to employ machinery for the dressing of woollen cloth. 'Mr. Cartwright was a very remarkable man, having, as I have been told, some foreign blood in him, the traces of which were very apparent in his tall figure, dark eyes and complexion, and singular though gentlemanly bearing. At any rate he had been much abroad, and spoke French well, of itself a suspicious circumstance to the bigoted nationality of those days.'[24] Mrs Gaskell gives no source for her information[25], and it is principally by his actions, rather than his character, that Cartwright is the part prototype of Robert Moore. But the fact that the rumour of a foreign strain in him, and his fluency in French, could be remembered as contributory causes of his unpopularity shows how much verisimilitude there is in the conception of the rôle.

Moore himself is proud of his foreign blood. 'Born and partly reared on a foreign soil', he counts himself more Belgian than British. He prides himself on being a native of Antwerp: 'Joe, I'm an Anversois; my mother was an Anversoise, though she came of French lineage, which is the reason I speak French.' (ch. 5). His appearance confirms the predominance of the foreign strain in him:

> He is what you would probably call, at first view, rather a strange-looking man; for he is thin, dark, sallow; very foreign of aspect . . . He seems unconscious that his features are fine, that they have a southern symmetry, clearness, regularity in their chiselling . . . his stature is tall, his figure slender. His manner of speaking displeases: he has an outlandish accent, which, notwithstanding a studied carelessness of pronunciation and diction, grates on a British, and especially on a Yorkshire ear. (ch. 2)

But Moore also has hereditary links with Yorkshire. Mr Yorke remembers his father, with whom he had had business dealings, and the overseer Joe Scott reminds him with characteristic forthrightness that he is the son of a Yorkshireman, and that there are natural affinities between the West Riding and Antwerp: 'But your father war Yorkshire, which maks ye a bit Yorkshire too; and onybody may see ye're akin to us, ye're so keen o' making brass and getting forrards.' Charlotte Brontë took some traits of Robert Moore from a Yorkshireman she herself knew well. In *Shirley* the Yorke family of Briarmains are largely a portrait of the Taylors of Gomersal. She used her recollections of the third son, Joe Taylor, as a schoolboy in the creation of young Martin Yorke, who has a rôle in the dénouement of the novel. Joe Taylor, as an adult, has certainly contributed to her portrait of the owner of Hollow's Mill.[26] He was concerned in carrying on the family business at Hunsworth. Like his father he was a linguist and had some business connections with Belgium. His original character is no doubt reflected in some of the variations of Moore's complex temperament. In his active resistance to the frame-breakers, however, Moore is modelled on the defender of Rawfolds Mill.

Moore's anomalous position as a semi-foreigner, half Belgian, half British, has a strong influence on his whole outlook on life, which is hinted at when he first appears:

> A hybrid in nature, it is probable he had a hybrid's feeling on many points — patriotism for one; it is likely that he was unapt to attach himself to parties, to sects, even to climes and customs; it is not impossible that he had a tendency to isolate his individual person from any community amidst which his lot might temporarily happen to be thrown . . . (ch. 2)

The truth of this is evident almost immediately in his dispute on the War in the Peninsula with the extreme Tory Helstone. He brings a European breadth of view into the discussion, but he is far from being the Jacobin Helstone thinks: he opposes the war party because his foreign market is blocked. His chief loyalty is to his trade, his mill, his machinery. Later he listens to Helstone advocating Government coercion of the disaffected workers, and to the Radical Yorke opposing it, without siding with either of them. But against the frame-breakers who have wrecked his machines, his cold anger and his determination to bring them to justice are implacable.

Moore's disinterested attitude to everything that does not concern his business is not incompatible with a strong sardonic vein in him. As the descendant of a line of patrician merchants he is thoroughly out of his element in Hollow's Cottage, and his impatience finds vent in the way he not only risks unpopularity by his actions but deliberately courts it by his almost contemptuous attitude to his work people. In his unbending pride in face of their demands, Caroline Helstone sees the same analogy with the pride of Coriolanus which Charlotte Brontë had seen in Wellington's disdain of the crowds at the time of the Reform Bill. Perhaps she is thinking of Wellington also when she shows Moore as having a cool courage which becomes exhileration in the face of danger. Here she is well served by the third person mode of narration in *Shirley,* which makes it possible to give an objective picture of the mill-owner defying the rioters. He is less sympathetic when, after successfully defending his mill, he hunts down the agitators who had been the leaders of the riot with relentless assiduity and conscious satisfaction, though he does not denounce their unfortunate followers.

But there is another side to his personality. He tells Caroline:

'. . . I find in myself . . . two natures: one for the world and business and one for home and leisure. Gérard Moore is a hard dog, brought up to mill and market; the person you call your cousin Robert is sometimes a dreamer, who lives elsewhere than in Cloth hall and counting-house.' (ch. 13)

He is perfectly aware of Caroline's devotion, and her type of beauty appeals to his fastidious taste, but he deliberately subordinates the dreamer in himself to the hard-headed man of business and plans to marry Shirley, the heiress, whose fortune can save him from impending bankruptcy. When she sees and denounces his mercenary motives, his vanity receives a severe blow. But the shock determines him never again to stoop to the rôle of fortune-hunter. It also proves to be the beginning of a mellowing process in him. When he returns to Yorkshire after an absence of several months, he tells Yorke, his only confidant: 'Something there is to look to, Yorke, beyond a man's personal interest: beyond the advancement of well-laid schemes; beyond even the discharge of dis-honouring debts. To respect himself, a man must believe he renders justice to his fellow-men . . .' (ch. 30). A few minutes later, he is shot and seriously wounded by a half-crazy weaver. During his illness he experiences the intense depres-sion natural to a man of his active temperament reduced to a rôle of passive endurance. But in this condition he comes to realise for the first time the extent of the suffering he has inflicted on Caroline, for he now learns of her illness and is too acute not to realise that his neglect of her had been a powerful contributory cause. He makes it clear to her that she has no rival in his heart, though the future is still clouded for him by the shadow of impending bankruptcy.

But Robert Moore is not called upon to endure bankruptcy. The repeal of the Orders in Council in the June of 1812 saves the owner of Hollow's Mill, like many others, from insolvency. In the final chapter of the novel he at last emerges from the shadow of commercial failure that has overhung him since its beginning, and can look forward both to success in business and domestic happiness, with a mill run on more paternalist lines than before, and a devoted wife to second him in every effort to create a model industrial community.

Robert Moore has a unique position among the foreigners in Charlotte Brontë's novels. He is indubitably the most modern of them. The least concerned with cultural values in themselves — it matters little to him whether Caroline reads Shakespeare or Chénier, provided she looks charming — he is first and foremost a merchant, the only representative in the novels of the commercial genius of the Netherlands, true son of Antwerp, the port on the Scheldt which so early became one of the major centres of European trade. But, as a merchant, with a whole-hearted interest in commerce, he is not by any means such a complete 'outsider' as at first appears. He is in fact far more at home in the industrial West Riding then the Parisian M. Pelet or M. Paul of *Villette* could possibly be. Had he failed in England, he would not have returned to Antwerp but have emigrated to America. For in virtue of his calling he is a citizen not simply of Europe but of the modern world. Helstone thought him a Jacobin. but he belongs rather to an international patrician caste. His ancestors had owned 'warehouses in this seaport, and factories in that inland town, had possessed their town-house and their country-seat,' just as the industrialist Yorke's family was 'the first and oldest in the district'. He is as proud of his 'bourgeois scutcheon', and as sensitive to its honour, as any feudal nobleman, and he loves his machinery as the feudal nobleman loved his land.

Charlotte Brontë would not have chosen a mill-owner for her hero, had she not been moved herself by the epic development of modern industry. She could not keep an industrialist, in the shape of the formidable Edward Percy, out of Angria. She has some hard things to say, in *Shirley*, of the mercenary nature of the mercantile classes and, in a famous passage, expresses the hope: 'Long may it be ere England really becomes a nation of shopkeepers!' But through the Taylors she was in close touch, for most of her life, with a mill-owner's family and she knew how to appreciate their vitality, their shrewdness, their originality. Yet she must often have felt out of her element among them. Mary Taylor remembered that at their house 'she had little chance of a patient hearing. We had a rage for practicality, and laughed all poetry to scorn.'[27] By giving her mill-owner hero a Belgian background, French for his native tongue and a foreign appearance, Charlotte Brontë combines the poetry she loves with the prose of the modern world. But she does not romanticise Robert Moore, and his day-dreams remain of a strictly utilitarian nature. They are also of the sort that quickly become solid fact. He plans to enlarge his mill and transform the quiet valley in which it stands into a thriving industrial colony. The prospect does not inspire the same enthusiasm in Caroline, who is moved to involuntary protest, even though she knows it will be ineffectual:

> '. . . You will change our blue hill-country air into the Stilbro' smoke atmosphere.'
> 'I will pour the waters of Pactolus through the valley of Briarfield.'
> 'I like the beck a thousand times better.'
> 'I will get an act for enclosing Nunnely Common, and parcelling it out into farms.'
> 'Stilbro' Moor, however, defies you, thank Heaven! . . .'
> (ch. 37)

Robert Moore's brother Louis does not make his appearance until the action of the novel is nearly two-thirds over. But his rôle is a structural necessity, for it is Shirley's love for him — unknown to the other characters — which largely accounts for the friendship she at once shows to his brother Robert, misleading him into thinking that she loves him, and Caroline into a similar belief. What little is known of him before he appears shows that he is different in character from his brother, though his youth, like Robert's, has been blighted by his family's financial ruin. Obliged to earn his living on leaving school, he has chosen teaching, not trade, as his profession and is now tutor in a private family. The family is that of Shirley's relatives the Sympsons, and when they come to stay with her the tutor accompanies them. Since the identity of his employers has not been revealed until this stage in the novel, his appearance is something of a coup de théâtre. Charlotte Brontë, however, deflates the romantic element, making his arrival at Hollow's Cottage to see his sister coincide with the disaster of burnt cherries in the preserving pan. The anti-climax is in keeping with the evident disappointment felt by Caroline, who is visiting the cottage, on her first sight of Robert's brother. Though like him in height, he is more like Hortense in feature, slower in speech and movement and calmer in temperament.

Louis Moore appears less of a foreigner than his brother or sister. '. . . he had been sent to England when a mere boy, and had received his education at an English school.' His resemblance to Hortense seems to be in feature only, and his quietness contrasts with his brother's alertness. The fact that he seems so much less of a foreigner than his brother or sister is, however, no reason why he should not be as living a character. His quietness is not intended to indicate lack of personality. In conception, his character belongs to the same order as Crimsworth's, taciturn but not unfeeling, tenacious, self-aware and self-controlled. Unfortunately, as tutor to a fifteen year old boy, he has little chance of demonstrating either force of mind or force of character. Even though it is the hope of seeing Shirley again that makes him endure his life as 'satellite of the house of Sympson', such an existence seems unworthy of the character he is meant to be, and he seldom comes to life as convincingly as his less patient sister or his more ambitious brother.

It is principally in the schoolroom that he is seen. He had taught Shirley French, his 'native language', in the past, when she was staying with her relatives. In the scenes where she visits him in the schoolroom, former French lessons are recalled. For Shirley, as pupil of the literary-minded Louis, they had taken a different course from the interminable 'analyses logiques' imposed by Hortense on the unwilling Caroline. Louis keeps in his desk a small bundle of copy-

books, which 'on scrutiny . . . proved to be French compositions, written in a hand peculiar, but compact, and
exquisitely clean and clear.' They had been written four years
before by Shirley, who is astonished to find them still in
existence, and even more astonished to find that Louis can
remember one of them, word for word.

The 'old copy-books' are of more significance than might
appear, for with their appearance the master-pupil relationship becomes a dominant theme. Like Crimsworth Louis
Moore combines male dominance and intellectual authority.
His brother Robert, with far more brilliant qualities, does not
dominate Caroline as Louis does the uninhibited and free-
dom-loving Shirley. The strange *devoir* 'La Première Femme
Savante', written by Shirley in adolescence and remembered
word for word by Louis Moore, expresses symbolically, in
highly rhetorical language, originally French but translated
into English, the ideal relationship of the sexes. In a primeval
forest setting, the girl Eva becomes the bride of Genius, and
so fulfils both her human destiny and the spiritual vocation
of which she is intuitively conscious. The pantheistic tone of
the essay recalls Emily Brontë, who helped to inspire the
portrait of Shirley, and so does the implication of the title
that 'the first blue-stocking' was wise enough to confine
herself to the school of Nature. But the atmosphere lacks the
austerity of Emily's mysticism and is more suggestive of a
Greek myth where gods descend to mortals. Genius is the
bridegroom of Eva and the being who tells her: '. . . I take
from thy vision, darkness: I loosen from thy faculties,
fetters! . . . I claim as mine the lost atom of life . . .' Translated into prose, this expresses the relationship of Louis
Moore and the brilliant Shirley as truly as that of Crimsworth
and the quieter Frances. In this context his social inferiority
ceases to be important. He is the 'master' Shirley looks for in
her lover, the 'man I shall feel it impossible not to love and
very possible to fear.'

In the schoolroom more emphasis is given than before to
the fact that French is Louis Moore's native language. That
his former pupil had begun to forget it was a symbol of their
estrangement. When at length he addresses her again in
French and she answers him, 'at first with laughing hesitation

and in broken phrase', it is a sign that communication between them has been restored. Passages from French literature once familiar are read or recited by Louis and repeated by her.[28] There are obvious overtones of Brussels in the nostalgic evocation of these recitations, especially of the passage from Bossuet, 'Le Cheval Dompté'.[29] But the recital comes to an abrupt end with 'Le Chêne et le Roseau' — 'that most beautiful of La Fontaine's fables' — and for an unexpected reason: French poetry is no longer of a calibre to satisfy them, now their enthusiasm has 'kindled to a glow'. It is Louis Moore who remarks: 'And these are our best pieces! And we have nothing more dramatic, nervous, natural!'

The criticism seems strangely out of place, coming from a man whose native language is French.[30] None the less, the literature of which he here speaks with noticeable lack of enthusiasm has had a decisive rôle in Shirley's intellectual formation. 'You read French. Your mind is poisoned with French novels. You have imbibed French principles', is the accusation of her indignant uncle, Mr Sympson, to which Shirley disdainfully replies: 'The ground you are treading on now returns a mighty hollow sound under your feet. Beware!' Something deeper is at issue here between uncle and niece than the question of the 'immorality' of French novels; it is the liberal belief in the equality of both sex and class, which was part of the republican ethos, and in which the half-Belgian Louis Moore believes as whole-heartedly as the wealthy Victorian Sympson rejects it. The pride of the heiress in her love for the tutor — the 'Usher', as her uncle scornfully calls him — is something more truly revolutionary in the Victorian novel than Jane Eyre's confession of her love for the patrician Rochester. It could be paralleled in the works of the French Romantics, most strikingly in the most extreme case, Victor Hugo's *Ruy Blas,* but more closely in some of the novels of George Sand, where an heiress finds no barrier to her love in the lover's lack of social or financial qualifications.[31] Louis Moore himself has no more doubts than Shirley of his ability to fill the rôle of squire of Fieldhead, with its farming land and its mill property, during the troubled era of the Industrial Revolution. And it is perhaps this confidence on the part of an intellectual, more than any other trait, that testifies to the foreign strain in him.

One element is absent from the study of the three Anglo-Belgians in *Shirley* which is normally prominent in Charlotte Brontë's study of foreigners, their attitude to religion. It is Dissenters, not Catholics, who come in for the most scathing criticism. Catholicism has no part in *Shirley,* though Robert Moore mentions once that it was his mother's religion. The owners of Hollow's Cottage have their pew in Briarfield Church, where Hortense at least is a regular attender, but their appearance there seems more in the nature of a social duty than an act of worship. Religion does not apparently enter into Robert Moore's thoughts when he is facing death, though it is Caroline's chief concern in similar circumstances.

With *Villette,* Charlotte Brontë returns to Brussels, but the character drawing, like the setting, is wider ranging, as well as more subtle in its technique, than in *The Professor.* As a famous author who had known lionising in London as well as heartbreak in Howarth, she had considerably more experience on which to draw. Memories of Brussels still help to suggest the central figures, but they are supported by a larger caste and seen in a more penetrating light. There is more maturity and more variety in the portraits drawn by Lucy Snowe than in those of Crimsworth, who only reaches the same standard of excellence in the charming study of Frances Henri. The frustrations and tensions of her difficult life sometimes influence Lucy's attitude to others, but she is willing to rectify errors of judgement where she sees them and frequently does so as she becomes more mature. It is scarcely necessary to add that she finds it more difficult to understand foreigners than her own countrymen. She would be in danger of idealising her compatriots, if there were not enough of them in the cosmopolitan milieu of Villette to remind her that they, too, have faults as well as virtues. In *The Professor* Crimsworth, when in Brussels, is isolated among foreigners, except for the meteoric appearances of Yorke Hunsden. In *Villette* the studies of foreigners are made more effective by the presence of a contrasting British group, the Brettons, whose name speaks for itself, and the Homes, who retain much of their British quality when they change their name to Bassompierre.

Once more the milieu is a school, and like Crimsworth

Lucy briefly sketches some of the individual pupils, but her method shows a far more finished art. She does not show 'specimens of the genus jeune fille' unrelated to the action, but limits herself to the leaders of the attempted classroom revolt in her first lesson. The 'three titled belles in the first row' are not described in detail like the three 'queens of the school' in the earlier novel, but 'Mesdemoiselles Blanche, Virginie and Angélique' are sufficiently characterised by the conjunction of their names and their disruptive activities. The most intransigent of the mutineers, 'Dolores by name, and a Catalonian by race', evidently drawn from the same original as the earlier Juanna Trista, is effectively etched in a couple of lines instead of a couple of paragraphs: 'She had a pale face, hair like night, broad strong eyebrows, decided features, and a dark, mutinous, sinister eye . . .'

A trio very different in character to the three 'titled belles' is presented by Madame Beck's children, who are Lucy's first pupils. It is usually thought that they were suggested by the three eldest Heger children, the only ones of the family of six whom Charlotte Brontë really knew.[32] When she arrived at the pensionnat, the eldest, Marie, was only four — a fact which precludes the possibility of her having served as a model, in any real sense, for Désirée Beck, who was old enough to 'translate currently from English to French' under Lucy Snowe's supervision. Louise and Claire, the two next in age, may have contributed something to the portraits of Fifine and Georgette Beck, who have hardly emerged from babyhood. It was of Louise that Charlotte Brontë retained the most vivid impression — 'elle avait tant de caractère, tant de naïveté dans sa petite figure.'[33] But whatever they may owe to reality, the Beck children play an effective rôle in the novel. Their presence helps to reveal the latent compassion and sympathy for young children in Lucy's nature. She has an evident fondness for Fifine, lively, honest, impatient and likely to blunder into difficulties, and for the 'puny and delicate but engaging' Georgette, and it is to her care that the clear-sighted Madame Beck entrusts her children in illness.

Another trio is furnished by the women teachers in the pensionnat. Crimsworth had already mentioned a similar trio. In number they correspond to Charlotte Brontë's colleagues at the pensionnat Heger, Mesdemoiselles Haussé, Sophie and Blanche, but two of them are so slightly characterised that they do not even receive individual names. The third, the Parisienne Zélie St Pierre, undoubtedly owes something to Mlle Blanche, whom Charlotte heartily disliked, especially during the unhappy final stage of her stay at the pensionnat Heger.[34] Crimsworth had anticipated this character in his summing up of Mlle Zéphyrine as 'a genuine Parisian coquette, perfidious, mercenary and dry-hearted'. Whatever she may owe to her prototype, Zélie is an autonomous artistic creation. She has the cool assurance and efficiency and the outward distinction of her compatriot Pelet, and she is an excellent disciplinarian, but she is in no other sense a good teacher, for she has none of Pelet's genuine interest in intellectual matters. She welcomes any opportunity of humiliating the English teacher, and her episodic appearances in the novel synchronise with such occasions. Her finest opportunity is provided by Lucy's failure to contribute the customary bouquet for M. Paul's 'fête', and she takes an evident pleasure in offering an 'explanation' of the omission which makes it almost an insult: 'For Meess Lucie Monsieur will kindly make allowance; as a foreigner she probably did not know our customs, or did not appreciate their significance. Meess Lucie has regarded this ceremony as too frivolous to be honoured by her observance.'

The staff of Mme Beck included, like Mme Heger's, visiting masters and mistresses. To this category evidently belongs Fräulein Anna Braun, who later gives private lessons in German to Lucy and Paulina de Bassompierre at the latter's home in the Rue Crécy. The brief sketch is interesting as the only one of a teacher of a nationality other than Belgian or French. It is hardly more flattering to the German character than the portrait of Zélie to the Parisian. Fräulein Anna Braun is recognised to be 'a worthy, hearty woman', but this hardly compensates for Lucy's patronising tone in speaking of her. Lucy and Paulina admire Schiller's ballads, but they appear to do so in the light of their own good taste, rather than through any assistance from their well-meaning but unpoetical teacher. The whole episode shows the peripheral importance of German as far as Lucy is concerned.

Teachers and pupils constitute the major part of the little community in the Rue Fossette. Its excellent organisation depends also on an efficient domestic staff. The most prominent member of this is the French 'portress', Rosine, who, from the little room which is her domain, controls the great street-door which connects the pensionnat with the world outside. Rosine is painted with an unfaltering touch. From the moment when she is seen in the little room 'dedicated to the portress's sole use', singing as she sews, she introduces into the pattern of the novel a refreshing quality of light-heartedness, which contrasts in its deliberate un-involvement with the intensity of the general atmosphere:

> . . . her voice, clear, though somewhat sharp, broke out in a lightsome French song, trilling through the door still ajar . . . There at the table she sat in a smart dress of 'jaconas rose', trimming a tiny blond cap: not a living thing save herself was in the room, except indeed some gold fish in a glass globe, some flowers in pots, and a broad July sunbeam. (ch. II)

Morally, Rosine appears to be another version of the French coquette, younger, more superficial and more harmless than Mlle Zélie, 'an unprincipled though pretty little French grisette, airy, fickle, dressy, vain and mercenary'. Lucy gradually comes to see her more as an individual and admits that she is 'on the whole, not a bad sort of person'. She is competent and versatile, able to combine her usual function with that of lady's maid when necessary. She is not easily intimidated but her temerity has its limits; when she has been obliged to interrupt one of M. Paul's lessons five times with urgent messages, she is unable to endure a sixth ordeal and Lucy is obliged to act as her substitute.

Rosine is obviously superior in status to the other domestics in the pensionnat, but Lucy Snowe seems to find more genuine kindness in the cook Goton, who wears 'a jacket, short petticoat and sabots'. She is the only servant left in the pensionnat during the long vacation, and it is no fault of hers that her excellent cooking can no longer tempt Lucy during her illness. Good nature also characterises Martha, the Brettons' Flemish-speaking bonne at La Terrasse, who proves an excellent nurse, although there is a language barrier between herself and Lucy. In contrast with Goton and Martha, the old servant Agnes, who belongs to the strange establishment in the Rue des Mages, is deliberately hostile to strangers. She becomes more tractable when spoken to in Flemish by the priest Père Silas, who intervenes on Lucy's behalf. But her only real merit is an artistic one: she is perfectly in harmony with her surroundings:

> ... had a young ruddy-faced bonne opened the door to admit me, I should have thought such a one little in harmony with her dwelling; but when I found myself confronted by a very old woman, wearing a very antique peasant costume, a cap alike hideous and costly, with long flaps of native lace, a petticoat and jacket of cloth, and sabots more like little boats than shoes, it seemed all right, and soothingly in character. (ch. 34)

By means of such rapid but vivid portraits, Charlotte Brontë gives life to the foreign milieu in the midst of which Lucy's destiny is played out. The community of the Rue Fossette has an active part in the drama. It was a stroke of genius to make the most highly individualized pupil in this community not a Belgian but an English girl, who has been wholly educated at foreign schools, but is still English enough to contrast with her continental contemporaries. Like most of the major characters of *Villette* she owes something to living models. Maria Miller, a boarder at the pensionnat Heger in the Brontës' day, and Susanna Mills, who was there at the same time, have both been mentioned as possible originals of Ginevra Fanshawe.[35] But she has her own rôle in the novel, and her heedless, provocative but not unattractive personality makes itself felt from the moment when Lucy Snowe first meets her till her last appearance in the Rue Fossette.

Ginevra is first seen during a Channel crossing, and from her conversation it is clear that she is largely the product of a continental education. Unlike most of the 'continental English' among Mlle Reuter's pupils as described by Crimsworth, she is not the child of 'broken adventurers' but of a snobbish and impecunious English family, whose daughters' education is paid for by a wealthy relative living

abroad. But some of Crimsworth's blighting criticism certainly applies to her in a modified form. Her formal schooling
has been negligible. 'I know nothing — nothing in the world
— I assure you; except that I play and dance beautifully, —
and French and German of course I know, to speak; but I
can't read or write them very well.' Her religion amounts to
no more than a superficial conformity with whatever form of
worship is practised in the milieu where she happens to find
herself. '. . . they call me a Protestant you know, but really I
am not sure whether I am one or not: I don't well know the
difference between Romanism and Protestantism.' In spite of
these results of a continental education, Ginevra remains to
some extent one of the 'British English' of Crimsworth's
second category. Her fair beauty is of the English type, and
she feels consciously superior to her foreign associates,
though she does not avoid them with the proud unsociability
Crimsworth approvingly notes as typical of the 'British
English'.

The greater maturity of *Villette* — as opposed to *The
Professor* — in the attitude to the foreign milieu becomes
evident in the portrait of Ginevra Fanshawe. Ignorant she
may be in scholastic matters, but her taste in dress, her grace
and social charm — qualities admired, not denigrated by Lucy
— owe something to continental influence. Conversely some
of her defects are undoubtedly of indigenous growth. Lucy,
who is frequently unconscious of her own insularity, is aware
that the same quality indicates prejudice in Ginevra. '. . . the
people about her, teachers and pupils, she held to be
despicable, because they were foreigners.' Her evident snobbery contrasts with the generally democratic atmosphere of
Labassecour. She uses the word 'bourgeois', as no Labassecourien would, to denote inferiority, saying scornfully of Dr
Bretton, 'he is only bourgeois', and considering that a reason
in itself for preferring his rival, Count de Hamal.

Insular and snobbish, Ginevra adds to these defects of her
English family background the general human failing of
selfishness, though she is good humoured enough as long as
nothing happens to annoy her. No marked virtues single her
out from her Labassecourien contemporaries, though, in
Lucy's eyes at least, she is physically more attractive than the

statuesque beauties of Villette. One moral quality she does possess, 'that directness which was her best point . . . the salt, the sole preservative of a character otherwise not formed to keep'. It is this that makes her not merely tolerate Lucy's plain speaking but like her all the better for it. In this she is evidently, in Lucy's estimation, distinctively English. Among the girls admitted to the Court circles at the concert in Villette, she stands out as 'the prettiest, or, at any rate, the least demure and hypocritical-looking of the lot'.

At the end of the novel Ginevra has the satisfaction of becoming the Countess de Hamal. Count Alfred de Hamal is one of the aristocracy of Labassecour. There is a French strain in him, and Ginevra does not fail to praise the Latin character of his good looks, as well as his other qualities: 'Colonel de Hamal is a gentleman of excellent connections, perfect manners, sweet appearance, with pale interesting face, and hair and eyes like an Italian.' Ginevra's praise is in itself a guarantee of triviality. De Hamal, for whom no known original exists, seems more of a type than a personality, the masculine equivalent of the 'French coquette', as seen by Charlotte Brontë. She emphasises this by stressing his affinity with the masculine rôle played by Lucy in the school vaudeville, where she takes the part of the 'butterfly, talker, traitor'. De Hamal's own rôle in the novel is that of a prolonged masquerade, since he is the 'nun' of the garden and the attic. With his gambling, his billets doux, his cult of fashion and his love of intrigue, he is reminiscent of a 'petit maître' from a comedy of Molière or a superficial version of a Musset character. So completely does his part belong to the comic register that he is incapable of understanding the suffering his 'romantic idea of the spectral disguise' has inflicted on Lucy, and sends her his apologies, through the medium of Ginevra's valedictory letter, in suitably flippant form: 'Alfred . . . hopes you won't miss him now that he has gone; he begs to apologise for any little trouble he may have given you.'

Ginevra is probably right in thinking that the 'Colonel-Count' will be a more congenial husband for her than Dr Bretton. She is none the less indignant when her bourgeois lover transfers his allegiance to her cousin Paulina. Paulina differs from her in every way, including racial background. Ginevra is a Continental by education only, till she eventually becomes one by marriage. Paulina's father is 'of mixed French and Scottish origin' and eventually inherits from the relatives of his French mother the title of Count de Bassompierre. His daughter is proud of their double nationality. 'We are Home and de Bassompierre, Caledonian and Gallic.'

Paulina's father has an intellectual bias — derived, according to his friends the Brettons, from 'a maternal uncle, a French savant' — and she has inherited something of this, though not his interest in science. She is cultured and intelligent. Her French is far better, if not more fluent, than Ginevra's: '. . . it was faultless, — the structure correct, the idioms true, the accent pure . . .' And when her father entertains a number of French savants to dinner she is at home in the salon-like atmosphere as Ginevra is not:

> Paulina was awed by the savants, but not quite to mutism:
> she conversed modestly, diffidently; not without effort,
> but with so true a sweetness, so fine and penetrating a
> sense that her father more than once suspended his own
> discourse to listen, and fixed on her an eye of proud
> delight . . . The grace and mind of Paulina charmed these
> thoughtful Frenchmen: the fineness of her beauty, the soft
> courtesy of her manner, her immature but real and inbred
> tact pleased their national taste; they clustered about her,
> not indeed to talk science, which would have rendered her
> dumb, but to touch on many subjects in letters, in arts, in
> actual life, on which it appeared she had both read and
> reflected. (ch. 27)

The main intention of this scene is no doubt to contrast the intelligence of Paulina with the shallowness of Ginevra, who finds such a milieu merely boring, and so gives Graham Bretton fresh cause to transfer his admiration to her cousin. But it is evident that, as the child of a scholarly father who is partly French, she has a natural affinity with those aspects of the French character which her creator whole-heartedly admired.

None the less Paulina and her father remain in essence more Caledonian than Gallic. Charlotte Brontë, as an ardent reader of Scott and *Blackwood's,* had admired the Scottish character since childhood and expressed her admiration in Angrian days in the creation of the Duke of Fidena, one of the few Angrian rulers of complete integrity. At the time when she was composing *Villette,* her early admiration had received fresh stimulus through her liking for George Smith, her publisher, himself a Scotsman in origin, and the brief but greatly enjoyed visit to Edinburgh which inspired such enthusiastic comment in her letters.[36] On first seeing Mr Home, Lucy thinks he looks very much a Scotsman, 'at once proud-looking and homely-looking'. When she meets him in Villette, after he has acquired a French title, she notices that 'there was still quite as much about him of plain Mr. Home as of proud Count de Bassompierre'. When his daughter dances, he asks: 'And is that a Scotch reel you are dancing, you Highland fairy?' Paulina seems to know Scotland only at secondhand through her father's reminiscences, but she evidently shares his pride in his native country.

Paulina Mary Home de Bassompierre, as she somewhat grandiloquently calls herself, seems intended to unite charm and thoughtfulness, a combination perhaps reminiscent of her double nationality. But 'the little Countess' is not so successful a creation as the little Anglo-Swiss lace-mender in *The Professor.* She is more attractive as the vulnerable and sensitive child of Bretton days than as the rather fastidious young aristocrat of the Hôtel Crécy. Charlotte Brontë recognised that she had not been entirely successful with this character, whose delicate charm she had meant to show as so superior to the more obvious beauty of Ginevra. 'I greatly apprehend . . . that the weakest character in the book is the one I aimed at making the most beautiful . . .'[37]

The reason for this comparative failure seemed clear to the author. '. . . if this be the case, the fault lies in its wanting the germ of the *real* — in its being purely imaginary.' Obviously no such fault invalidated the creation of the directrice of the pensionnat in the Rue Fossette, Mme Beck. But it was only the germ of the real that was required. At the time of the publication of *Shirley,* when 'originals' were being eagerly sought by the Yorkshire public, Charlotte Brontë had already emphatically denied that any of the characters were intended as literal portraits: 'It would not suit the rules of art, nor my own feelings, to write in that style. We only suffer reality to *suggest,* never to *dictate.* The heroines are abstractions, and the heroes also . . .'[38] Nothing is more certain than that the character of Mme Beck is an abstraction, an autonomous artistic creation, like any other leading figure in the novels. Yet because of the unique significance of the Hegers in Charlotte Brontë's life, she, like M. Heger, has been identified with a living model to a degree which has been manifestly unfair to both, and which justifies some consideration of the position in the light of present knowledge.

All the evidence confirms that Mme Heger was essentially a very different person from the scheming directress of the Rue Fossette. After the publication of *Villette,* her conduct was totally unlike what might have been expected of Mme Beck in similar circumstances. Mme Beck would doubtless have been greatly concerned by the publication of a novel likely to suggest such an unflattering picture of herself, and would have employed all her craftiness to denigrate its author. Mme Heger simply continued, as before, to devote herself to her husband and family, and to her school. Her success in both spheres was something which could not have been achieved by any amount of Machiavellian scheming, only by genuine qualities of heart as well as mind. Six years after the publication of *Villette,* an English pupil at the pensionnat found her presence there 'an abiding influence of serenity that reassured one . . .'[39] But the same pupil also discovered that this serenity, unlike the passionless calm of Mme Beck, had not always been maintained without cost to herself. Once when she was complaining bitterly of unfair treatment, Mme Heger countered her passionate protests with the quiet question: 'Seriez-vous la seule personne au monde qui ne connaîtrait pas l'injustice?'

The kindness she showed to all her pupils did not cease when they left the pensionnat. They remained then, and always, her 'chères élèves'. Some of the letters she wrote in later years to members of a Yorkshire family who had been at the pensionnat have been preserved. They have been truly described as 'those of a kindly and sympathetic woman, with a fine appreciation of the joys and burdens of motherhood'.[40]

Unlike Mme Beck, who seemed to have little maternal feeling, she evidently considered a woman's life as best fulfilled in caring for a family or, if unmarried, in doing so vicariously like her daughter Claire, who succeeded her in the pensionnat and of whom she said: '. . . she is not, as you know, married; but she is the mother of a family in the finest sense of the word . . .'[41] She was a woman to whom her religion meant far more than to Mme Beck, who was content with outward observance and some rational philanthropy and capable of laughing at her cousin M. Paul for being a 'dévot'. Religion was for her the most important consideration in the bringing up of children: 'To turn a child into a good man or woman is to make one's life fruitful in time and eternity.'[42] She was a sincere and practising Catholic, and when Mrs Gaskell referred to Charlotte Brontë's dislike of Romanism as one of the chief causes of the silent estrangement between the two women during the second year of her stay in Brussels, she was stating a tragic truth. Her religion in fact meant as much to Mme Heger as her own faith did to Charlotte Brontë. In a letter written shortly before her death to one of the former Yorkshire pupils she said: 'I am glad to hear that you often read from "The Imitation". It is chiefly from there that my husband and I draw light and consolation.'

For Mme Heger religion and maternity were the two most important things in life. But Charlotte Brontë's deep distrust of Romanism made it impossible for them to meet on the common ground of their religious faith. And Mme Heger with her strongly Catholic background probably considered that the unmarried woman would find the most satisfying substitute for her natural vocation in the vicarious maternity of the teacher or the nun. It is likely that — on far more disinterested grounds — she shared Mlle Reuter's disapproval of a literary career for women. With her lucid common-sense and her wide knowledge of the adolescents with whom she was primarily concerned, she was probably as much aware of the potential dangers of the novelist's art as of its intrinsic value. It must have been a shock to her to realise, as she no doubt did, in the course of Charlotte Brontë's second year at the pensionnat, that the shy little English teacher, whose admirable *devoirs* showed such satisfactory progress in the mastery of French, cherished literary ambitions. She was anxious, as she had always been, to encourage her in the teacher's career which had been her declared objective in coming to Brussels — even to the point of being willing to send one of her own daughters to the projected school in Yorkshire. She could hardly have been expected to know that for Charlotte Brontë teaching was not a natural vocation, and that this woman of twenty-seven, with an apparently uneventful life behind her, was the possessor not merely of literary talent, but of a genius which was now beginning to demand its definitive expression.

Still less was it likely that with her practical nature and her common sense she should understand the romantic devotion to her 'master' by which Charlotte Brontë was increasingly dominated during her second year in Brussels. Secure in her husband's love, she knew she had no cause for jealousy. But she did not believe, as Charlotte Brontë did, in the possibility of a friendship that was both passionate and Platonic, on the part of a still young woman for a married man whom she frequently met. It is probable that in the circumstances she did try to diminish the opportunities for meeting between them. Had she had a deeper understanding of Charlotte's temperament, she might have acted differently and let her continue to enjoy his friendship freely for what could only have been a limited period, but unlike Mme Beck she certainly believed she was acting in Charlotte's best interest, as well as taking the wisest course, and was never motivated by a cold self-interest like the crafty directress of the school in the Rue Fossette.

But even had Mme Heger been as much like the wily Mme Beck as she was basically unlike her, the radical difference between her situation and that of Mme Beck in the novel would make any real analogy impossible. The directress of the school in the Rue Fossette is a widow of several years' standing. She has no special affection for her mercurial cousin M. Paul, and it is quite unjustifiably that she tries to put a stop to the friendship, which finally grows into love, between him and the young English teacher. Though she does not love M. Paul, she wants to marry him so that she can bind him to her interests. Since she cannot do so, she joins in the conspiracy to send him abroad to act as agent for the property of a wealthy old relative, part of whose estate she hopes to inherit. She thus becomes responsible for preventing the marriage between two people admirably suited to each other.

But it is only in the last part of the novel, when it is clear that Lucy and M. Paul are falling in love, that Mme Beck becomes the active antagonist of the English teacher. Till then she is by no means a wholly unsympathetic figure. Physically, like the earlier portrait of Mlle Reuter, she was modelled on Mme Heger; the resemblance was still evident to Frederika Macdonald when she compared Charlotte Brontë's description with her own recollections of Mme Heger in middle age.[43] As in the case of Mlle Reuter, she is attractive without being beautiful, because of her fresh colouring, graceful movements and the general impression of serenity she conveys:

> When attired, Madame Beck appeared a personage of a figure rather short and stout, yet still graceful in its own peculiar way; that is, with the grace resulting from propor- tion of parts. Her complexion was fresh and sanguine, not too rubicund; her eye, blue and serene; her dark silk dress fitted her as a French sempstress alone can make a dress fit . . . I know not what of harmony pervaded her whole person . . . (ch. 8)

The same harmony is reflected in her apparently effortless management of the pensionnat 'without bustle, fatigue, fever, or any symptom of undue excitement: occupied she always was — busy, rarely.' Her efficiency is compatible with a concern for the health and happiness of her pupils reminis- cent of the constant watchfulness of Mme Heger, remem- bered with gratitude by Frederika Macdonald, for the community in her care:

> No minds were overtasked: the lessons were well dis- tributed and made incomparably easy to the learner . . . She never grudged a holiday . . . her method in all these matters was easy, liberal, salutary, and rational: many an austere English school-mistress would do vastly

well to imitate her — and I believe many would be glad to do so, if exacting English parents would let them. (ch. 8).

But the moral portrait of Mme Beck, even from the start, is Janus-faced. Her efficiency is rooted in the craftiness which is her dominant characteristic and which stamps her as the novelist's creation — a very different personality from Mme Heger in essentials. ' "Surveillance", "espionage", — these were her watchwords.' The first was part of the normal discipline of continental schools, though distasteful to Charlotte Brontë. But 'surveillance' is not the same thing as 'espionage', and the latter is the more accurate definition of Mme Beck's activities, from the moment when Lucy watches her, on the night of her arrival in Villette, carefully making a cast in wax of the keys she has found among the stranger's few possessions. This spying is made highly ironic by the fact that Mme Beck herself regards it in the light of a stern and exacting duty. In the case of the keys, she wishes to provide herself with the means of finding out all she can about the Englishwoman she has engaged without references as nursery governness for her children. 'The end was not bad, but the means were hardly fair or justifiable.' There is also a source of potential comedy in the situation, for spying is an activity which can never be acknowledged, even when it has obviously been detected. When Mme Beck eavesdrops and is betrayed by a sneeze out of season, she acts with her usual aplomb: '. . . she came forward alert, composed, in the best yet most tranquil spirits: no novice to her habits but would have thought she had just come in, and scouted the idea of her having been glued to the key-hole for at least ten minutes.'

The tranquillity which characterises Mme Beck, like her efficiency, has another side to it, not at once obvious to the observer. Her skill in management was based on espionage. Her unshakeable calm is made possible by her incapacity for any deep feeling. She is not naturally callous, any more than she is naturally dishonest. Just as she likes honesty when it does not interfere with her interests, so she likes to diffuse an atmosphere of serenity about her. But she distrusts emotion, looking on it as a disruptive influence, for 'la Convenance et la Décence were the two calm deities of Madame's worship'.

The portrait of Mme Beck is, with that of M. Paul, Charlotte Brontë's most complete study of a foreigner. Their racial inheritance is not the only influence that has helped to form their complex personalities, but it is a vital part of them. Mme Beck does not only show her continental origin in her trim dress and social flair, and her astonishment at the intrepidity of 'les Anglaises'. She also shows it in her reaction to situations which would have provoked a different response from an Englishwoman. It is not likely a contemporary English schoolmistress would have felt the same alarm at Lucy's studiousness, or 'often and solemnly' warned her not to study too much, lest the blood should all go to her head. But there are differences also in her responses on a deeper level. She subscribes to the ethics of her milieu in general, not only from self-interest but because she obviously finds them acceptable. Her worship of 'la Convenance et la Décence' is not something peculiar to herself: it is characteristic of the tradition in which she has been brought up. It is alien to Lucy, whose irony on the subject betrays in fact her partial incomprehension of the issue involved, an incomprehension probably shared by Charlotte Brontë herself. For these 'calm deities' represented a standard of civilisation first established in the classic age of French culture and by no means as incompatible with deep feeling as Lucy supposed. From this source Mme Beck derives in fact a certain dignity, but in her case it remains superficial, precisely because there is not enough feeling behind it to give it its true significance.

The lasting dichotomy in Charlotte Brontë's attitude to French culture reappears in this brilliant and complex portrait. The capacity of Mme Beck for subtle diplomacy — her most outstanding characteristic — is viewed by her with mingled admiration and distrust. It is significant that she feels such a capacity should have had, as its true sphere of activity, not a scholastic milieu in Labassecour, but the turbulence and the intrigues of revolutionary or of imperial France:

> That school offered her for her powers too limited a sphere; she ought to have swayed a nation: she should have been the leader of a turbulent legislative assembly. Nobody could have browbeaten her, none irritated her nerves, exhausted her patience, or over-reached her astuteness. In

her own single person, she could have comprised the duties of a first minister and a superintendent of policy . . . (ch. 8)

Mme Beck is not Lucy's only enemy in the final stages of the action. She is one of a 'secret junta' of three, of whom the other members are Père Silas and Mme Walravens. Père Silas is unique in Charlotte Brontë's novels as the portrait of a Catholic priest. He is a much more sympathetic, if not by any means as subtle a study as Mme Beck. It is not till he grows alarmed by his former pupil's love for a heretic that he is in any sense Lucy's enemy. The first contact between them takes place when she visits the confessional, when he shows the same sympathy as the priest at Ste Gudule to Charlotte Brontë in a similar crisis. Later, in conjunction with Mme Beck, he does his best to convince her of the impossibility of marriage with M. Paul. But he none the less remains basically sympathetic in his attitude to her.

The portrait of Père Silas is another proof that Lucy's insularity has become modified since her arrival in Villette. She admits that he is 'naturally kind, with a sentimental French kindness' — for he is a Frenchman, not a Labassecourien. Dr Bretton knows him as 'a man I have often met by the sick beds of both rich and poor: and chiefly the latter'. Lucy pays him the high compliment of saying: 'There was something of Fénelon about that benign old priest.' But when he shows himself anxious to convert her to his faith, all her entrenched suspicion of Catholicism reasserts itself. She believes that to respond would be to abandon her will and conscience to his direction and lose the power of moral choice. When he tells her, 'Protestantism is altogether too dry, cold, prosaic for you,' he shows a complete misunderstanding of her nature and background, not knowing her distrust of mysticism in a religious context.[44] When he next appears in the Rue des Mages, it is in an atmosphere saturated with superstition. But his natural kindness reasserts itself later when, though he fails to persuade her to abjure Protestantism, 'through every abortive experiment, under every repeated disappointment' he remains patient. Lucy does not scorn or dislike him as she does the other members of the 'secret junta', and acknowledges that he is 'not a bad man, though the advocate of a bad cause'.

In introducing Mme Walravens, the remaining ally of Mme Beck, Charlotte Brontë adopts a method of presentation which makes her seem less a person than an evil force. She is strange enough in herself — a hunch-backed dwarf who persists in wearing the elaborate dress and the magnificent jewels she flaunted as the wife of a rich jeweller in her distant youth. But what Lucy first sees in the strange house in the Rue des Mages is her shadow, as she comes down the winding staircase, and then an appearance which can scarcely be called a human form:

> She might be three feet high, but she had no shape . . . Her face was large, set, not upon her shoulders but before her breast; she seemed to have no neck; I should have said there were a hundred years in her features, and more perhaps on her eyes — her malign, unfriendly eyes . . . This being wore a gown of brocade, dyed bright blue, full-tinted as the gentianella flower . . . But her chief points were her jewels . . . Hunchbacked, dwarfish and doting, she was adorned like a barbarian queen. (ch. 34)

Mme Walravens, like her household, seems to belong, in this crucial moment, to a new dimension in which fact and fancy are fused in a visionary reality. There is a clue to her almost mythical significance in her sinister name. It has been pointed out that Walravens is a medieval variant of *wal rabens,* 'slaughter ravens', a reference to the grim function of the birds sacred to Odin on the battlefield, and that the germanic name, not inappropriate to the mixed linguistic background of Belgium, is peculiarly appropriate to the old woman who battens on the living as well as the dead happiness of M. Paul.[45] Her mysterious and sinister nature is made even clearer by the other names Lucy instinctively applies to her when she appears: 'Distincter even than the scenic details stood the chief figure — Cunegonde, the sorceress! Malevola, the evil fairy.'

There could be no more fitting setting for the second and final appearance of Mme Walravens than the midnight fête in the park, that 'woody and turfy theatre' where a shadow of mystery reigns which is still more potent than the spell which lay over the Rue des Mages. Enthroned on her rustic bench, she is an even more startling incarnation of the grotesque than before:

> Père Silas stooped over the seat with its single occupant, the rustic bench and that which sat upon it: a strange mass it was — bearing no shape, yet magnificent. You saw, indeed, the outline of a face and features, but these were so cadaverous and so strangely placed, you could almost have fancied a head severed from its trunk, and flung at random on a pile of rich merchandise . . . Hail, Madame Walravens! I think you looked more witchlike than ever. (ch. 38)

The almost surrealist quality of the imagery is in keeping, like the former image of the malevolent fairy, with Lucy's state of heightened awareness, now raised by the influence of the narcotic to dream-like proportions. It expresses her sense of Mme Walravens' inhumanity, but it has a wider significance as well, suggesting the cruelty of the useless sacrifices exacted by fanaticism, greed and self-interest in general. Yet this grotesque is also a human figure; Mme Walravens suddenly proves she is 'no corpse or ghost, but a harsh and hardy old woman' by marking her annoyance with Mme Beck's noisy eldest child by 'a resounding rap with her gold-knobbed cane'.

Around Mme Walravens and the two other members of the 'junta', Mme Beck and Père Silas are grouped, in the climactic scene in the park, a circle of relations and friends, minor figures whose number accentuates the solitary condition of Lucy in a foreign city. The most prominent is the young Justine Marie, whom Lucy wrongly suspects of being the intended bride of M. Paul. She is a handsome good-humoured girl, with the type of beauty indigenous to the country and is in fact betrothed to the fair-haired young Heinrich Muller, whose German nationality seems to emphasise the Germanic element in the Walravens' circle. No description is given of Mme Beck's brother, Victor Kint. Josef Emanuel, the half-brother of M. Paul, a noted pianist and the principal music-teacher in Villette, had already been described when he appeared at the concert attended by Lucy and the Brettons.

The probable prototype for this character was M. Heger's brother-in-law M. Chapelle, who taught music at the pensionnat, as well as being a professor at the Brussels Conservatoire Royal.[46] He impresses Lucy chiefly by his general unlikeness to M. Paul, whose dynamism he lacks, but he is a gifted musician. Another representative of Villette society present in the park on the night of the fête, though not a member of the circle round Mme Walravens, is M. Miret, the pensionnat bookseller, who later becomes her landlord in the Faubourg Clotilde. He is said to have been modelled on 'the excellent bookseller to the pensionnat Heger'.[47]

The microcosm of Villette society in the park would not be complete without M. Paul. He is one of the last to arrive, but is seen to be 'the true life of the party . . . proving indisputably his right of leadership'. His rôle here coincides with his rôle in the novel, where it is only in the later stages that his true stature becomes apparent. Until then the part of the hero apparently belongs to Graham Bretton, rather as Ginevra — though with less solid qualifications — for long usurps the place that ultimately proves to belong to Paulina. And like Paulina, M. Paul can only be appreciated as he merits when the strength and the weakness of his more conventionally attractive rival have been seen and understood.

The contrast between the two is accentuated by the difference in nationality. The surname Bretton obviously suggests 'a variation of Britain'.[48] Until they moved to the Continent the Brettons had lived in the ancient English town of which they bore the name, but they have some Scottish blood, as their distant relation 'Mr Home' recalls when he tells Graham: '. . . you descended partly from a Highlander and a chief, and there is a trace of the Celt in all you look, speak and think.' It is because of their financial losses that they move to the Continent, where Graham Bretton soon becomes known as a doctor in Villette, but they remain very British in their new environment.

On his first appearance as a schoolboy of sixteen, Graham Bretton shows the mixture of charm and egoism which is always to characterise him. He is kind to a forlorn child because kindness is part of his genial nature, but he can say good-bye to her without in the least understanding what the parting means to her. The same qualities will be evident at a later stage in his relations with Lucy. But when he reappears as an adult in Villette he is a more attractive and impressive figure than before, for in Lucy's eyes he incorporates, in the foreign milieu, some of the best qualities of her compatriots. When he comes to her aid on the night of her arrival showing 'a nature chivalric to the needy and feeble, as well as the youthful and fair', she pronounces him 'a true young English gentleman'. When the stranger who has come to her assistance reappears as the 'Dr John' of the Rue Fossette, and is finally recognised by her as Graham Bretton, he continues to appear to advantage in the continental setting. His chivalric love of Ginevra is contrasted with the intrigues of the amorous de Hamal. He shows a more disinterested chivalry in his kindness to Lucy herself when Père Silas draws his attention to her plight, taking her to be nursed at his own home before he realises that the English teacher is the Lucy Snowe of Bretton days.

It is at this stage of closer acquaintance that Lucy begins to be conscious that the adult Graham has his weak points. She does not regret the termination of his infatuation with Ginevra, whom he suspects of intriguing with his rival, but she is startled at its abruptness. Even in his growing friendship for herself she is aware of a self-indulgent quality, 'pleasure in homage, some recklessness in exciting, some vanity in receiving the same . . .' He writes her friendly letters to cheer her solitude, but seems amused as well as touched when he discovers what their value is for her. And the letters cease abruptly when Graham renews his acquaintance with the Bassompierres and falls in love with Paulina. She is a worthier object for his love than Ginevra, but it is clear that there is a certain snobbishness in his selection of a bride. For 'little Polly Home' he had at best a patronising affection, but he has quite a different attitude to the 'little Countess'. 'The pearl he admired was in itself of great price and truest purity, but he was not the man who in appreciating the gem, could forget its setting . . . there was about Dr John all the man of the world; to satisfy himself did not suffice; society must approve . . . .' He reveals his limitations in another direction when he takes Lucy to see Vashti act and, unlike her, remains singularly unmoved in the presence of genius:

> . . . it amused and enlightened me to discover that he was watching that sinister and sovereign Vashti, not with wonder . . . nor yet dismay, but simply with intense curiosity . . . Cool young Briton! The pale cliffs of his own England do not look down on the tides of the Channel more calmly than he watched the Pythian inspiration of that night. (ch. 23)

His response is equally insensitive when Lucy at last is induced to tell him of the apparition of the nun. He refuses to believe in the possibility that she can have seen anything supernatural, insisting that 'it was all optical illusion — nervous malady, and so on'. But a practical emergency like the threatened fire at the theatre finds him completely adequate, and confirms the truth of Lucy's judgment: 'Dr John *could* think and think well, but he was rather a man of action than of thought . . .'

Handsome, gifted, with no faults serious enough to diminish the charm of his attractive personality, Dr Bretton has all the obvious qualifications for the hero of the novel. But the action of *Villette* is not conventionally schematic, and in its later stages he is unquestionably overshadowed by that superficially less impressive figure, M. Paul. When Charlotte Brontë's publisher protested at the shifting of the centre of interest, she recognised the justice of the complaint, but affirmed that the change was 'in a sense compulsory on the writer', and compatible with truth to life, if not with 'the spirit of romance'.[49] It is only gradually and almost reluctantly that Lucy Snowe herself begins to comprehend that the foreign 'professor of literature' possesses qualities lacking in her brilliant young compatriot, and to recognise the true stature of the man she eventually comes to prefer 'before all humanity'.

M. Paul has been identified with M. Heger as inevitably as Mme Beck with his wife, and in this case the artist's creation is nearer the personality that helped to suggest it. The technique used in the drawing of M. Paul seems to confirm Charlotte Brontë's own description of her borrowings from real life sources in the portraits of her heroes and her heroines. 'Qualities I have seen, loved, and admired, are here and there put in as decorative gems, to be preserved in that setting.'[50] Yet it remains true here, as always, that she only suffers reality to *'suggest,* never to *dictate'*. M. Paul differs from the man who helped to suggest him as surely, if not as completely, as Mme Beck from Mme Heger. In this case too the identification does less than justice to the creative power of the artist. And it is equally certain that contemporaries of M. Heger would not have found in the literary creation all the qualities that characterised one of the leading teachers of his generation in Belgium, the man to whom, as to his wife, his country recognised that it owed much.

At the time of the Brontës' stay in Brussels, Constantin Heger was already a highly gifted teacher, with very definite views on his profession, and on the methods to be employed in it. He expressed these views in the two speeches he gave at the prize-giving of the Athénée Royal in 1834 and 1843. He was only twenty-five when he was first invited to give the prize-giving address in 1834 — a great honour, since the occasion was one of the events of the Brussels year. Perhaps his colleagues were honouring by their choice not only the professional gifts of a former pupil of the Athénée but the courage of the young man who had fought in the Belgian Revolution of 1830 and had lost his wife and child in the cholera epidemic of 1833. It was in his teaching vocation that he had found solace and power to face life again after this crushing calamity.

In the speech of 1834 he gives lucid expression to his passionate belief in the function of education, speaking as one who has chosen it as his life's work: '. . . quoi de plus palpitant d'intérêt pour moi, qui ai voué à l'instruction tout ce que Dieu m'a donné d'intelligence, tout ce qu'il me donnera de jours!'[51] but the personal note is, from the start, subordinated to a generous concern with wider interests. He believes that education should be the State's primary concern, convinced as he is that it is the best safeguard of society, far better than penal action because it is preventive instead of merely punitive. He is conscious, like Victor Hugo, of the tragedy of illiteracy condemned for transgressing laws

it does not understand. He sees, too, how vital education is in
the era of Belgium's industrialisation. But his ideal of education includes something more than the formation of law
abiding and efficient citizens; it is above all moral education
that he considers indispensable, and never more so than in an
increasingly scientific age:

> Que le professeur se hâte de montrer aux jeunes gens
> qu'il y a quelque chose de plus impérieux que l'intérêt, le
> devoir . . . que l'instituteur se hâte de donner le corps pour
> contrepoids à l'esprit, la conscience au calcul; qu'il se hâte,
> l'avenir de la société en dépend!

> Donner une instruction purement scientifique fut, en
> tout temps, une grande faute; de nos jours, ce serait un
> crime, car sans l'éducation morale, la science n'est pas
> seulement insuffisante, elle est nuisible . . . Il est bien
> coupable, messieurs, celui qui s'occupe de remplir la tête et
> laisse le coeur vide: c'est faire de la science l'auxiliaire de
> l'égoïsme, c'est voiler cette difformité morale sous des
> dehors séduisants . . . enfin, c'est armer l'égoïsme de toutes
> pièces et rendre irrésistible son action dissolvante sur la
> société.[52]

The moral education he sees as the primary necessity is the
function not only of the teacher but of the father, and its
basis is a religious one:

> Préservé par la sollicitude de son père et de son maître,
> l'enfant ne passera aux études savantes, qu'après avoir été
> initié à la connaissance des devoirs, aux vérités de la
> Religion. [53]

As a man of action as well as of convictions, Constantin
Heger did not hesitate to implement the principles he
formulated in this speech, which might be considered as the
programme of his life's work. He was predominantly occupied with his pupils at the Athénée Royal, but he also
found time to help those less fortunate than this privileged
minority, and to extend to them, too, as far as he could, the
benefits of education, which he felt the State owed to all its
citizens, by classes given in his scanty leisure. After his

second marriage in 1836, lessons in literature at his wife's school were added to his teaching programme. In the years that followed, as the father of a young family, he had personal experience of the privileges and duties he had already recognised as belonging to the 'chef de famille'.

In 1843 he was again invited to give the address at the Athénée prize-giving. He had no need to repeat, in the presence of the burgomaster of Brussels, the belief in the dignity of his profession to which he had already given definitive expression. This time it is a practical aspect of teaching that concerns him, the question of the advisability of prizes from an educational standpoint. The speech reveals him as a highly gifted teacher, with methods very much his own, for his treatment of the apparently pedestrian subject develops into a brilliant study of the use the teacher can make, in the pupil's best interests, of the instinct of emulation. With Pascalian insight he shows how fatal it would be to crush this quality, inborn in every child, which witnesses to a desire of perfection divine in origin, as well as to the human desire for power and personal triumph. In his opinion the teacher can and should utilise this instinct to encourage his pupils to develop their gifts and to make them aware of those of others, whose achievements they can take as models to rival and if possible surpass. He admits, however, that the critics of emulation have some ground for their distrust; it is a source of energy potent both for good and evil, which must never be allowed to degenerate into pride or vanity. The teacher must guide and train it. Here, too, religion is the supreme safeguard. '. . . il faut qu'elle (l'émulation) soit refrénée et gouvernée par la Religion.'[54]

In the conclusion of his speech M. Heger depresses undue pretensions on the part of the prizewinners by unexpectedly reminding them how much they owe to sources other than their own still immature powers: '. . . à votre âge, on ne fait encore que recevoir . . . Songez-y bien, vous avez déjà beaucoup reçu et de tout le monde; de Dieu, de vos parents, de votre patrie . . .'[55] Speaking of the parents' contribution, he now rates the mother's as the more important, thinking surely in the first place of the mother of his own children when he says: 'Enfants, tout ce que vous avez, tout ce que l'avenir vous réserve, vous le devez à votre mère. — Après Dieu, c'est elle qui vous a tout donné . . .'[56] Finally, with the days of the 1830 Revolution no doubt in his mind, he reminds his pupils what they owe to 'cette autre vénérable mère . . . la patrie'.

It is clear from these masterly speeches — copies of which were among the most treasured possessions of Charlotte Brontë — that, at the time when she knew him, M. Heger was already a mature thinker, for whom teaching was a way of life, closely integrated with his religious, moral and political beliefs. His world was evidently an altogether wider one than that of the fictional M. Paul. As in the case of Mme Beck, there are also crucial differences of situation between the 'professor of literature' of the Rue Fossette and the prominent Brussels figure with whom he has sometimes been identified. M. Paul is only seen, in his magisterial capacity, as a visiting teacher in a girls' school. He is not a happily married man with a young family but a bachelor, still faithful to his dead love of twenty years ago, until his friendship with Lucy slowly and hesitatingly develops into a dominant interest and finally into a love more mature than his youthful passion. In the end he sacrifices his prospect of happiness and his chosen profession to a quixotic sense of duty which makes him leave Europe for no very convincing motive and with a passivity very unlikely to have been shown by M. Heger. Yet memories of Brussels have contributed much to the portrait of M. Paul. But so integrated in this study are fiction and reality that it lives as a perfect entity, the undoubted masterpiece among Charlotte Brontë's masculine portraits.

In physical appearance M. Paul at first sight appears almost insignificant. The adjective 'little', which is constantly applied to him, emphasises his difference to the conventional image of the hero: 'A dark little man he certainly was; pungent and austere . . .' But he is too vital to be insignificant, and as she comes to know him better, Lucy Snowe realises that he can appear physically impressive through the sheer force of his personality. His form, 'not tall but active', is 'alive with the energy and movement of three tall men' and, in a crowd, his face stands out because it possesses:

> ... certain vigorous characteristics ... rendered con-
> spicuous now by the contrast with a throng of tamer
> faces: the deep, intent keenness of his eye, the power of
> his forehead, pale, broad, and full — the mobility of his
> most flexible mouth. He lacked the calm of force, but its
> movement and fire he signally possessed. (ch. 20).

As their friendship ripens, she finds that his face can also
express a kindness that transforms it:

> ... I cannot affirm that I had ever witnessed the smile of
> pleasure, or content, or kindness round M. Paul's lips, or in
> his eyes before. The ironic, the sarcastic, the disdainful,
> the passionately exultant, I had hundreds of times seen
> him express by what he called a smile, but any illuminated
> sign of milder or warmer feelings struck me as wholly new
> in his visage. It changed it as from a mask to a face ... I
> know not that I have ever seen in any other human face an
> equal metamorphosis from a similar cause. (ch. 27).

Lucy's changing attitude to M. Paul's physical appearance
is symptomatic of her changing opinion of him in general,
during her eighteen months at the pensionnat. Although it is
on his advice that Mme Beck engages her as nursery governess, for long she only sees this 'vague arbiter' of her destiny
at a distance. She first experiences the force of his personality when he turns to her for help in his dilemma over the
school play he is directing. His autocratic quality comes to
the fore again when the examination-day approaches and he
is reluctantly obliged to let Lucy undertake the examination
in English. Half mockingly he accuses her of cherishing
ambitious dreams of her coming triumph. The accusation is
certainly unfounded, as far as scholastic ambitions are concerned, but it shows his insight into the true personality
beneath Lucy's external coldness: 'Other people in this house
see you pass, and think that a colourless shadow has gone by.
As for me, I scrutinised your face once, and it sufficed.'

At first Lucy is present at M. Paul's lessons merely in her
capacity of surveillante. It is not till she herself becomes his
pupil that his full stature is revealed. It is significant that the
chapter called *M. Paul* is the one in which she describes how
she comes to know him as a teacher. He shows endless

patience with her difficulties in the initial stages of any task, but becomes ironic and exacting as soon as her real talents begin to assert themselves. The result of his arbitrariness is, paradoxically, to incite her to further effort: '. . . his injustice stirred in me ambitious wishes — it imparted a strong stimulus — it gave wings to aspiration.' To stir dormant faculties into action, while at the same time taking good care that achievement did not breed complacency, was very much the method of M. Heger, as his speech of 1843 shows. Frederika Macdonald wrote years later that he excelled 'in calling out one's best faculties; in stimulating one's natural gifts; in lifting one above satisfaction with mediocrity . . .'[57]

M. Paul, that born teacher, gives lessons 'on any and every subject that struck his fancy', but it is in teaching literature that he is at his best and awakes most response in Lucy. His knowledge of it is wide and deep, and he soon discovers that her background is very limited in comparison with his own, though everyone else in the Rue Fossette thinks 'Meess Lucie' learned. The theme of the *devoirs* recurs in this context, but instead of being used, as in *The Professor* and *Shirley*, primarily to illustrate the gifts of the pupil, it is interwoven with the revelation of the powers of the master. To his wide knowledge of literature M. Paul unites a remarkable gift for the dramatic interpretation of it. He sometimes interrupts the evening study hour at the pensionnat by substituting for the usual 'lecture pieuse' some 'tragedy made grand by grand reading, ardent by fiery action' or 'passages from some enchanting tale, or the last witty feuilleton which had awakened laughter in the salons of Paris . . .' The effect is enhanced by the range and flexibility of his voice, 'remarkable for compass, modulation and matchless expression'. The same power of verbal interpretation characterised M. Heger. Many years later, when he had ceased to give regular lessons, his occasional readings could still delight the assembled school, as another English pupil remembered: 'He read sometimes a drama, sometimes a narrative poem, and we absolutely lived in it for those two or three hours. He was a magnificent reader . . .'[58]

In addition to reading books, M. Paul is a persistent and penetrating student of human nature, both in the classroom and out of it. He tells Lucy: 'My book is this garden; its contents are human nature — female human nature. I know you all by heart . . .' In Lucy's eyes he appears at first to be a ruthless observer and certainly, on the surface, his criticism of herself can be blatantly unjust; after the school play, he accuses her of ambition, after her nervous illness of egotism and, when the Brettons introduce her to some social life, of becoming volatile and pleasure-loving. Yet these accusations are far more flattering in reality than the calm verdict of Graham Bretton: 'Lucy's disadvantages spring from over-gravity in tastes and manner — want of colour in character and costume.' They act as a healthy stimulus, rousing her to self-defence. Beneath their half-teasing exaggeration is a real understanding of her nature, its strength and its dangers, such as no one else in Villette possesses. M. Heger was also a keen observer, and one who used his powers of penetration in the interests of his profession, for he believed it was essential to success in teaching 'to study the pupils, to know each one of them, to neglect none, and above all never to allow an aversion towards any one even to enter into the heart of the teacher'.[59]

The schoolroom is M. Paul's domain. But he is sociable by nature, and as much at ease outside its walls as within them. He can change from austerity to geniality with light-ning speed, when he wants his company — usually still his pupils — to enjoy themselves. This side of his nature is evident at the school fête:

> No sooner was the play over and *well* over, than the choleric and arbitrary M. Paul underwent a metamor-phosis. His hour of managerial responsibility past, he at once laid aside his magisterial austerity; in a moment he stood amongst us, vivacious, kind and social . . . (ch. 14)

He is equally genial when he fulfils his promise to take the boarders to breakfast in the country. 'He was a man whom it made happy to see others happy; he liked to have movement, animation, abundance and enjoyment around him.' He is often to be seen in the pensionnat garden, for gardening is one of his favourite occupations:

> ... He liked to tend and foster plants ... it was a re-
> creation to which he often had recourse ... His lips mean-
> time sustained his precious cigar, that (for him) first
> necessary and prime luxury of life ... (ch. 36)

These means of relaxation were also characteristic of M.
Heger; years later, when a boarder at the pensionnat,
Frederika Macdonald encountered him in the garden clipping
and thinning the vines and, when invited to accompany him
to his library, found that the room was:

> in this beautifully clean and orderly house, a model of
> disorder; clouded as to air, and soaked as to scent, with the
> smoke of living and the accumulated ashes of dead cigars.
> But the shelves laden from floor to ceiling with books
> made a delightful spectacle.[60]

The turning point in Lucy's relations with M. Paul is the
discovery that he has the capacity for enduring and self-
sacrificing love, shown by his devotion to the memory of the
dead Justine Marie and to her unattractive relations. Up to
this time she had not thought him capable of such depth of
feeling: 'What means had I, before this day, of being certain
whether he could love at all or not? I had known him jealous,
suspicious; I had seen about him certain tendernesses, fitful-
nesses — a softness which came like a warm air, and a ruth
which passed like early dew, dried in the heat of his
irritabilities: *this* was all I had seen.' With her new confidence
in the potentialities of his nature, Lucy does not hesitate to
show how much she likes and admires him. The chapter
called *Fraternity* raises their relationship to the level of a
close and trusting friendship, which seems to Lucy worthy to
be compared to love itself: 'I envied no girl her lover, no
bride her bridegroom, no wife her husband; I was content
with this my voluntary, self-offering friend.'

This relationship, the most stable to which they had
attained, is immediately threatened by the use Lucy's
enemies make of their difference of religion. Influenced by
Père Silas, M. Paul fears there may be something almost
pagan about Lucy's Protestantism, while she continues to
think Romanism 'wrong, a great mixed image of gold and

clay'. Yet the sincerity of M. Paul's belief compels her admiration, and he is a man who translates it into action. '. . . the self-denying and self-sacrificing part of the Catholic religion commanded the homage of his soul.' He devotes most of his income to the dependent household in the Rue des Mages and 'a host of nameless paupers'. Misfortune is a sure passport to his compassion. Lucy herself first attracts his sympathy because of her solitary condition. 'Pauvrette!' is his involuntary exclamation when she says she likes a friend better than a triumph. This side of M. Paul's nature is reflected in his surname of Emanuel, suggestive of the choice of name for a member of a religious order and evidently considered by Charlotte Brontë as appropriate in this context.[61] His conduct obliges Lucy to recognise that Catholicism is not incompatible with the truest Christian virtues:

> Whatever Romanism may be, there are good Romanists: this man, Emanuel, seemed of the best; touched with superstition, influenced by priestcraft, yet wondrous for fond faith, for pious devotion, for sacrifice of self, for charity unbounded. (ch. 34)

The self-sacrificing devotion to the interests of others which characterised M. Paul was also present in Constantin Heger and was inspired by the same source. 'Catholique, il l'était, et croyant, et profondément chrétien . . .'[62] At the time of Mrs Gaskell's visit to Brussels he was well known in the city as an active member of the Société de St Vincent de Paul and a pioneer of Christian socialism in his work among the poor. He was also capable of showing self-abnegation to a heroic degree, as later events proved, though in a different way from the over-docile pupil of Père Silas. After teaching for years at the Athénée he was promoted to be Préfet des Études — a post he filled brilliantly — but resigned the headship after two years because he disagreed in principle with the directives of the Inspector of Education, and because he felt his teaching was most valuable with the very young.[63] He voluntarily returned to teaching the most elementary class (the seventh), which had been his original function. His love and understanding of children made him as successful in this obscure but endlessly influential rôle as he was when using his knowledge and love of literature in teaching higher classes. Patience and sympathy with children were outstanding characteristics of this temperamentally impatient man who had said at the outset of his career: 'L'enfance est ce que je connais de plus respectable.'[64] This side of M. Heger's character is not reflected in any striking manner in M. Paul, but it can be glimpsed in certain episodes of *Villette;* it is through the youngest child in the school that he sends a message to Lucy, and during the day's holiday in the country, it is the children — 'those who liked him more than they feared' — who are the first to gather confidently round him when he begins to tell a story.

In *Villette,* where integration of personality is, in the last analysis, more important than the enjoyment of love, though only to be achieved through love, M. Paul is given very little time to reveal himself in the role of lover. The idyllic climate of the Faubourg Clotilde is not his natural element, and his indulgence, his 'silent, strong, effective goodness' are impressive mainly by contrast with his usual whirlwind vitality. For all his indulgence he is still 'the master' and Lucy is content to shape her wishes in accordance with his own. When he had once provocatively affirmed that a 'woman of intellect' was 'a sort of "lusus naturae"', a luckless accident, a thing for which there was neither place nor use in creation, wanted neither as wife nor worker', he had not spoken entirely in jest, even though it was unlikely that 'lovely, placid, and passive feminine mediocrity' represented in fact his ideal. The house in the Faubourg Clotilde, with the modest schoolroom as its centre, seems to him the appropriate setting for his love. For her it is a temporary refuge, where she can be happy not so much in the development of her own powers as in the hope of his return. When he leaves, she lives for his letters, as she had formerly lived for Graham Bretton's. This time she is not disappointed. M. Paul's letters are the final expression of his personality: in them is its essence, the quality which most surely unites him to Lucy Snowe, his impassioned and generous sincerity. 'By every vessel he wrote . . . He wrote because he liked to write . . . because he was faithful and thoughtful, because he was tender and true. There was no sham and no cheat, and no hollow unreal in him.'

M. Paul, Charlotte Brontë's finest masculine portrait, comes to life first and foremost in virtue of his humanity, but in painting this portrait she was helped and not hindered by his foreign nationality. Just because his background is foreign, his qualities ultimately stand out in stronger relief. The unexpected ways in which they are manifested frequently provoke her to satire and even to caricature, but the satirical quality gives added verve to the portrait, and ultimately it combines with the wonder of metamorphosis, as the features of the man are discovered where insularity had first seen a mask.

The satire which is rarely absent from her account of him, till the later stages of the novel, is usually provoked by the same quality: the freedom with which he abandons himself to the mood of the moment. The reserve that controls the Englishwoman is perfectly unknown to him. He is well aware that in her eyes he often seems lacking in 'desirable self-control', but when she reproaches him with lack of dignity, he replies by challenging her insular attitude:

> 'My dignity! . . . when did you ever see me trouble my head about my dignity? It is you, Miss Lucy, who are 'digne'. How often, in your high insular presence, have I taken a pleasure in trampling upon what you are pleased to call my dignity; tearing it, scattering it to the winds, in those mad transports you witness with such hauteur, and which I know you think very like the ravings of a third-rate London actor.' (ch. 31)

Yet however undignified these 'mad transports' may appear in Lucy's eyes, she is compelled to recognise the genuineness of the feelings they express. M. Paul may seem absurd as he darts from his desk to vent his irritation in a violent attack on the fuel in the stove because the class, and particularly the foreign surveillante, seem to him inattentive; he ceases to be so when the depth of his indignation becomes evident: '. . . there certainly was something in M. Paul's anger — a kind of passion of emotion — that specially tended to draw tears. I was not unhappy, nor much afraid, yet I wept.' Occasionally M. Paul is so much irritated by what he thinks Lucy's insular reserve that he is provoked into being as

unfair to 'les Anglaises' as she can be to the Labassecouriennes. Her failure to participate in the present-giving
ceremony on his fête day provokes a violent tirade against
their minds, morals, manners and personal appearance, 'their
tall stature, their long necks, their thin arms, their slovenly
dress, their pedantic education, their impious scepticism(!),
their insufferable pride, their pretentious virtue'. The diatribe
need not be taken too seriously, as Lucy herself knows. M.
Paul is a man of too wide sympathies to be guilty of lasting
injustice. He does however believe that Englishwomen err on
the side of too much independence. And just as Lucy sees a
causal connection between what she criticises in the Labassecouriennes and their Catholic background, so M. Paul thinks
the temerity of 'les Anglaises' is due to the fact that they are
'nurslings of Protestantism'. Though he detests prudery, he is
genuinely shocked to find Lucy unchaperoned in the picture
gallery considering the 'Cleopatra'. He remains suspicious of
the independence nurtured by her 'strange, self-reliant, invul-
nerable creed' until at last the complete understanding
between them gives him a clearer insight into the nature of
her belief and he accepts her Protestantism as part of herself,
'the sole creed for "Lucy"'.

As might be anticipated, it is on the subject of politics that
the difference of nationality between M. Paul and Lucy
provokes the most acrimonious exchange. Normally he is no
more a chauvinist than he is a bigot. It is only on the
unfortunate occasion when Lucy withholds her present for
his fête that his temporary disgust with 'les Anglaises'
overflows into a comprehensive denunciation of England and
the English, 'fastening not only upon our women, but upon
our greatest names and best men . . .' The 'greatest names'
could hardly fail to include Wellington. In the circumstances
it is not surprising that Lucy finally loses her insular calm and
issues a challenge in return:

> At last I struck a sharp stroke on my desk, opened my
> lips, and let loose this cry —
> 'Vive l'Angleterre, l'Histoire et les Héros! A bas la
> France, la Fiction et les Faquins!' (ch. 29)

Into this alliterative formula is condensed the fundamental

cause of her distrust towards France, the association in her mind between the French character and artificiality and perfidy. The heritage of the Napoleonic wars still speaks here, and what M. Paul himself calls 'the old quarrel of France and England'.

The indictment is the more serious because falsehood is what Lucy most fears and truth what she most ardently seeks. Yet by the time she uttered these explosive words she had really reached a degree of maturity where truth was no longer synonymous with England nor falsehood the predominant characteristic of France. Her quarrel on this occasion is with M. Paul rather than with France. He has been unjust and he knows it, as his rapid return to equanimity shows. 'He now thought he had got the victory, since he had made me angry. In a second he became good-humoured.' Lucy's own anger is only 'a strange evanescent anger', and not an hour later she is able to smile in retrospect at the whole scene and regret the initial misunderstanding which had caused it.

It is noticeable that it is France, not Labassecour, that Lucy attacks. M. Paul thus becomes by implication the representative of France. Later, and in a very different mood, when she has personally experienced his dominance as a teacher, she expresses her combined amusement and admiration of his dynamism in a daring parallel with Napoleon Bonaparte:

> I used to think, as I sat looking at M. Paul, while he was knitting his brows or protruding his lips over some exercise of mine . . . that he had points of resemblance to Napoleon Bonaparte. I think so still.

> In a shameless disregard of magnanimity, he resembled the great Emperor. M. Paul would have quarrelled with twenty learned women, would have unblushingly carried on a system of petty bickering and recimination with a whole capital of coteries, never troubling himself about loss or lack of dignity. He would have exiled fifty Madame de Stäels, if they had annoyed, offended, outrivalled, or opposed him . . .

> To pursue a somewhat audacious parallel, in a love of

power, in an eager grasp after supremacy, M. Emanuel was
like Bonaparte. He was a man not always to be submitted
to. Sometimes it was needful to resist; it was right to stand
still, to look up into his eyes and tell him that his
requirements went beyond reason — that his absolutism
verged on tyranny. (ch. 30)

The tone of the comparison, with its mixture of appreciation
and reservation, reflects her attitude to France — as represented by one of her greatest men — much more accurately
than her previous outburst. Through the veil of satire some of
the qualities emerge which help to constitute, in Lucy's
opinion, M. Paul's affinity with the French character: his lack
of inhibitions, his dynamism, his interest in the things of the
intellect and his confidence in his intellectual powers.

The family origins of M. Paul were in fact, neither Frénch
nor Labassecourien. Having remarked that on his fête day he
had 'dressed for the "situation" and the occasion' like a true
Frenchman, Lucy instantly adds in parenthesis: 'though I
don't know why I should say so, for he was of strain neither
French nor Labassecourien'. That his political loyalties,
however, belong first and foremost to Labassecour is clear
from his speech to the youth of the Athénée. It is noticeable
that, though his authoritarian qualities may have helped to
suggest a Napoleonic comparison, he is as much opposed to
tyranny as he is to anarchy:

> . . . with all his fire he was severe and sensible; he trampled
> Utopian theories under his heel; he rejected wild dreams
> with scorn; — but when he looked in the face of tyranny —
> oh, then there opened a light in his eye worth seeing; and
> when he spoke of injustice, his voice gave no uncertain
> sound . . . (ch. 27)

In the fact that his ancestors came from another country,
as in his loyalty to the land where his family settled, M. Paul
resembled M. Heger. The Heger family came originally from
the Rhineland but emigrated to Belgium, where they had
been settled for three generations before his birth.[65] He was
passionately devoted to the land for whose independence he
had fought, and his patriotism found eloquent expression in
his speech at the Athénée in 1843, when he reminded his
pupils of the debt they owed to their country:

La Patrie! ah! c'est avec d'indicibles douleurs aussi qu'elle vous a enfantés à la liberté . . .

Longtemps avant que vous fussiez au monde, cette autre mère avait tout préparé pour vous avec amour; rien ne lui a coûté. Pour vous léguer intact et brillant ce nom de Belges, dont nous pouvons être fiers, elle a intrépidement combattu toutes les tyrannies depuis César jusqu'à Napoléon. Elle a prodigué son or et son sang pour chacun des droits dont vous jouissez; durant dix-huit siècles, elle a incessamment travaillé et lutté pour grossir votre patrimoine de gloire, de science et de liberté . . .

M. Paul, however, does not belong to Labassecour in the same way as M. Heger did to Belgium. Though she could not omit his patriotism from her portrait of him, Lucy is less concerned with this than with his affinities with the French character. But she gives no exact indication of his racial origin. That there is a meridional element in it is clear from his physical appearance, 'that swart, sallow, southern darkness which spoke his Spanish blood . . .', as well as from the fact that Carlos is one of his Christian names. In this way the Latin heritage which is undoubtedly his is coloured with a southern fire which sometimes kindles into a strange beauty of its own, and the portrait acquires that touch of mystery which is the hall-mark of all true art. Neither a Frenchman nor a Labassecourien in origin, M. Paul has the Frenchman's breadth of mind and intellectual alertness, with the Labassecourien tenacity. He stands in Lucy's eyes for something more than either — a citizen of Europe, the continent which she had first seen 'like a wide dreamland, far away'.

# 6 The use of the French language and stylistic echoes of French in the novels

The use of the French language in Charlotte Brontë's novels is essentially functional. She used French as Scott used dialect, and as Emily Brontë uses it in *Wuthering Heights*, because without it the painting of character and milieu would lack an essential element. In the Angrian cycle she had taken the first steps towards the utilisation of the native idiom which she had seen in the Waverley novels, as well as in the pages of *Blackwood's*. She had, however, to live in a French-speaking milieu before she could become attuned to the intimate rhythms of the language. By the time she wrote *The Professor*, French had become for her a valued medium of expression, and one to which her nostalgic memories gave an indestructible charm.

The French she introduces is mainly the language she heard in the everyday life of the pensionnat. The passages she memorised daily after her return from Brussels were chosen for their conversational style, and the foreign newspapers sent to Haworth helped to keep her in touch with the language in current use. Much of the French in the novels occurs in conversation, or in reported speech, and has the naturalness and immediacy that this implies.

This, however, does not remove, though it may mitigate, the practical difficulty encountered by all writers who introduce an idiom which is not that of their readers, the question of intelligibility. Charlotte Brontë could, it is true, assume some familiarity with the French language among her public, for French novels were much read in England in the 1840s.[1] But the extent to which she used it caused some uneasiness to her publishers, when they read her work in manuscript, and was considered with misgiving by more than one of her early critics.[2] The subsequent inclusion, as an appendix to the

Everyman edition of *The Professor* and *Villette,* of translations of the French phrases used, shows that publishers
continued to be aware of the possible obstacle they might
present. Yet it seems unlikely that readers often pause to
consult these translations. And it is certain that modern
critics never make a major and seldom even a minor issue of
the difficulty caused by the amount of French in the text. It
is evident that in general Charlotte Brontë has solved the
problem of intelligibility with a dexterity no less effective
because it was probably largely intuitive.

A number of the words she introduces occur in isolation.
Many belong to the vocabulary of the pensionnat environment and are easily understandable from the context.
Charlotte Brontë does not hesitate, however, to give an initial
explanation when she thinks it necessary. The 'carré' is 'a
large square hall between the dwelling-house and the pensionnat', the teacher's 'estrade' 'a low platform raised a step
above the flooring'. Occasionally the regional use of a word
has to be explained: 'the morning pistolets, or rolls, which
were new-baked and very good'. Abstract terms might be
expected to present more difficulty, but the majority, words
like amour-propre, sang-froid, aplomb, belong to an international currency. More skill was needed to introduce entire
phrases in such a way as to be easily intelligible. They vary
from passages of dialogue to phrases intercalated in speeches
otherwise in English. Here, too, the context often provides a
clue to the general meaning: 'A bell rang' forms the natural
prelude to 'Voilà pour la prière du soir!' Or a French phrase
may be immediately followed by its English equivalent: 'Je
vis dans un trou! I inhabit a den, Miss — a cavern, where you
would not put your dainty nose.' The reader accepts the
blend of the two languages almost unconsciously because of
the skill with which Charlotte Brontë has succeeded in fusing
them momentarily for the purposes of her art.

For those purposes, clarity is essential. But in making it
easy for the reader to assimilate the French she uses, she has
aims which go far beyond the question of intelligibility. Her
use of the language makes a powerful contribution to the
atmosphere of the novel as a whole. The descriptions of the
Belgian milieu both in *The Professor* and *Villette* owe much

of their authenticity to the skilful use of French terms. The foreign school would not stand in such complete contrast to the English scholastic milieu without this difference of terminology. The noisy 'pensionnaires' and 'externes' of the Rue Fossette obviously belong to a different world from the subdued pupils of Lowood, and the schoolroom itself undergoes a metamorphosis when it becomes a 'classe', whose glass door opens into a 'vast and vine-draped berceau'. By the same means the details of day to day life in a foreign milieu, as Lucy Snowe and Crimsworth experience it, are made visible and tangible. The strong light admitted by '*croisées* that opened like doors' shines on the furniture that belongs to such a milieu: 'lustre', 'guéridon', 'console'. When Mme Beck's pensionnaires take their walks into the country, they are regaled with '*gaufres* and *vin blanc,* or new milk and *pain bis,* or *pistolets au beurre* and coffee'. Lucy Snowe shows, perhaps unconsciously, how closely idiom and milieu are associated in her mind when, on recovering from her fainting-fit, she wonders if she is still in Villette or back in Bretton, and looks out from the window 'fully expectant of a town view somewhere, a rue in Villette, if not a street in a pleasant and ancient English city'.

The use of French is closely integrated with the action. Charlotte Brontë has succeeded in making French phrases as much a part of the drama of the novel as French terms are of the setting. The fact that the reader's attention is inevitably drawn to them within the framework of an English text means that they are peculiarly suited to throw into relief the crucial moments of the emotional drama. The latent antagonism between Lucy and Mme Beck is momentarily revealed when she shrinks from the ordeal of giving her first lesson, but is goaded into doing so by Madame's challenge:

'Dites donc,' said Madame sternly, 'vous sentez-vous réellement trop faible?' (ch. 8)

In *The Professor* French and English sometimes alternate in dialogue in a pattern which mirrors the harmony between the lovers:

'Monsieur sera-t-il aussi bon mari qu'il a été bon maître?' 'I will try, Frances.' (ch. 23)

In *Villette* the stormier relations of Lucy and M. Paul are reflected in a less successful attempt to achieve a harmony between the two languages:

> 'Let me hear you say, in the voice natural to you, and not in that alien tone, "Mon ami, je vous pardonne." ' . . .
> 'Monsieur Paul, je vous pardonne.'
> 'I will have no monsieur: speak the other word, or I shall not believe you sincere: another effort — *mon ami,* or else in English, — my friend!' (ch. 27)

Much of the humour, as well as the drama, of the novels is similarly emphasised by the skilful use of French phrases. Faced with the fearful duty of interrupting M. Paul's classes to fetch pupils for their music lesson, that accomplished soubrette Rosine expresses her sense of the situation with her customary verve:

> 'Mon Dieu! Mon Dieu!' cried she. 'Que vais-je devenir? Monsieur va me tuer, je suis sûre; car il est d'une colère!'
> Nerved by the the courage of desperation, she opened the door.
> 'Mademoiselle La Malle au piano!' was her cry.
> Ere she could make good her retreat, or quite close the door, this voice uttered itself:—
> 'Dès ce moment! — la classe est défendue. La première qui ouvrira cette porte, ou passera par cette division, sera pendue — fut-ce Madame Beck elle-même!' (ch. 28)

The most essential use to which French is put in the novels is in the service of the characterisation. Several of the principal characters are French-speaking. Much of their conversation must necessarily be given in English, but something is inevitably lost in the passage from one idiom to another. All the more effective are the moments when a sentence in their native idiom comes like a flash of light to illumine the hidden springs of their nature.

Charlotte Brontë introduces such phrases with an unerring sense of timing. Most of Mlle Reuter's speeches are reported in English. But on the one occasion when she allows Crimsworth a glimpse of her real nature, the revelation of her wily diplomacy is prefaced by a sentence in her own idiom:

'Allons, Monsieur le professeur — asseyons-nous; je vais vous donner une petite leçon dans votre état d'instituteur.' (ch. 18)

Before reproducing the lesson in strategy which follows, Crimsworth comments regretfully: 'I wish I might write all she said to me in French — it loses sadly by being translated into English.' When subsequently her infatuation for Crimsworth temporarily distorts her judgment, the change is underlined by her misguided attempt to express her feelings in the 'style noble':

> 'Que le dédain lui sied bien!' I once overheard her say to her mother: 'il est beau comme Apollon quand il sourit de son air hautain.'
> And the jolly old dame laughed, and said she thought her daughter was bewitched . . . (ch. 20).

In *Villette,* where the French-speaking Mme Beck and M. Paul share with Lucy Snowe the leading rôles, the use of French as a means of characterisation is more fully developed. Since Mme Beck's command of insular speech is in fact exhausted when she has said 'You ayre Engliss,' most of what she says has to be given in translation, but the judicious use of her own idiom seems to crystallise those qualities which make her most herself. A few sentences are enough to convey her perfect awareness of the differences in outlook between herself and Lucy:

> 'Il y a,' said she, 'quelque chose de bien remarquable dans le caractère anglais.'
> 'How, Madame?'
> She gave a little laugh, repeating the word 'how' in English.
> 'Je ne saurais vous dire "how"; mais, enfin, les Anglais ont des idées à eux, en amitié, en amour, en tout. Mais au moins il n'est pas besoin de les surveiller.' (ch. 26)

There is in Mme Beck's use of her native a cool efficiency language, as there is about her whole personality. She wastes words no more than she wastes time. 'C'est bien. Ça ira,' is all she says when Lucy has successfully surmounted the ordeal of her first lesson. Her wit never loses its urbanity, but it

acquires different overtones in the later stages of the action. Her friendly reception of Lucy, on her return from her visit to the strange household in the Rue des Mages, culminates in an ostensibly light-hearted phrase, which is probably, of all her remarks, the one best remembered by readers of *Villette:*
'. . . oubliez les anges, les bossues, et surtout, les Professeurs . . .'

M. Paul's capacity for speaking English is nearly as limited as Mme Beck's. His dynamic nature, however, demands expression in its native idiom more frequently and more imperatively than hers. The authoritative tone he instantly assumes in his relations with Lucy is reflected in frequent commands which gain added force when given in his own tongue:

> 'Brava!' cried he . . . 'J'ai tout entendu. C'est assez bien.'
> 'Encore!'
> A moment I hesitated.
> 'Encore!' said he sternly. 'Et point de grimaces! À bas la timidité!' (ch. 14)

The wit and humour which are very much a part of him gain, like the witticisms of Mme Beck, when they are expressed in his own language. They cover a wider range of tone and feeling. They may be simply a safety valve for his irritability, as when he calls 'Williams Schackspire' 'le faux dieu de ces sots païens, les Anglais'. But more often his humour has sympathy and understanding behind it. On the eve of the dreaded day when Lucy has to act as examiner in English, his provocative reference to her supposed ambition is just what is needed to provoke discussion and a better understanding between them:

> 'Ainsi,' he began, abruptly fronting and arresting me, 'vous allez trôner comme une reine; demain — trôner à mes côtés? . . .' (ch. 15)

But he has other moods beside the humorous, and French is as much the natural idiom of his emotions as it is of his wit. When exasperated by his pupils' incomprehension of the 'grand tragedy' he is trying to rehearse, he can use the rhetorical resources of the language with telling effect:

'Vous n'êtes donc que des poupées,' I heard him thunder. 'Vous n'avez pas de passions — vous autres. Vous ne sentez donc rien! Votre chair est de neige, votre sang de glace! Moi, je veux que tout cela s'allume, qu'il ait une vie, une âme!' (ch. 14)

Even more telling is the quiet melancholy of his reply when Lucy assures him that the letter which has so much delighted her is only that of a friend: 'Je conçois, je conçois: on sait ce que c'est qu'un ami.'

The effectiveness of the rôle depends not only on what M. Paul says but on the way he says it. He has a Frenchman's mastery of intonation and gesture. The tragi-comedy of his anger when Lucy contributes no flowers on his fête day owes its effect to the variations of intonation and movement which accompany the repetition of one simple sentence:

> Voiceless and viewless, stirless and wordless, he kept his station behind the pile of flowers.
> At last there issued forth a voice, rather deep, as if it spoke out of a hollow: —
> 'Est-ce là tout?' . . .
> 'Est-ce là tout?' was reiterated in an intonation which, deep before, had now descended some notes lower.
> 'Monsieur,' said Mademoiselle St. Pierre . . . 'I have the honour to tell you that, with a single exception, every person in class 'has offered her bouquet . . .'
> The answer vouchsafed to Mademoiselle St. Pierre from the estrade was given in the gesticulation of a hand from behind the pyramid . . .
> A form, ere long, followed the hand. Monsieur emerged from his eclipse, and . . . demanded a third time, and now in really tragic tones —
> 'Est-ce là tout?' (ch. 29)

Spoken by M. Paul and Mme Beck, French is an admirable medium for the expression both of lucid common sense and of a wide range of mood and feeling. It is used in a different way by Ginevra Fanshawe, that product of a continental education, for whom it provides convenient substitutes for anything that does not sound entirely respectable in English: 'I . . . send lessons *au diable* (one daren't say that in English, you know, but it sounds quite right in French).' Under the cover of this linguistic protection she does not hesitate to confess to her impatience with the 'sterling qualities and solid virtues' she neither has nor intends to have:

> 'Les penseurs, les hommes profonds et passionnés ne sont pas à mon goût . . . Va pour les beaux fats et les jolis fripons! . . . A bas les grandes passions et les sévères vertus! . . .
>
> J'aime mon beau colonel . . . je n'aimerai jamais son rival. Je ne serai jamais femme de bourgeois, moi!' (ch. 9)

The use of the foreign idiom which is so much a part of *The Professor* and *Villette* is naturally less in evidence in the novels with English settings. Yet its function is not negligible in *Jane Eyre,* and it makes an indispensable contribution to the complexities of *Shirley.* In the former, its rôle is clearly defined and artistically satisfying; in the latter, where it is used more widely, the effect is not always so successful but, without these echoes of French, Hollow's Cottage and its owners would lose much of their original character.

In *Jane Eyre* French is the native tongue of the child Adèle, and the use she makes of it is perfectly in keeping with her part in the novel. The predominant concern with 'matters of dress', which Jane regrets, is reflected in her delight when her 'cadeau' proves to be a dancer's dress of rose-coloured satin:

> 'Est-ce que ma robe va bien?' cried she, bounding forwards; 'et mes souliers? et mes bas? Tenez, je crois que je vais danser!' (ch. 14)

The effect of this is in fact charming, the language echoing the lightness of the movement. But Adèle is primarily, in Rochester's eyes, 'a miniature of Céline Varens', and when he occasionally speaks to her in French, his own tone is usually ironic. French is also occasionally used by the members of the house party at Thornfield, notably by Blanche Ingram who likes to show off her fluency and her good accent, and by her equally snobbish mother, who remarks 'Tant pis!' when warned that her remarks on governesses must necessarily be heard by Jane Eyre. In this context the language is debased to becoming simply a status symbol.

In *Shirley*, with its Belgian born heroes and its Yorkshire setting, the language situation presents anomalies not found in the other novels. Special care was needed here, if the use of French was to be satisfactorily integrated, but Charlotte Brontë, who began *Shirley* with a confidence induced by the success of *Jane Eyre*, seemed from the start to be insufficiently aware of the need for caution as well as audacity in this respect. It was à propos of *Shirley* that her publishers observed that the French might be a matter of criticism and she evidently admitted that their objection was reasonable, modifying the text of one chapter in consequence and owning to some apprehension herself on the subject.[3]

The French of *Shirley* is naturally most convincing when it is spoken by the Belgian born Moores, but it is only Hortense who uses it normally as her natural means of expression. She is chiefly concerned with the domesticities of Hollow's Cottage and her idiom is effective and easily intelligible within this context, whether she is denouncing the Yorkshire servant as 'coquine de cuisinière, fille insupportable' or praising the café au lait as 'un breuvage royal'.

Robert Moore is bilingual, though as the owner of a mill in an out of the way district of Yorkshire he normally speaks more English than French. He is quite willing, however, to gratify Hiram Yorke's liking for dropping into French — the tongue which reminds the manufacturer of his youth — in the course of one of the arguments which they both enjoy:

> '. . . Go back to Antwerp, where you were born and bred, mauvaise tête!'
>
> 'Mauvaise tête vous-même; je ne fais que mon devoir; quant à vos lourdauds de paysans, je m'en moque!'
>
> 'En revanche, mon garçon, nos lourdauds de paysans se moqueront de toi; sois en certain,' replied Yorke . . . (ch. 3)

French seems to come most readily to his lips in moments of impatience or sardonic amusement. 'Ma foi! mon ami, ce sont vraiment des enfants terribles que les vôtres!' is his comment to Yorke after listening to the conversation of the family at Briarmains. Occasionally he uses gallicisms but shows his practical sense by promptly adding an explanation of their meaning. He tells his overseer Joe Scott: '. . . the 'classe ouvrière' — that is, the working people in Belgium — bear themselves brutally towards their employers; and by *brutally,* Joe, I mean brutalement — which, perhaps, when properly translated, should be *roughly.'* In talk with Caroline, he says of his sister: 'Hortense, you know, is exquisitely susceptible — in our French sense of the word — and not, perhaps, always reasonable in her requirements . . .' But there seems to be no emotional compulsion to motivate his use of his native tongue. He may use it when ironically amused or even in his rare moments of genuine gaiety, but English is the language of the 'confessional' at Rushedge and of the love scenes with Caroline.

His brother Louis, who earns his living by teaching his native language, might be expected to employ it more frequently than the owner of Hollow's mill. But he is normally a man of few words, roused from his taciturnity only by the presence of Shirley. When he tries to analyse the attraction her rebellious nature has for him, it is partly in words from his own language that he does so: '. . . the moment her "minois mutin" meets my eye, expostulatory words crowd to my lips . . . the more crâne malin, taquin is her mood . . . the more I seek her, the better I like her.' She had been his pupil when she shared her cousin's French lessons, and French continues to play its part in their relationship when she revisits the schoolroom. His recital of a passage familiar to them both in the past is enough to restore contact between them: 'When he ceased, she took the word up as if from his lips, she took his very tone; she seized his very accent . . . she found lively excitement in the pleasure of making his language her own . . .' For Louis Moore, his language is above all a precious asset in his relations with Shirley. His mastery of French is the medium through which he asserts his mastery of her.

The Moore family are the principal French speakers in the novel, but not the only ones. Hiram Yorke's obvious pleasure in talking with Robert Moore in his own idiom is purely nostalgic in origin — 'he had heard, in Parisian cafés and theatres, voices like his; he was young then, and when he looked at and listened to the alien, he seemed young again.' That there is neither snobbery nor affectation in his attitude is proved by the fact that far more often he expresses himself in dialect. The combination of French and Yorkshire dialect is interesting. That it also appears natural shows that for Charlotte Brontë they are both means to the same end, the expression of Yorke's complex personality; the first contains echoes of his cosmopolitan youth, the second matches the rugged originality of his maturity.

The introduction of foreign terms in *Shirley* is justifiable on the part of the half Belgian Moores and of Yorke with his continental background. It is another matter when they are used by the narrator. *Shirley* is the only one of the novels which is a third person narration. Charlotte Brontë uses the form with her customary independence, by no means always observing the detachment it normally presupposes. Her personal involvement is evident enough in passages which voice her own deeply held convictions, but it is also manifested from time to time in less obvious ways. It is her own preference, rather than any artistic necessity, that explains the occasional intrustion into the narrative of French terms, where the context offers no evident reason for it. There is some justification for their use in incidents involving Hortense Moore, where they have practically the effect of reported speech: 'Caroline knew well that "chapeau en soie jaune" . . . that "robe de soie noire" . . . that "schal gris de lin" . . .' but there is no obvious reason for saying, in describing Caroline's clerical guests, that Malone was 'all in "grande tenue" ' or that Boultby spoke in a 'round sound "voix de poitrine" '. It is still more unexpected to find French words used to describe the schoolboy diplomacy of Martin Yorke: 'Martin paused "interdit" one minute . . . the next he knew his ground . . . With the true perspicacity "des âmes élites" (sic), he at once saw how this — at first sight untoward event — might be turned to excellent account . . .' Such arbitrary use of French terms can only be explained on the grounds of the author's personal predilection. For Charlotte Brontë, as for her own Hiram Yorke, such echoes of the language recalled 'old, perhaps pleasurable associations'.

More than a nostalgic pleasure is in question, however, in other cases, where the choice of a French word is explicitly justified by Charlotte Brontë in her capacity of narrator. It may be required to define a subtle shade of meaning. After referring to the 'bonté' that characterises Hortense Moore, she explains in a parenthesis: 'I use this French word, because it expresses just what I mean; neither goodness nor good nature, but something between the two.' The grace of a gesture is caught by the French term in the sentence: 'She took those thin fingers between her two little hands — she bent her head "et les effleura de ses lèvres".' This is followed by the parenthesis: 'I put that in French because the word "effleurer" is an exquisite word.' Pictorial values are in question when 'reflets' occurs in the description of a winter landscape. Again the choice of the foreign term is defended, this time in an unexpected footnote: 'Find me an English word as good, reader, and I will gladly dispense with the French word. "Reflections" won't do.'

Artistically such interpolations can scarcely be justified, yet they throw light on the evolution of Charlotte Brontë as an artist. The lessons of Brussels had taught her a more exacting appreciation of the 'mot juste'. In reading French literature, and especially the French Romantics, she realised with what exactness the language of its masters could reproduce not only thought but feeling and sensation. She was already aware, before she went to Belgium, of the resources of the 'universal language' in portraying the social comedy, though her life abroad greatly increased this awareness and gave verve and finish to the dialogue she introduces in *The Professor* and *Villette*. But the French Romantics showed her that this infinitely flexible language could present shape, sound and colour with the same veracity as ideas. Their consummate word painting played its part in her apprenticeship as a writer, a part which deserves some recognition when the resources of her style are considered.

The Romantic writers to whom M. Heger introduced her naturally come to mind particularly in this connection. Romanticism, however, had its eighteenth-century predecessors, and one of these deserves mention as well. Charlotte Brontë's collection of books given her by M. Heger included the complete works of Bernardin de Saint-Pierre. They had not been forgotten when she wrote *Shirley*. Louis Moore invites his former pupil, who is forgetting her French, to read, by way of practice, 'a few pages of the "Fragments de l'Amazone" '. But it was not Bernardin's Utopian theories that attracted Charlotte Brontë, who would probably have said, as Moore does, when he puts away the book: 'I approve nothing Utopian'. His attraction for her, as for most readers, no doubt lay in his passionate interest in the natural beauties of the universe and his power of reproducing them with an attention to detail and an artistry which were revolutionary for the literary vocabulary of his time. One of the salient characteristics of his art was his vivid use of colour and form, based on the result of first hand observation recorded in his travel notes. His colours were often borrowed from those of the sky and associated with the form and movement of the clouds to produce skyscapes that before him had been unknown, except on the painter's canvas:

> J'ai aperçu dans les nuages des tropiques, principalement sur la mer et dans les tempêtes, toutes les couleurs qu'on peut voir sur la terre. Il y en a alors de cuivrées, de couleur de fumée de pipe, de brunes, de rousses, de noires, de grises, de livides, de couleur marron, et de celle de gueule de four enflammé . . .[4]

Such skyscapes must have had a particular appeal for Charlotte Brontë, familiar from childhood with 'the shape of the clouds and the signs of the heavens'. She told Mrs Gaskell 'what a companion the sky became to anyone living in solitude − more than any inanimate object on earth − more than the moors themselves'.[5] It is noticeable that the passage of *Shirley* in which 'reflets' is used is a description of the subtle colouring of a winter evening:

> A calm day had settled into a crystalline evening: the world wore a North Pole colouring: all its lights and tints looked like the 'reflets' of white, or violet, or pale green gems. The hills wore a lilac blue; the setting sun had purple in its red; the sky was ice, all silvered azure; when the stars rose, they were of white crystal − not gold; gray, or cerulean, or faint emerald hues − cool, pure and transparent − tinged the mass of the landscape. (ch. 32)

It has been said of this passage that it is 'as much Bernardin de Saint-Pierre as if he had written it himself'.[6] The affinity with Bernardin has also been recognised in the most vivid sunset in *The Professor:*[7]

> . . . a balmy and fresh breeze stirred the air, purified by lightning; I felt the West behind me, where spread a sky like opal; azure immingled with crimson: the enlarged sun, glorious in Tyrian tints, dipped his brim already; stepping, as I was, eastward, I faced a vast bank of clouds, but also I had before me the arch of an evening rainbow — a perfect rainbow, high, wide, vivid . . . (ch. 19)

The sunset in this case is the prelude to a dream, but one which is based on the natural scene: 'then in a dream were reproduced the setting sun, the bank of clouds, the mighty rainbow.' As often with Bernardin, the sky is here complemented by sea, a sea of 'changeful green and intense blue'. Beneath the rainbow appears a visionary figure symbolising Hope, whose beauty is evidently derived from the colours of the evening sky: '. . . the soft but dusk clouds diffused behind . . . pearly, fleecy, gleaming air streamed like raiment round it; light, tinted with carnation, coloured what seemed face and limbs . . .'

Bernardin de Saint-Pierre had a direct influence on two of the leading French Romantics, Chateaubriand and Lamartine. Not only did they share his belief in the 'harmonies' between nature and Providence but they realised the possibilities opened up by his new approach to descriptive writing, which combined such exactitude of detail with such conscious artistry. Both were known to Charlotte Brontë, and there are obvious echoes of Chateaubriand's landscape painting in the Brussels *devoirs*.[8] In scope and power he is superior to Bernardin, combining vividness of detail with panoramic breadth of vision and rising to poetic heights the earlier writer only reached in *Paul et Virginie*. Among his favourite themes was the moonlit landscape. The seascape from the *Génie du Christianisme* which figures among Charlotte Brontë's Brussels transcriptions is followed, in the same chapter of the *Génie,* by an incomparable description of a moonlit night.[9] One wonders if something of his skyscape, vaster and more dynamic than Bernardin's, is reflected in the brilliant and sensuous painting of moonlight and storm in Louis Moore's journal in *Shirley:*

> This night is not calm: the equinox still struggles in its storms. The wild rains of the day are abated: the great single cloud disparts and rolls away from heaven, not passing and leaving a sea all sapphire, but tossed buoyant before a long-sounding, high-rushing moonlight tempest. The Moon reigns glorious, glad of the gale; as glad as if she gave herself to his fierce caress with love. No Endymion will watch for his goddess to-night: there are no flocks out on the mountains; and it is well, for to-night she welcomes Æolus. (ch.29)

The French Romantics not only desired a plastic and colourful language; they also wanted flexibility, expressiveness and rhythm. The 'mot juste' depended for its effect on its placing in the sentence. During the classical period the French sentence had become largely standardised; the Romantics introduced changes into the pattern which were all the more effective by contrast.[10] The balanced phrases of classical rhetoric were often replaced by a more rapid succession of shorter clauses, whose symmetry depended on more complex relationships. Word order as a whole became more varied. Inversion was used not only when it was a grammatical necessity but optionally, for stylistic reasons. Chateaubriand often introduced it with telling effect, as in his description of Niagara, where the inversion focuses attention on the centre of the picture: 'Entre les deux chutes s'avance une île, creusée en dessous, qui pend avec tous ses arbres sur le chaos des ondes.'[11] This flexible language was rich in imagery inspired by the Romantic outlook on nature and on life. Their consciousness of the primordial importance of contrast is mirrored in their love of antithesis, both structural and syntactical. Chateaubriand's painting of Niagara contrasts the two falls of the cataract, one in brilliant sunshine and the other in frightening shadow. Hugo contrasts Mirabeau as a writer with Mirabeau in his element as an orator: 'Après Mirabeau, écrivain, Mirabeau orateur, quelle transfiguration!' Metaphor and simile are frequent, since they reflect the Romantics' sense of the relationship between all things in the physical and moral universe. Chateaubriand compares the spray of the cataract to the smoke of some vast conflagration. Nodier compares old age to a stream whose windings brings it back to the neighbourhood of its source, so that the scenes of childhood and youth can be effortlessly recalled, like reflections in tranquil water.[12]

Such were the qualities of the style Charlotte Brontë found in the passages from the French Romantics which she read with M. Heger, and in their work in general. They all contributed to the same end, the awakening in the reader of a heightened awareness, analogous to that aroused by poetry. Such a conception of style was naturally congenial to her. Her own shows, in a different idiom, many of the same essential qualities, the dynamism and the rhythm, the frequency of inversion and antithesis, the wealth of imagery.[13] In her case, too, they were the natural result of a temperament and a conception of art in which feeling, though not uncontrolled, is allowed a latitude of expression unknown to classical objectivity. The 'echo of a style' which is sometimes perceptible in the Brussels *devoirs* would have had little significance for so individual an artist, had it not harmonised with the voice of her own genius, already becoming articulate.

The style of the French Romantics made it possible for them, as novelists, to achieve, in the great emotional crises of their works, a heightened mode of prose unknown to the novel before them. The improvisation of Corinne, the apostrophe of René to the Autumn storms, Atala's song of exile seem neither forced nor unnatural in their context. Hugo, Balzac and George Sand could all operate the transition from the natural world to a visionary one with its own appropriate language. George Sand's *Lélia* which, like Balzac's *Peau de Chagrin,* orchestrates most of the dominant themes of Romanticism, makes frequent use of this heightened language. It is sometimes associated, as often in George Sand's *Consuelo,* with states in which the consciousness functions at an unusual depth, such as dreams and hallucinations. But its effect is most powerful when it is restricted to the imaginative summits of the narration.

A similar mode of prose is sometimes used by Charlotte Brontë. In *The Professor* the vivid description of a sunset, widening into vision, is completely different from the other descriptions in the novel. Its brilliant colours owe something, as has been seen, to the resplendent tropical skyscapes of Bernardin de Saint-Pierre. The transition from natural to supernatural is marked by an increased gravity of style, in line with the same quality shown by the French novelists in their prose poems: 'I stood, methought, on a terrace; I leaned over a parapeted wall . . .' The failure of the whole in this case to produce a satisfying effect comes from lack of integration with the personal narrative. Crimsworth is normally too restrained for this sudden revelation of a highly imaginative temperament to be acceptable.

A great advance in the use of the same technique is evident in *Jane Eyre*. It is clear that the three extraordinary drawings Jane shows to Rochester represent in the imagery of dreams the essence of her inner life. They are thus of vital importance, both for him and for the reader. They are clearly linked with memories of an unhappy childhood: Bewick's sometimes macabre vignettes and the apparition of Death in *Paradise Lost* find their natural correlatives in shipwreck and polar sky. The central picture shows a woman's figure rising from a wind-swept hill. Long before a similar figure had been painted by Charlotte Brontë in an early poem, but she had then received the name, Nature.[14] By calling this painting 'a vision of the Evening Star', Jane Eyre shows that it is rather the night side of nature with which she feels in communication. The hill-top, painted with a mobile touch Bernardin de Saint-Pierre would have approved to show 'grass and some leaves slanted as if by a breeze', is recognised by Rochester as Latmos. The Evening Star is also the moon goddess, and in contrast to the swollen sea and the ghastly apparition of the other paintings, this one has for foreground the favoured soil of Greece.

After the strange paintings, it comes as a surprise to find Charlotte Brontë, in her next visionary passage — the dream of Jane Eyre after the interrupted marriage — substituting a human figure for the moon goddess. Jane dreams the moon is about to burst from the clouds, but what she then sees is the apparition of her mother's spirit. It is clear from this that for her the universe is not a closed system of impersonal forces but one in which intercommunication is possible between the natural and the spiritual. This vision is closely related to the action of the novel, for it is the source from which Jane draws the strength to leave Thornfield.

*Shirley,* intended to offer the reader 'something unromantic as Monday morning', seems unlikely to give much scope for the style appropriate to moments of poetic vision. It is not till half-way through the novel that the first of such moments occurs. Once more at the centre of it is the archetypal woman figure. In the warmth of an early summer evening Shirley sees her 'kneeling at her evening prayers', not at a Grecian altar but before the ridge of Stilbro' Moor.[15] This figure, called by Shirley alternatively Nature, Eve — but not Milton's Eve — and a 'woman-Titan', mother of rebels — 'she bore Prometheus' — is a disturbing one to Caroline. Her dismay has some similarity with that of the poet Sténio in George Sand's *Lélia* when the heroine, after gazing in adoration at the evening sky, refuses to kneel when they enter a church, though it is to Milton's fallen archangel rather than to Eve that Sténio compares Lélia, who is too proud to condescend to observe the terrestrial beauty of nature herself.[16]

With the arrival on the scene of Louis Moore, the mode of heightened prose occurs more frequently in *Shirley.* The essay written by Shirley in adolescence, which he can still repeat word for word, is, as Charlotte Brontë reminds the reader, the translation of a *devoir:* '. . . he gave it in French. but we must translate on pain of being unintelligible to some readers.' Its thematic importance is unquestionable.[17] 'Eva' symbolises the destiny of woman, which is the real subject of the novel, and she does so more completely than the earlier 'woman-Titan', for Caroline as well as Shirley speaks here. But artistically the more extended passage is less successful than the former one: the pupil is too near to her Romantic models. Faced like Chateaubriand with the necessity of showing that her 'desolate young savage' is really a highly intelligent being, torn by spiritual conflict as well as passion, she relies too much on rhetoric. Eva lacks the charm of Atala and, in the later stages of this strange rhapsody, where she becomes the personification of Humanity, wedded to Genius, she lacks the power of the towering symbolic figures in *Lélia*. Yet to dare to introduce this mixture of allegory and poetry into a work as full of realistic detail as *Shirley* is in itself a striking proof of the originality of Charlotte Brontë's style.

Louis Moore shows himself, in his journal, to be a better master of the poem in prose than his pupil. Though there is undoubtedly too much sentimental reverie, there is some true poetry as well. He excels in his painting of 'the dark-blue, the silver-fleeced, the stirring and sweeping visions of the autumn night-sky'. It is doubtful whether a lover's jealousy is justification enough for dramatising Sir Philip Nunnely's courtship of Shirley into 'the fable of Semele reversed'. But in itself the vision of the catastrophe which destroys the priest of Juno in the temple at Argos is charged with imaginative power. Subconsciously at least, Louis Moore understands better than his pupil the consequences of an attempted union between humanity and genius.

In *Villette* Charlotte Brontë is in full possession of the varied resources of her style. A fidelity to significant detail as exquisitely meticulous as in Flemish painting is shown to be compatible with a mode of poetic prose which is lyrical in its intensity, for both are expressions of the same sensibility. Because the inner tension is greater in *Villette,* the novel of solitude, than in any of the previous novels, the moments of heightened prose are more impassioned. The hallucinations induced by Lucy Snowe's nervous illness cannot be described otherwise than in poetic language: suffering 'brewed in temporal or calculable measure, and mixed for mortal lips, tastes not as this suffering tasted'. The euphoria produced by the total release of Lucy's imaginative power during the moonlit fête makes possible the beautiful recitative which is the greatest stylistic achievement in *Villette.*

Charlotte Brontë's success in this field was no doubt helped by her familiarity with biblical language and by her acquaintance with Bunyan's poetic allegory and with the work of De Quincey.[18] But the works of the French Romantics showed her how this mode of language could be used as an integral part of the novelist's art. The ending of *Villette* provides a final example of the affinities between their heightened style in climactic scenes and that of Charlotte Brontë at her most lyrical.

The resemblance here is one of situation as well as of style. The ship in which M. Paul sailed to Guadeloupe was the *Paul et Virginie.* He sets sail for Europe at the time of the equinoctial gales, just as Virginie for Mauritius in the season of hurricanes. In both cases the doom of the ship is foretold by the signs of the sky. Bernardin de Saint-Pierre gives more detail, but the sense of impending disaster is equally strong in Charlotte Brontë's 'The skies hang full and dark — a wrack sails from the west; the clouds cast themselves into strange forms . . .' In both cases the forces of nature strike with terrible swiftness; the hurricane brings chaos to the tropical sea; the Atlantic is convulsed by 'a wild south-west storm'. Bernardin, who had known many storms at sea, gives an account of the shipwreck as it was seen by eye-witnesses. Charlotte Brontë does not do this, but in her lyric finale she personifies the forces of destruction with an intensity that lifts the scene at once to the visionary plane reached later by the narrator of *Paul et Virginie:*

> That storm roared frenzied, for seven days. It did not cease till the Atlantic was strewn with wrecks; it did not lull till the deeps had gorged their full of sustenance. Not till the destroying angel of tempest had achieved his perfect work would he fold the wings whose waft was thunder — the tremor of whose plumes was storm.

That the novel does not end on this plane, but moves back to the prosaic reality which Lucy Snowe has learned to accept, is the final proof of the artist's mastery in *Villette.*

# 7 Conclusion

Foreign settings, foreign characters and the artistic utilisation of the French language made an important contribution to Charlotte Brontë's art, but so perfectly was it assimilated in a work whose foundations were laid 'deep in the rich main soil of English life and letters'[1] that English readers accepted it without question. In a surprisingly short time her novels found appreciative readers on the Continent as well. It was as an outstanding English novelist that they acclaimed her, but the sympathetic treatment she received from the first from French critics would hardly have been possible had her art not belonged also in part to a common European background. They accepted the continental settings and characters, and the use of the French language, sometimes almost without comment, and so confirmed their authenticity. At times they even showed more discernment than their English contemporaries. This was felt by Charlotte Brontë herself when she read Eugène Forcade's reviews of *Jane Eyre* and *Shirley*. Traces of insularity and manifestations of anti-Catholicism could not lastingly affect their admiration of Charlotte Brontë, though it was not till recently that the essential ambivalence of her attitude seems to have been recognised. Such discerning criticism, still continued, deserves a place in the study of Charlotte Brontë's foreign vision and bears eloquent testimony to its essential truth.

The most outstanding of the first French critics was Forcade, whose reviews appeared in the authoritative *Revue des Deux Mondes*. Charlotte called his article on *Jane Eyre* 'one of the most able, the most acceptable to the author, of any that has yet appeared . . .'[2] She was even more appreciative of his review of *Shirley:* 'Comparatively few reviewers even in their praise — evince a just comprehension of the author's meaning — Eugène Forcade . . . discerns every point, discriminates every shade . .. . With that man I would shake hands if I saw him. I would say "you know me, Monsieur — I shall deem it an honour to know you", I could not say so much to the mass of London critics . . .'[3] What she particularly valued in his estimate of her work can be deduced from another reference in her correspondence of the same date: 'I do not find that Forcade detects any coarseness in the work — it is for the smaller critics to find that out. The master in the art — the subtle-thoughted, keen-eyed, quick-feeling Frenchman knows the true nature of the ingredients which went to the composition of the creation he analyses — he knows the true nature of things, and gives them their right name.'[4]

It was in fact the moral censure that had not been spared her by some English critics that hurt her, as no criticism based purely on aesthetic criteria could have done. Eugène Forcade, on the contrary, was filled with admiration for the courage with which Jane Eyre confronted her difficult life: '. . . ce que je ne cesserai de louer, c'est l'inspiration mâle, saine, morale qui anime *Jane Eyre* à chaque page.'[5] The possibility that her passion and individualism could be considered coarse and unfeminine never occurred to him,and in the conclusion to his review of Charlotte Brontë's first novel he again praises its fundamental integrity.

It was not only coarseness of which Charlotte Brontë was accused by some English critics. According to the famous article in *The Quarterly*, *Jane Eyre* was both anti-religious and anti-social, representative of 'the tone of mind and thought which has overthrown authority and violated every code human and divine abroad, and fostered Chartism and rebellion at home'.[6] By contrast, Forcade praised the author of *Jane Eyre* for *not* 'fulminating an apocalypse against society' in a work where society played almost as implacable a rôle as the fatality of antiquity. By the time he reviewed *Shirley,* however, he was aware that discordant voices had been heard in England in opposition to the chorus of praise with which most critics greeted *Jane Eyre,* and he considered explicitly whether Currer Bell's second novel gave evidence of anti-social tendencies. His defence of her position here must also have been in Charlotte Brontë's mind when she praised his 'just comprehension of the author's meaning'.[7] He recognises that the accent of revolt sometimes heard in the earlier novel has become stronger, and that if the belief in self-assertion which is at times advocated as a duty, even by the 'douce Caroline', were adopted as a ruling principle, it could become a potential danger. But he feels the note of revolt in *Shirley* is in essence the expression of powers which have not yet found their true outlet.

His estimate of the characterisation in the novels emerges chiefly from his choice of passages to translate. Jane Eyre and Rochester both seem to the Frenchman distinctively English characters. Jane has the stoical courage to be expected of the heroine of 'un livre tout anglais'. Rochester is the English aristocrat, at once sophisticated and primitive. He is also victim of 'l'amère ivresse du spleen' — the Byronic qualities with which Charlotte Brontë endowed her hero certainly help to explain his interest for the French critic. *Shirley,* with its wider canvas, gives him even more strongly the sense of being transported in imagination to a different country and he affirms he would be willing to spend a month in Yorkshire for the sake of meeting 'des personnes aussi aimables, aussi originales, aussi curieuses'. Since Forcade is so conscious of the fundamentally English quality of the society in *Jane Eyre* and *Shirley,* it is all the more noteworthy that he accepts without criticism the introduction of French speaking characters, and recognises them at once as his compatriots. Adèle is 'un bijou de Parisienne'. Hortense Moore is 'plus française qu'anglaise, une espèce de provinciale de chez nous transplantée dans ce qu'il y a de plus anglais en Angleterre'. At the same time he endorses Charlotte Brontë's own analysis of the hybrid quality in Robert Moore: 'Né d'une mère presque française, il est ni Anglais ni Français . . .'

The French critic's appraisal of Charlotte Brontë's last novel was considerably less eulogistic, and it is noticeable that she makes no allusion to it in her correspondence. He does not pay *Villette* the compliment of undivided attention but considers it in conjunction with a novel by another English woman writer, Lady Fullerton, and the grounds of the comparison are made clear in the title of his article: *Un roman protestant et un roman catholique en Angleterre.*[8] It is the importance of the religious issue in *Villette* which explains his change in attitude. Charlotte Brontë had found the pensionnat milieu pervaded by 'a subtle essence of Romanism'. He is conscious that the author of *Villette* is 'protestante jusque'à la dernière fibre du coeur'. His declared preference for the 'roman catholique' is primarily on ethical grounds. He admits more artistic talent may have been needed to compose *Villette,* but this concession can hardly have made his verdict more acceptable to Charlotte Brontë. In view of his evident lack of enthusiasm for the book, it is all the more noticeable that he does not question the authenticity of the foreign setting. Though he finds no intrinsic interest in the life of a pensionnat, he recognises the success with which Charlotte Brontë has evoked the world of the Rue Fossette, so new and so perplexing in the eyes of Lucy Snowe.

Forcade was the most perceptive contemporary reviewer of Charlotte Brontë's work in France, but *Jane Eyre* attracted the attention of others as well and was twice translated into French in the author's lifetime.[9] After her death, Mrs Gaskell's *Life of Charlotte Brontë* received a good deal of notice in France and introduced, as in England, a new critical approach. It was in the light of this that Émile Montégut published, in the *Revue des Deux Mondes,* a 'portrait général' of the novelist, in which the focus has shifted from her works to her personality, seen against her racial and family background.[10] He is more interested in Charlotte as the potential heroine of a novel than as a novelist in her own right, but the few pages he spares for a consideration of *Jane Eyre, Shirley* and *Villette* show remarkable insight. He appreciates their poetic quality and sees the protagonists in *Jane Eyre* as epic figures. Jane herself is 'la Charlotte idéale et poétique'. Rochester, who combines the patrician with the potential rebel, belongs to the same spiritual race as Mirabeau. St John Rivers, 'coeur tranquille et âme inquiète', is of the family of Calvin and Knox. Montégut adds that these characters are so English that it takes some time to pierce through their defences to their essential human qualities, but it is noticeable that these, once found, can suggest European counterparts.

Thanks to the interest her work aroused in critics of the calibre of Forcade and Montégut, and to the translation of *Jane Eyre*, Charlotte Brontë became known in France almost as soon as in England. She would have been proud to know that her early readers included the artist Eugène Delacroix. Among contemporary English novels only *Jane Eyre* shared with *Vanity Fair* the honour or pleasing his fastidious taste, but it was from the former that he transcribed two passages in his *Journal*, one reflecting Rochester's impatience with the hollowness of society and the other the 'sense of mutual affection' which, no less than passion, seemed to surround the lovers at Thornfield.[11]

The interest Charlotte Brontë had aroused in France did not disappear with time, but the impact made by Mrs Gaskell's biography determined, as in England, the direction it would take for years to come, and critics followed Montégut in considering her work in terms of her life, and that of her family. As the greatness of *Wuthering Heights* came to be realised, the enigmatic figure of Emily attracted increasing attention. In future, instead of literary biographies of Charlotte, there were to be, as in England, biographical studies of the Brontë family, though she was always to occupy the central place. The later critics benefitted from being able to consult a more comprehensive collection of Charlotte's letters, and subsequently from the publication of the four letters to M. Heger. As a result the Brussels period received more comprehensive treatment. The biographical studies of Ernest Dimnet, Émilie and Georges Romieu and Robert de Traz all recognise the importance of M. Heger in Charlotte's life.[12] The chief emphasis is on the emotional situation, but the value of the intellectual interchange with a man of wide culture is also appreciated in varying degrees, especially by Émilie and Georges Romieu.[13]

The novels themselves are viewed mainly in a biographical context, and the two with foreign settings have a special interest because of their association with the Brussels period. But *The Professor*, though translated into French the year after its publication, remains overshadowed by *Villette*, though it earns praise from Dimnet for its style. The more complex art of the final masterpiece is increasingly appreciated. Since Lucy Snowe's experience in the Rue Fossette is now seen as related to Charlotte Bronte's in the pensionnat of the Rue d'Isabelle, it is surprising that the ambivalence of the novelist's attitude to foreign culture and to foreigners should still be largely ignored. That an apparently insular writer could paint insularity so well in Lucy Snowe, and give the other leading rôles in the drama to two people so un-English as M. Paul and Mme Beck without prejudice to the success of her characterisation, is a paradox that seems to pass unnoticed. Its explanation is implicit, none the less, in Robert de Traz's comment that the mature Charlotte sometimes speaks in Lucy Snowe — 'la Charlotte qui écrit le roman, après avoir souffert et médité bien plus que son modèle.'[14]

Writing in the first half of the twentieth century, these critics all profited from the increased biographical material available. The latest in date, Robert de Traz, also refers to the discovery of the true significance of the juvenilia. He wrote, however, before Fannie Ratchford's comprehensive evaluation of the Angrian and Gondal cycles had appeared. The most recent French biography of the Brontës, by Charlotte Maurat, gives more attention than any previous one to the importance of the epic cycles which dominated their imagination throughout childhood and adolescence.[15] In the light of her fuller treatment the subsequent stay in Brussels is seen in a wider perspective, as the experience thanks to which Charlotte Brontë emancipated herself from what was unreal in the climate of Angria, while still retaining its imaginative richness.

The Brontë story has not lost its charm in the retelling, in France any more than in England, but it has now become sufficiently familiar for separate studies to be made of the family's two outstanding members. Emily's enigmatic personality and astonishing genius have been sympathetically considered.[16] No separate full-length study of Charlotte's art has yet been published in France, but an important contribution towards it has been made by Professor Sylvère Monod in the introduction to his translation of *Jane Eyre*.[17] He has the intimate understanding of his subject that can only come through a long and close encounter with the text, and his appreciation of Charlotte Brontë's work is both profound and clear-sighted. He is aware of its imperfections,[18] but far more aware of its outstanding merits. He is also aware, as her translator, of the ambiguity of her attitude to 'la France, les Français et le français'. Conscious that she seems to have deliberately erected, between her French readers and herself, a barrier of prejudice and misunderstanding, he determines to clarify the situation by explicit reference to the ambivalence of her position.

It is interesting to see with what sureness of touch the French critic handles this complex question. In illustration of the imperfections she finds in his nation, he quotes a selection of caustic comments, from Pelet's revelation of 'la caractéristique nationale de la férocité' to Ginevra Fanshawe's habit of dropping into French 'when about to say something specially heartless and perverse'. But her anti-French prejudices are, as he knows, often coloured by her prejudiced attitude to Catholicism, developed by residence in a predominantly Catholic country. And he also stresses the contradictions in her attitude, indicated by her evident pride in her familiarity with Belgium and with the French language, which she makes a salient feature of her books. His attention is particularly attracted to the use this 'ardent champion of anti-France' makes of French words and he recalls how Crimsworth, on first hearing French spoken in Brussels, said that it was music in his ears. Charlotte Brontë's utilisation of his language seems to him, as indeed it is, an 'indirect homage', and he is anxious to point out this aspect of her art to his French readers, who would not otherwise be aware of it through the medium of a translation. He might have adduced proof from her own remarks, and from the character drawing in her novels, that she knew how to recognise valuable moral qualities in the French. If he prefers to keep the discussion chiefly on the linguistic plane, it is perhaps because he knows, as a translator, that there is no surer evidence of an artist's predilection than his choice of words. But the best proof of the real sympathy with France underlying Charlotte Brontë's attitude is surely the sympathy she inspires in her translator, as in her previous French critics, and his generous refusal to allow any superficial misunderstanding to interfere with it: 'Malgré la piètre estime où elle nous tient, nous ne pouvons lui marchander l'hommage de notre admiration et de notre affection.'

No consideration of Charlotte Brontë's attitude to 'France' — and all that she understands by that term — would be adequate if it were not finally considered in the context of her Romanticism. All Romanticism is in a sense an exile. Writers on the Brontës have often spoken of the Celtic heritage of these children of an Irish father and a Cornish mother as a predisposing cause of the moral solitude that seemed to surround them. Certainly there are traces of nostalgia for Ireland in Charlotte's affection for 'the West, the sweet West' in the Angrian tales. They were none the less at home in Yorkshire, as they would probably have been nowhere else, because Haworth offered them what they most needed, the freedom of the moors and of wide horizons and the solitude of the parsonage, which was not loneliness because they could share their dreams. For they were artists, richly endowed with the quality which Charlotte called 'my darling, my cherished-in-secret, Imagination, the tender and the mighty . . .', and the nature of imagination is never to be satisfied with what actually exists. The young Brontës, like Jane Eyre, found solace in listening to a tale their imagination 'created and narrated continuously', quickened with all the 'incident, life, fire, feeling' that was lacking in their actual existence. Such a tale demanded a setting as splendid as itself, a blend of all the scenes that had charmed them in their reading, Shakespeare's Illyria and Byron's Levant, the North of Scott and Ossian, and the Orient of the *Arabian Nights.* Such were the origins of the foreign vision that was ultimately to lead to the territory of Villette.

In this mosaic of imagined beauty, visions of the South have a privileged place. The exotic decorations of the rooms where she sits are a solace to Mary Percy in her loneliness:

. . . The walls were painted with sweet Italian scenes — groups of figures amidst the gleaming statues and blushing roses of some stately garden. A lake with a sweep of sunny shore in the distance, and the sky of a southern clime canopying all. Then in each niche of the Saloon there stood a figure of delicate sculpture, a laughing Bacchante crowned with vine leaves, or a radiant Muse leaning on her silent shell . . .[19]

This Mediterranean climate is the most equable in the wide and varied domain of Angria. The moors of the North and the burning sands of the East are the setting for war, lust and murder. There is most serenity and harmony in the scenes that borrow their colouring from an imagined Italy or Greece. Verdopolis, that 'splendid city rising with such graceful haughtiness from the green realms of Neptune', is planned in the imagination of Charlotte and Branwell as another Athens. France is too closely associated, in the minds of the young Brontës, with the Napoleonic Wars to belong as completely as Greece or Italy to this enchanting climate. But, on the lips of Mina Laury or Caroline Vernon, the mention of Provence or the gardens of Fontainebleau suggests a paler but authentic sunlight. Above all, France makes an important contribution to the culture of Angria, which is thought of as complementary to the contribution of Greece.

Even in Angria Charlotte Brontë is not unaware of the dangers of Romanticism. In the Palladian mansions, and under skies as blue as in Italy, disaster still takes place when the rational side of life is too completely subordinated. The love of truth was as much a part of Charlotte's nature as her worship of imagination and the time inevitably came when she felt obliged to say a reluctant 'Farewell to Angria'. When she finally crossed the Channel to visit the Continent she had often dreamed of, it was with the common-sense intention of acquiring additional qualifications as a schoolmistress. But the impetus to make the decision had been given by Mary Taylor's description of the artistic glories of Brussels and, like Lucy Snowe, she still saw the Continent in anticipation partly in Angrian colours, even while reminding herself that 'day-dreams are delusions of the demon'.

The reality was different from the 'wide dream-land' she had half hoped for, yet not so different that her ardent imagination could not find nourishment in scenes so indisputably new: '. . . to me, all was beautiful, all was more than picturesque . . .' The plains of Brabant could not offer 'snow-gleaming towers' or 'serrated heights', but they had space and light and wide horizons. The streets of Brussels had their magic, seen in a glow of festal illumination or moonlit splendour or in the flashing lightning of a 'spell-wakened tempest'. Even the pensionnat garden had its fascination as 'a little plot of ground in the very core of a capital', an oasis of trees and flowers where all was stone around. In the art galleries, the placid Madonnas, the opulent beauties of Rubens, the 'exquisite little pictures of still life' interpreted the spirit of their environment in line and colour, and it became vocal in the chime of bells and in tumultuous choruses from which 'the ear drank a satisfying sense of power'.

But Brussels opened up wider vistas than these. Charlotte Brontë, more fortunate than her heroine Shirley, encountered her 'professor of literature' at the time when Romanticism in France had reached its height. She never learned, even from M. Heger, to appreciate the literature of the classical period at its true value. Her reactions to Corneille and Racine were probably similar to those of Caroline Helstone, who showed herself so apathetic when reading 'those esteemed authors'. The masterpieces of 'the French romantic tradition, which had evidently flowed in full tide through the teaching of that Brussels classroom',[20] awoke in her a very different response. Much that she had already found in the Romantic literature of her own country — above all in Byron — she found again in the French Romantics: individualism, feeling, passion, the belief in genius — no literary movement has used the word more often than this one, born of Revolution and ineffaceably marked by the climate of the Napoleonic era. But in French Romanticism these qualities manifested themselves in varying ways and with shifts of emphasis that made the experience a revelation as well as a recognition of deep-rooted affinities. The Romantic intensity of feeling was reflected not only in the rebirth of poetry but in a prose which was itself another form of poetry. The initiator was Chateaubriand, creator of Réne and Atala as well as author of the *Génie du Christianisme,* and it was the novelists above all who benefitted from this discovery. Hugo himself as novelist, Balzac and George Sand were able in this medium to combine their gifts for narration and drama with a form of vision which was essentially poetic. This conception of the novel was particularly congenial to Charlotte Brontë. It was in the Romantic poets of her own country that she had first recognised the blend of feeling and self-revelation which was to form the basis of her art.[21] But verse was not her true medium, and though Scott, whom she so much admired, could offer her the example of prose narrative with an epic resonance, it was only shot through at intervals with the lyricism of individual feeling. In French Romanticism, however, she found abundant confirmation of her inborn sense that the novelist may also be a poet. It was the union of both that she admired in George Sand and that, in her mature judgment, constituted the greatness of the French writer: '... It is *poetry*, as I comprehend the word, which elevates that masculine George Sand, and makes out of something coarse something godlike.'[22]

But French Romanticism was organically linked with the classic tradition. The masterpiece of the forerunner Bernardin de Saint-Pierre, *Paul et Virginie*, was in essence an eglogue, not a melodrama. The artists whom M. Heger offered to Charlotte Brontë as models, when he gave her the advice: 'Étudiez donc la forme', were predominantly Romantics, but there was in them a conciliation rather than a break between the Greco-Latin heritage and the new freedom. This was most evident in the writers who heralded the dawn of the movement, Chénier and the lesser Millevoye, above all Chateaubriand, but Hugo himself acknowledged Virgil as one of his masters. The symmetry and harmony which Charlotte Brontë had associated, in Angrian dreams, predominantly with Greece and Italy, she rediscovered in the French Romantics. In *Atala* passion is never allowed to distort purity of line or harmony of colour; calm succeeds storm and tragedy becomes elegy. The teaching of Brussels did more than confirm Charlotte Brontë in her belief in the power of genius; it pointed to the way in which genius could be controlled. *Athenes sauvée par la poésie,* incomparably the finest of her writings in Brussels, shows how much she gained from contact with the Greco-Latin heritage. She was too much of an individualist ever to remain for long completely in tune with it, as the satirical conclusion of her essay reveals. But she had never been nearer to the heart of France than when she reconstructed the Parthenon, though she saw it by moonlight and not by the light of day.

She was still insular in some respects when she returned from Brussels; she was also what she had always wished to be, a European. It has been observed that she uses the word 'French', 'continental' and 'foreign' interchangeably,[23] and the association shows that in European culture it was primarily the Greco-Latin heritage that attracted her, the meridional blend of passion and harmony, as it had done since Angrian days. Although she also studied German while in Brussels, German literature never held the same interest for her, though she appreciated Schiller's Ballads. Few, however, can have understood better than she the longing behind Mignon's song:

> Kennst du das Land wo die Zitronen blühn . . .

She returned to England a Romantic still, but her Romanticism had been enriched by the contact with European authors. Paradoxically it was the contact with Classicism in its most uncompromising aspect, the cult of reason, that first bore fruit in her writings. The traumatic emotional experience of Brussels played its part here, and she came back with an increased awareness of the perils of the imagination and a determination to emphasise the rational side of life in her art. *The Professor* admitted the importance of feeling, but feeling is so firmly held in check by reason that it remains curiously muted. But *The Professor* was a necessary discipline that set her free to risk the full deployment of her powers in *Jane Eyre*. In *Jane Eyre* Romanticism is again in the ascendant and feeling is expressed with a frankness that startled contemporary English readers. But it manifests itself in alliance with that more complex and mysterious faculty imagination, and this was the salient quality of English Romanticism, to which Charlotte Brontë needed no fuller introduction through the medium of a foreign literature, for she had known and understood its importance for the artist since Angrian days. Its magic is superbly illustrated in *Jane Eyre*. With her first published novel she took her place among the Romantic artists of her own country. Echoes of the European heritage are there: 'Where did you see Latmos?' asks Rochester, 'for that is Latmos.' But such echoes combine with the other elements of her art to form a living unity.

The fusion of European overtones with the art of an English novelist is realised again in *Shirley*. The action of *Shirley* is firmly located in an English and a Yorkshire setting. It is fundamentally a Yorkshire novel, but such overtones contribute to the richness of its dominant themes. Belgium has given something of the colours of a Flemish painting to the domesticity of Hollow's cottage, and the accent of French Romanticism can be heard in the impassioned rhetoric of Shirley's apostrophe to Genius, the bridegroom of Humanity.

*Villette,* which has an English heroine in a continental setting, is the most mature of the novels. In its greatest scenes Charlotte Brontë's Romanticism acquires at times an almost transcendental quality. In *Villette* the Angrian dream has finally become the artist's vision. Belgium and France have contributed to its poetry, as well as Lucy Snowe's beloved England, but at the most inspired moments of the narration they are absorbed in a wider whole. The mature artist knows that the creative imagination does not depend in the first place on any material source but on a vision which can be described only in symbolic terms. In this sense, all vision is foreign. Lucy Snowe came as near as she could to evoking this immaterial yet real territory in her apostrophe to Imagination: 'A dwelling thou hast, too wide for walls, too high for dome — a temple whose floors are space — rites whose mysteries transpire in presence, to the kindling, the harmony of worlds!'

# References

## ABBREVIATIONS

* Quotations from Haworth edition.


## INTRODUCTION

1. See Phyllis Bentley, *The Brontë Sisters*, p. 16 and Kathleen Tillotson, *Novels of the Eighteen Forties*, pp. 277–80.


## CHAPTER ONE

1. 'The History of the Year', 1829; SHBMU I, p. 2.
2. 'A Romantic Tale', 1829; SHBMU I, p. 12.
3. See F. E. Ratchford, *The Brontës' Web of Childhood*, p. 3.
4. 'Characters of the Celebrated Men of the Present Time', 1829; SHBMU I, p. 38.
5. 'History of the Young Men', 1831; SHBMU I, pp. 92–3.
6. See Ratchford, op. cit., p. 33.
7. 'The Swiss Artist', Nov 1829, BST V, pt 29, ed. C. K. Shorter.
8. 'A Frenchman's Journal', Nov 1830, transcript in BST X, pt 52.
9. 'Albion and Marina', 1830; SHBMU I, p. 31.
10. 'A Peep into a Picture Book', 1834; SHBMU I, p. 358.
11. 'Visits in Verreopolis', 1830; SHBMU I, p. 44.
12. See Donald Hopewell, 'Cowan Bridge'; BST VI, pt 31.
13. See introduction to Clement Shorter's privately printed edition of Charlotte Brontë's translation of *La Henriade*, 1919. BM.
14. She is known to have used Porny's French Grammar (M. Porny, *Grammatical Exercises in English and French*, London, 1810). Inside the cover she scribbled an Angrian poem, the tone of which suggests that it was written just before she left home for Roe Head and that the date 'January 17, 183–' (the last figure is undecipherable) stands for 17 January 1831. See note on poem beginning 'On the bright scenes around them spread . . .', SHBP, p. 243.
15. E. Nussey, 'Reminiscences of Charlotte Brontë', *Scribner's Magazine*, May 1871. Reprinted BST II, pt 10.
16. CB to EN, 18 Oct 1832; SHB I, p. 107.

17. 'The Pirate', 1833; SHBMU I, p. 174.
18. 'Napoleon and the Spectre' is included in *The Twelve Adventurers and other Stories*, ed. C. W. Hatfield.
19. 'The Foundling', 1833; SHBMU I.
20. Ibid., p. 226.
21. 'The Bridal', SHBMU I, p. 208.
22. Lady Julia Sydney, suffering from boredom, '... ordered the carriage and as a *dernier ressort* drove to the Theatre-Royal.' 'My Angria and the Angrians', 1834; SHBMU II, p. 6.
23. Ibid., p. 25.
24. 'A Peep into a Picture Book,' 1834; SHBMU I, p. 362.
25. CB to EN, 21 Jul 1832; SHB I, p. 103.
26. CB to EN, 26 Sep 1836; SHB I, p. 146.
27. 'The Return of Zamorna', Dec 1836 or Jan 1837; SHBMU II, p. 298.
28. 'And when you left me . . .', 1836; SHBMU II, p. 245.
29. Quoted by Ratchford, op. cit., p. 116.
30. 'A Peep into a Picture Book', 1834; SHBMU I, p. 359.
31. 'Caroline Vernon', *Legends of Angria*, p. 246.
32. Ibid., p. 263.
33. 'The Last of Angria', undated fragment in Bonnell collection, BPM: quoted in BST VI, pt 34. Transcript by C. W. Hatfield.
34. Transcript by C. W. Hatfield in 'Charlotte Brontë and Hartley Coleridge'; BST X, pt 50.
35. CB to EN, 20 Aug 1840; SHB I, p. 215.
36. 'Balzac was for me quite a new author . . .' CB to G. H. Lewes, 17 Oct 1850; SHB III, p. 172.
37. See CB to G. H. Lewes, 12 Jan 1848; SHB II, p. 180. 'Now I can understand admiration of George Sand . . .'
38. Referring to the 'box of forty French novels that arrived in 1840', Sir William Haley said: 'I think we should know much if we only knew the exact works it contained. I am sure that "Mauprat" was among them.' See Sir William Haley, 'Three Sisters'; BST XI, pt 57. It seems probable that Emily Brontë also was attracted by *Mauprat*. Cf. Patricia Thomson, 'Wuthering Heights and Mauprat', *Review of English Studies*, Feb 1973.
39. Cp. the *Quarterly*, 1836. 'We have had, and we still have, some conscientious doubts whether we should mention this author at all . . .'
40. Cp. Jacques Blondel, *Emily Brontë. Expérience spirituelle et Création poetique*, p. 124.
41. Mrs Humphry Ward, Introduction to *Jane Eyre*, Haworth edition, p. xxxvii.
42. CB to EN, 7 Aug 1841; SHB I, p. 240.

CHAPTER TWO

1. See Gérin, pp. 191–2.
2. Ibid., pp. 192–4.

3. Gaskell, ch. XI, p. 218.
4. Ibid., ch. XI, p. 221.
5. CB to EN, May 1842; SHB I, p. 260.
6. Ibid.
7. See Gérin, p. 204.
8. Gaskell, ch. XI, p. 227.
9. Ibid., p. 226.
10. CB to EN, May 1842; SHB I, p. 261.
11. First exercise book of Charlotte Brontë at the Pensionnat Heger. BPM.
12. CB to EN, May 1842; SHB I, p. 261.
13. Gaskell, ch. XI, p. 228.
14. Ibid.
15. Gaskell, ch. XI, p. 231.
16. J. Hewish, *Emily Brontë*, p. 63.
17. BPM, Bonnell Collection. For complete list, see pp. 231—2.
18. 'La jeune fille malade', 18 Apr 1842; BST XII, pt 62. Translation by Jean P. Inebnit. Original in the Morris L. Parrish Collection at Princeton University Library.
19. 'Portrait de Pierre l'Hermite,' 31 Jul 1842, cit. Gaskell, ch. XI, pp. 232—5.
20. Gaskell, p. 231.
21. Victor Hugo, *Étude sur Mirabeau* in *Littérature et Philosophie Mêlées*, 1834. M. Heger has quoted from sections III and VI.
22. Gérin, p. 193.
23. Joseph-François Michaud, *Histoire des Croisades*, 1819, Vol. I, p. 4.
24. 'Le Roi Harold avant la bataille de Hastings,' Jun 1842, trans. Dorothy Cornish; BST XI, pt 57. French text given by Gérin, *Emily Brontë*, Appendix A. Original in BPM. Bonnell Collection.
25. *The Professor*, ch. 16, pp. 136—7.
26. Ibid., p. 139.
27. Ibid.
28. 'La Chenille', 11 Aug 1842; BST XII, pt 65, with trans. by Phyllis Bentley. Original in possession of the Heger family. 'Le Papillon', 11 Aug 1842; BST XI, pt 60, trans. L. Nagel. Reprinted from *Five Essays in French*, 1948, trans. L. Nagel with intro. and notes by F. E. Ratchford. French text given by Gérin, loc. cit. Original in the Henry W. and Alfred A. Berg Collection, New York Public Library.
29. Chateaubriand had painted the same metamorphosis in a famous sentence: 'Ver, chrysalide et papillon, l'insecte rampa sur l'herbe, suspendit son oeuf d'or aux forêts, ou trembla dans le vague des airs.' *Génie du Christianisme*, I, 5, ch. 5. The touch of exotic colour in Charlotte's description of the butterfly: '. . . ses ailes vibrantes brillent au soleil des couleurs du colibri . . .' suggests the exotic descriptions of *Atala*. Charlotte Brontë's Brussels transcriptions include a passage from the *Génie du Christianisme*, 'Prière du soir à bord d'un vaisseau', and one from *Atala*, 'La cataracte de Niagara'.

30. I Corinthians XV, verse 42.
31. Abel Villemain, *Tableau de la littérature au dix-huitième siècle*, 1828—9. See *The Professor*, ch. 4.
32. Carlyle, *Heroes and Hero Worship*, 1840; Guizot, *Histoire de la Révolution d'Angleterre*. (The first part, *Histoire de Charles Ier*, appeared 1826—7.)
33. See Gaskell, ch. XI, p. 237.
34. CB to EN, July 1842: SHB I, p. 267.
35. Margaret Lane, *The Brontë Story*, p. 146.
36. CB to EN, May 1842; SHB I, p. 260.
37. CB to EN, Jul 1842; SHB I, p. 267.
38. Gérin, op. cit., p. 209.
39. See Gustave Charlier, 'Brussels Life in Villette'; BST XII, pt 65 and Gérin, loc. cit.
40. MT to EN, 24 Sep 1842; SHB I, p. 272.
41. 'La Justice humaine', 6 Oct 1842; BST XII, pt 62, trans. Dorothy Cornish. Original in BPM. Bonnell Collection.
42. *Villette*, ch. 35, p. 480.
43. CB, 'Le Palais de la Mort', 16 Oct 1842; BST XII, pt 62, trans. Dorothy Cornish. Original in BPM. EJB, 'Le Palais de la Mort', 18 Oct 1842; BST XII, pt 64, with trans. by Margaret Lane. Original in BPM.
44. See J. C. Maxwell, 'Emily Brontë's "The Palace of Death" '; BST XV, pt 77. He indicates as fairly close to M. Heger's version, 'La Mort', in the *Fables* (1792) of Jean-Pierre Florian (I, ix).

  Buffon also associates Intemperance and Death: 'L'intempérance détruit et fait languir plus d'hommes, elle seule, que tous les autres fléaux de la nature humaine réunis.' *Nature des animaux*.
45. M. Heger to Mr Brontë, 5 Nov 1842; SHB I, pp. 278—80.
46. See Gérin, p. 214.
47. CB to EN, 14 Oct 1846; SHB II, p. 115.
48. CB to EN, 30 Jan 1843; SHB I, p. 291.
49. MT to EN, 18 Feb 1843; SHB I, p. 293.
50. CB to EN, 6 Mar 1843; SHB I, pp. 293—4.
51. Ibid.
52. Charles-Hubert Millevoye, *Élégies*, 1812.
53. 'La Chute des Feuilles', 30 Mar 1843; BST VI, pt 34, essay with corrections and comments of M. Heger, introduced by M. H. Spielmann; text and M. Heger's corrections and comments, and trans. by Phyllis Bentley; BST XII, pt 65. Original in possession of Heger family.
54. 'Je crois que toute poésie réelle n'est que l'empreinte fidèle de quelque chose qui se passe, ou qui s'est passé dans l'âme du poète . . .' Ibid.
55. *The Orphans* (trans. from the French of Louis Belmontet), SHBP, pp. 72—4. Original MS dated Feb 1843. First printed in *The Manchester Athenaeum Album*, 1850, with the exception of the first stanza.

56. Auguste Barbier, *Iambes*, 1831. Translated with title *Napoleon*, SHBP, pp. 229—30. Original MS dated Mar 1843. The fourth stanza, of eight lines, has been omitted. Trial lines for part of poem (two versions) BPM. Bonnell Collection.

57. Bossuet, 'Le Cheval dompté'; Buffon, 'Le Cheval'.

58. SHBP, pp. 59—60. Original MS 29 Jan 1838. Copied at Brussels, 1843. See note, loc. cit.

59. Ibid., p. 42. Original MS 26 Mar 1839. Copied at Brussels 1843. See note, loc. cit.

60. Volume in BM. See G. E. Maclean, 'Unpublished Essays in Novel Writing by Charlotte Brontë'; BST V, pt 26.

61. CB to EN, 1 Apr 1843; SHB I, p. 295.

62. Ibid., p. 296.

63. CB to PBB, 1 May 1843; SHB I, p. 297.

64. Ibid.

65. 'La Mort de Napoléon', 31 May 1843; BST XII, pt 64, text and trans. Margaret Lane. Text (incomplete) also given by Mrs Gaskell, ch. XII. Original in BPM.

66. 'Two Brussels Schoolfellows of the Brontës'; BST V, pt 23 (letter from Mlle L. de Bassompierre).

67. CB to EJB, 29 May 1843; SHB I, p. 299.

68. Ibid.

69. See draft of letter in German, 5 Jun 1843; SHB I, p. 300. Cf. Gérin, p. 235.

70. 'La Mort de Moïse', 27 Jul 1843; text and trans. Phyllis Bentley, BST XII, pt 65. Original in possession of the Heger family.

71. Gaskell, ch. XI, p. 236.

72. Casimir Delavigne, *Les Messéniennes*, Livre I, V, 1818.

73. For example she calls the plain a sea of verdure, into which the forests on its fringe extend their long avenues of trees like promontories into the ocean. In *Atala* Chateaubriand describes the wooded foothills stretching into the savannah as 'des coteaux qui formaient des golfes de verdure en avançant leurs promontoires dans la savane.'

74. Deuteronomy, ch. 34.

75. CB to EN, 6 Aug 1843; SHBI, pp. 311—12.

76. Cf. Gérin, p. 237.

77. Cf. Auguste Slosse, *Paul Heger*, 1846—1925, p. 8.

78. Cf. Gérin, p. 240.

79. CB to EJB, 2 Sep 1843; SHB I, p. 303.

80. CB to EJB, 1 Oct 1843; SHB I, p. 305.

81. 'Athènes sauvée par la Poésie', 6 Oct 1843, trans. Dorothy Cornish, BST XII, pt 62. Original in BPM. Bonnell Collection.

82. This incident from Plutarch's *Life of Lysander* is referred to by M. Baron, a colleague of M. Heger at the Brussels Athénée Royal, in his introduction to the edition of Casimir Delavigne's *Les Messéniennes*, published in Paris by Dufey and A. Vezard in 1831 and specially intended for scholastic use. It was no doubt known to M.

Heger, who admired Delavigne, and this, rather than Plutarch's text, may well have been the immediate source.

83. *The Violet*, 14 Nov 1830; *The Complete Poems of Charlotte Brontë*, ed. C. K. Shorter & C. W. Hatfield, 1923, pp. 107—12.

84. Chapman's translation of the *Iliad* was in the Ponden House Library.

85. *Villette*, ch. 35. pp. 479—80.

86. *Iliad*, Book 9. It seems probable Charlotte Brontë read the *Iliad* in Chapman's translation. See editor's note to trans. by Dorothy Cornish of 'Athènes sauvée par la Poésie'; BST XII, pt 62.

87. Draft of a letter in French. Original in BPM. Bonnell Collection.

88. It is marked 'Abercrombie', a name which she perhaps associated with the Scottish general Sir Ralph Abercromby, commander-in-chief of the expedition to Egypt in 1801.

89. CB to EN, 13 Oct 1843; SHB I, pp. 306—7.

90. Ibid.

91. CB to EN, 15 Nov 1843; SHB I, p. 309.

92. Cf. Gérin, pp. 248—52.

93. CB to EJB, 19Dec 1843; SHB I, pp. 309—10.

94. See MT to Mrs Gaskell, 18 Jan 1856; SHB I, p. 276.

95. Cf. Gaskell, p. 271.

96. CB to EN, 23 Jan 1844; SHB II, p. 3.

97. *Lès Fleurs de la Poésie Francaise depuis le commencement du XVIᵉ Siècle*, published at Tours in 1841. See Gérin, p. 254

98. CB to EN, 23 Jan 1844; SHB II, p. 3.

99. See H. E. Wroot, 'The Persons and Places of the Brontë Novels'(*Villette*); BST III.

100. See M. H. Spielmann, 'An early essay by Charlotte Brontë'; BST VI, pt. 34.

101. Frederika Macdonald, *The Secret of Charlotte Brontë*, p. 221.

## CHAPTER THREE

1. CB to EN; SHB II, p. 3.

2. Ibid.

3. See Gérin, p. 263.

4. Mrs Gaskell to EN, 9 Jul 1856; SHB IV, pp. 201—3.

5. CB to M. Heger, 24 Jul 1844; BST V, pt 24, which contains the four letters to M. Heger (reprinted from *The Times* of 29 Jul 1913, with explanatory article by M. H. Spielmann).

6. See pp. 40—1.

7. Janet Harper, 'Charlotte Brontë's Heger Family and their school', *Blackwood's Magazine*, Apr 1912.

8. Southey to CB, Mar 1837; SHB I, pp. 155—6.

9. CB to EN, 14 Nov 1844; SHB II, p. 21.

10. CB to M. Heger, 8 Jan 1845; BST V, pt 24.

11. See introduction by Margaret Lane to the Everyman edition of *Villette*.
12. BST V, pt 24.
13. See for discerning comments C. W. Hatfield's note, quoted by F. E. Ratchford, *The Brontës' Web of Childhood*, pp. 164—5 and Kathleen Tillotson, *Novels of the Eighteen-Forties*, p. 279.
14. The previous one, which she remembers as dated 18 May, cannot have been preserved.
15. CB to M. Heger, 18 Nov 1845; BST V, pt 24.
16. M. Heger to EN, 7 Sep 1865; SHB IV, pp. 247—9.
17. See Edith M. Weir, 'New Brontë Material comes to Light (Letters from the Hegers)'; BST XI, pt 59.
18. Quoted in M. H. Spielmann's trans. in his explanatory article accompanying the text and trans. of the Brontë letters in *The Times*, 29 Jul 1913; reprinted in BST V, pt 24.
19. CB to Mrs Gaskell, 26 Sep 1850; SHB III, p. 162.
20. SHBP, p. 239.
21. SHBP, p. 26.
22. Ibid.
23. See Gérin, p. 281.
24. SHBP, p. 240.
25. SHBP, pp. 231—5. The first draft is in an exercise book which had been used by Charlotte Brontë in Brussels in 1843, but the reference to the parting in the closing verses makes it probable that it was actually written, or at least completed, after her return.
26. SHBP, p. 56.
27. SHBP, pp. 26—8.
28. SHB II, p. 52.
29. CB to W. S. Williams, Sep 1848; SHB II, p. 256.
30. 'Biographical Notice', 1850 edition of *Wuthering Heights* and *Agnes Grey*.
31. CB to Messrs Aylott & Jones, 6 Apr 1846; SHB II, p. 87.
32. CB to W. S. Williams, 14 Dec 1847; SHB II, p. 161.
33. Gérin, p. 316.
34. Biographical notice to the second edition of *Wuthering Heights*. Cit. SHB II, p. 140.

CHAPTER FOUR

1. Preface written by Charlotte Brontë with a view to the publication of *The Professor* in 1851. The 'crude efforts' were no doubt the transitional fragments written after her farewell to Angria in 1839.
2. C. W. Hatfield, 'The Early Manuscripts of Charlotte Brontë; A Bibliography'; BST VI, pt 34.
3. See Gaskell, ch. XI.
4. See H. E. Wroot, 'The Persons and Places in the Brontë Novels (*Villette*)', BST III (Supplementary Part); Edgar de Knevett,

'Charlotte Brontë's School in Brussels'; BST VI, pt 33; M. H. Spielmann, 'Charlotte Brontë in Brussels', in *A Centenary Memorial: Charlotte Brontë*, ed. Butler Wood. Facsimiles of two plans of the school and its surroundings made by Louise Heger for M. H. Spielmann are in the BPM.

5. See M. H. Spielmann, loc. cit.

6. This window obviously corresponds to the single casement in the back of the boarding house of the boys' Athénée, which over-looked the garden of the Heger pensionnat. See Gérin, p. 314.

7. See Spielmann, loc. cit. The music was suggested by the sound of a French horn, on which a footman in the Errara mansion, at the corner of the Rue Royale and the opening to the Belliard steps, was a talented performer.

8. The Brontës chose an equally unobtrusive position in the classroom at the pensionnat. 'On the last row, in the quietest corner sat Charlotte and Emily, side by side, so deeply absorbed in their studies as to be insensible to any noise or movement around them.' Gaskell, ch. XI, p. 241.

9. Built from 1818 to 1840 on the site of the fourteenth-century fortifications.

10. Cf. Gérin, pp. 198–200.

11. CB to EJB, 2 Sep 1843; SHB I, p. 303.

12. For the position of the old Rue Notre Dame aux Neiges, see Gérin, p. 221 and H. E. Wroot, 'The Persons and Places of the Brontë Novels (*The Professor*)', BST III (Supplementary Part).

13. CB to G. H. Lewes, 6 Nov 1847; SHB II, p. 152.

14. Gérin, p. 494.

15. Spielmann, loc. cit. See *Villette*, ch. 27 ('The carriage-wheels made a tremendous rattle over the flinty Choseville pavement . . .').

16. Cf. Georgia S. Dunbar, 'Proper Names in *Villette*', *Nineteenth-Century Fiction*, vol. xv, no. 1, Jun 1960.

17. Spielmann, loc. cit.

18. Gérin, p. 188.

19. Gaskell, ch. XI, p. 223.

20. In a German exercise book used in Brussels in May 1843 she wrote a poem *The Nun*, in which a veiled figure becomes a symbol of deepening twilight in a lonely house. SHBP, p. 235.

21. The slab actually existed; in the days of the cross-bowmen it covered the entrance to an underground passage, probably intended as a way of escape in case of attack from surrounding heights. See Chadwick, *In the Footsteps of the Brontës*, p. 206.

22. Cf. Gérin, *Emily Brontë*, p. 133.

23. See H. E. Wroot, loc. cit. He also recalls that there had previously been a church belonging to the community of the Béguines in the Rue d'Isabelle.

24. See Spielmann, loc. cit.

25. See Gérin, pp. 202–3. She also points out that the manor itself was probably identical with the Taylors' school, the converted château de Koekelberg.

26. See Gustave Charlier, 'Brussels Life in *Villette*' (extracts trans. Phyllis Bentley from an essay in Professor Charlier's volume *Passages*); BST XII, pt 65. See also Gérin, pp. 209—10.
27. Ibid.
28. Ibid.
29. Ibid.
30. Gustave Charlier, loc. cit.
31. Gérin, pp. 248—52.
32. Ibid.
33. Cf. 'The Tragedy and the Essay', 1833; SHBMU I, p. 314.
34. See Gustave Charlier, loc. cit.
35. CB to Amelia Taylor, 7 Jun 1851; SHB III, pp. 244—5. 'To-night . . . I expect to see and hear Rachel at the French theatre. I wonder whether she will fulfil reasonable expectation — as yet it has not been my lot to set eyes on any serious acting for which I cared a fig . . .'
36. CB to James Taylor, 15 Nov 1851; SHB III, p. 290.
37. Ibid.
38. See Gérin, p. 221.
39. Louise Heger speaks of '. . . St. Jean-Baptiste (i.e. St. Jean-Baptiste au Béguinage), église qui se trouve à l'autre côté de la ville près du canal: quartier du Père Silas dans "Villette".' See Frederika Macdonald, *The Secret of Charlotte Brontë*, note to p. 205.
40. See Gustave Charlier, loc. cit.
41. Gérin, pp. 238—9.
42. Nearly a fortnight after the fête, in *Villette*, comes the Feast of the Assumption (see ch. 41).
43. See Robert B. Heilman, 'Charlotte Brontë's "New Gothic" '.

## CHAPTER FIVE

1. CB to Margaret Wooler, 31 Mar 1848; SHB II, p. 202.
2. Cp. Byron, *The Age of Bronze:*
      A single step into the right had made
      This man the Washington of worlds betrayed . . .
3. The Brussels transcriptions include Hugo's *La Pologne(Les Chants du Crépuscule)* and Lamartine's *Épitaphe des Prisonniers Français morts pendant leur captivité en Angleterre (Recueillements Poétiques).*
4. CB to W. S. Williams, 25 Feb 1848; SHB II, p. 190.
5. CB to W. S. Williams, 11 Mar 1848; SHB II, p. 198.
6. CB to W. S. Williams, 11 Mar 1848; SHB II, p. 198.
7. CB to Margaret Wooler, 31 Mar 1848; SHB II, p. 203.
8. CB to W. S. Williams, 25 Feb 1848; SHB II, p. 190.
9. CB to Margaret Wooler, 17 Feb 1852; SHB III, p. 318.
10. Thackeray, 'Little Travels and Roadside Sketches', cit. Gérin, p. 222.
11. CB to E. Nussey, 28 Dec 1846; SHB II, p. 119.

12. CB to W. S. Williams, 6 Nov 1852; SHB IV, p. 18.
13. Gérin, p. 314.
14. Spielmann, loc. cit.
15. 'A Leaf from an Unopened Volume', 1834.
16. Mrs Humphry Ward. Introduction to *The Professor*.
17. Ch. 23. Included in SHBP (section *Posthumous Poems*) with title, *Master and Pupil*. See note, p. 219.
18. 'Lucia has trodden the stage . . . You never seriously thought of marrying her; you admired her originality, her fearlessness, her energy of mind and body; you delighted in her talent, whatever that was, whether song, dance or dramatic representation; you worshipped her beauty, which was of the sort after your own heart: but I am sure she filled a sphere from whence you would never have thought of taking a wife.' (ch. 25).
19. See *Jane Eyre*, Clarendon edition, ed. Jane Jack and Margaret Smith, for note on this passage, p. 599, where it is commented on as 'a particularly clear Byronic reminiscence'.
20. *Jane Eyre*, ch. 28. The play is *Die Räuber*. See note p. 603, Clarendon edition.
21. 'They (the Wheelwrights) would . . . have known that *Shirley* was by a Brussels pupil . . . from the absolute resemblance of Hortense Moore to one of their governesses — Mlle Hausse (sic).' C. K. Shorter, *Charlotte Brontë and her Circle*, p. 442.
22. H. E. Wroot, 'The Persons and Places in the Brontë Novels (*Shirley*)'; BST III (Supplementary Part).
23. Ibid.
24. Gaskell, ch. VI, p. 109.
25. The rumour of a foreign strain in Cartwright is rejected by Edward Taylor, grandson of Joshua Taylor, in his marginal annotations to his copies of *Shirley*. 'Moore was Mr. Cartwright in so far as the story of the Luddite disturbance fits him . . . The foreign extraction and family are pure romance and of course his sister and brother are mythical.' See Joan Stevens, 'Sidelights on "Shirley": Brontëana in New Zealand'; BST XV, pt 79.
26. See Gérin, p. 389. '. . . the Taylors (accurately portrayed in the Yorke family) holding the forefront of the stage with an unmistakable evocation of Joe Taylor as the mill-owner hero, Robert Moore.' See also Ivy Holgate, 'The Structure of Shirley'; BST XIV, pt 72.
27. Mary Taylor to Mrs Gaskell, 18 Jan 1856; SHB I, p. 91.
28. Passages from Bernardin de Saint-Pierre, Bossuet, Corneille, Racine and La Fontaine.
29. 'Le Cheval Dompté' is one of the Brussels transcriptions.
30. In a footnote in the first, three-volume edition of *Shirley*, 1849 (vol. 3, p. 106), deleted in subsequent editions, Charlotte Brontë reminds the reader that when Louis Moore expressed this opinion, the 'modern French school of poetry' was 'yet unknown' and quotes in illustration of the dynamic qualities he would have

appreciated several stanzas from Hugo and Barbier. But Moore's criticism remains an anomaly, coming from a French-speaking reader of Corneille, Racine and La Fontaine.

31. Cp. *Valentine*, 1832; *Le Compagnon du Tour de France*, 1840; *Le Meunier d'Angibault*, 1845.

32. The Heger family consisted of: Marie, born 1837; Louise, born 1839; Claire, born 1840; Prospère, born 1842; Victorine, born 1843; Paul, born 1846.

33. CB to M. Heger, 24 Jul 1844; BST V, pt 24.

34. Cp. CB to EJB, 2 Sep 1843; SHB I, p. 303. '. . . Mlle Blanche's character is so false and contemptible I can't force myself to associate with her. She perceives my utter dislike and never now speaks to me — a great relief.'

35. See SHB I, pp. 255–6 and Charles Lemon, 'The Origins of Ginevra Fanshawe', BST XVI, pt 81.

36. CB to W. S. Williams, 20 Jul 1850; SHB III, p. 126. '. . . who indeed that has once seen Edinburgh, with its couchant crag-lion, but must see it again in dreams waking or sleeping? . . . You have nothing like Scott's Monument . . . and above all you have not the Scotch National character — and it is that grand character after all which gives the land its true charm, its true greatness.'

37. CB to George Smith, 6 Dec 1852; SHB IV, p. 23.

38. CB to EN, 16 Nov 1849; SHB III, p. 37.

39. Frederika Macdonald, *The Secret of Charlotte Brontë*, p. 157.

40. Edith M. Weir, 'New Brontë Material comes to Light (Letters from the Hegers)'; BST XI, pt 59.

41. Ibid.

42. Ibid.

43. Macdonald, op. cit. p. 194.

44. See Dr J. B. Baillie, *'Religion and the Brontës'*; BST VII, pt 37.

45. Georgia S. Dunbar, 'Proper Names in *Villette*', *Nineteenth-Century Fiction*, XV (Jun 1960).

46. See Gérin, *Emily Brontë*, p. 133.

47. Spielmann, op. cit.

48. Dunbar, loc. cit.

49. CB to George Smith, 6 Dec 1852; SHB IV, p. 22.

50. CB to EN, 16 Nov 1848; SHB III, p. 17.

51. Discours prononcé à la distribution des prix de l'Athénée Royal de Bruxelles, le 16 aôut 1834.

52. Ibid.

53. Ibid.

54. Ibid., le 15 aôut 1843.

55. Ibid.

56. Ibid.

57. Macdonald, op. cit., p. 217.

58. Janet Harper, 'Charlotte Brontë's Heger Family and their School', *Blackwood's Magazine*, Apr 1912.

59. See H. E. Wroot, 'The Persons and Places of the Brontë Novels' (*Villette*); BST III (Supplementary Part).
60. Macdonald, op. cit., p. 208.
61. See Dunbar, op. cit. Charlotte Brontë's spelling of the name Emmanuel is always as above.
62. *L'Indépendance Belge*, 9 May 1896, quoted by Chadwick.
63. See Macdonald, op. cit., p. 46, and Gérin, p. 228.
64. Discours de 1834.
65. Gérin, p. 192.

## CHAPTER SIX

1. Cf. Kathleen Tillotson, *Novels of the Eighteen Forties*, p. 7.
2. Including George Smith himself ('The Brontës', *Cornhill Magazine*, vol. 28, 1873).
3. 'You observe that the French of "Shirley" might be cavilled at. There is a long paragraph written in the French language in that chapter entitled "Le cheval dompté". I forget the number. I fear it will have a pretentious air. If you deem it advisable and will return the chapter, I will efface and substitute something else in English.' CB to W. S. Williams, 15 Sep 1849; SHB III, p. 21. 'I return the Proof-sheets — Will they print all the French phrases in italics? I hope not; it makes them look somehow obtrusively conspicuous.' CB to W. S. Williams, 17 Sep 1849; SHB III, p. 21.
4. *Études de la Nature*, 1784, étude X (section *Des Couleurs*).
5. Mrs Gaskell to friend, Aug 1850; SHB III, p. 147.
6. J. N. Ware, 'Bernardin de Saint-Pierre and Charlotte Brontë', *Modern Language Notes*, vol. XL, Jun 1925. 'Reflets' occurs several times in the *Harmonies de la Nature*, e.g.: 'Il n'est pas douteux que les reflets de la terre n'augmentent la chaleur du soleil.' 'Ce tableau est rempli de reflets physiques et moraux.'
7. Ware, loc. cit.
8. See pp. 29, 47 above.
9. *Génie du Christianisme*, 1, 5, ch. 12, *Deux perspectives de la nature*.
10. See Stephen Ullmann, *Style in the French Novel*, Cambridge University Press, ch. 4.
11. *Atala*. (Brussels transer.)
12. *Séraphine (Souvenirs de Jeunesse)*. 'À cet âge de repos, le cours de la vie ressemble à celui d'un ruisseau que sa pente rapproche, à travers mille détours, des environs de sa source. (Brussels transer.)
13. See Margot Peters, *Charlotte Brontë: Style in the Novel.*
14. *The Violet*, Nov 1830. See p. 53 above.
15. *Shirley*, ch. XVIII.
16. George Sand, *Lélia*, Part I, 2.
17. See p. 141. Cf. Inga-Stina Ewbank, *Their Proper Sphere*, p. 200. '... the position of this curious essay as the thematic centre of

*Shirley*, and its profound relation to the other novels, is indisputable.'

18. De Quincey was one of the authors who received, in 1847, a copy of the *Poems by Currer, Ellis and Acton Bell*, in acknowledgement of the 'pleasure and profit' they had received from his works.

## CHAPTER SEVEN

1. Mrs Humphry Ward, Introduction to *Jane Eyre*, Haworth edition.
2. CB to W. S. Williams, 16 Nov 1848; SHB II, p. 271.
3. CB to EN, 22 Nov 1849; SHB III, p. 42.
4. CB to W. S. Williams, 22 Nov 1849; SHB III, pp. 40—1.
5. Eugène Forcade, 'Jane Eyre', *Revue des Deux Mondes*, 1 Nov 1848.
6. Elizabeth Rigby, 'Vanity Fair', 'Jane Eyre' and 'Governesses' Benevolent Institution — Report for 1847', *Quarterly Review*, Dec 1848.
7. Cf. Eugène Forcade, 'Le Roman Contemporain en Angleterre — *Shirley*', *Revue des Deux Mondes*, 15 Nov 1849.
8. *Revue des Deux Mondes*, 15 Mar 1853. The novels are: *Villette*, by Currer Bell and *Lady-Bird*, by Lady Georgiana Fullerton. Lady Fullerton had already published *Ellen Middleton*, 1844; *Grantley Manor*, 1847.
9. See Émile Langlois, 'Early critics and translators of "Jane Eyre" in France'; BST XVI, pt 81.
10. Emile Montegut, 'Charlotte Brontë. Portrait general', *Revue des Deux Mondes*, Jul 1857.
11. Delacroix, *Journal*, 15 Sep 1858. See E. L. Duthie, 'Delacroix and "Jane Eyre" '; BST XIII, pt 66.
12. Cf. Ernest Dimnet, *Les Soeurs Brontë*, 1910; Émilie and Georges Romieu, *La Vie des Soeurs Brontë*, 1929; Robert de Traz, *La Famille Brontë*, 1939.
13. Cf. Emilie and Georges Romieu, op. cit., p. 112.
14. Robert de Traz, op. cit., p. 285.
15. Charlotte Maurat, *Le Secret des Brontë*, 1967.
16. Cf. Jacques Debu-Bridel, *Le Secret d'Emily Brontë*, 1950, and Jacques Blondel, *Emily Brontë. Experience spirituelle et création poétique*, 1956.
17. Sylvère Monod, Introduction to translation of *Jane Eyre*, 1966.
18. Cf. Sylvère Monod, 'L'imprécision dans "Jane Eyre",' *Etudes Anglaises*, XVII, 1 (1964).
19. 'The Return of Zamorna', SHBMU II, p. 287.
20. Mrs Humphry Ward, Introduction to *Villette*, Haworth edition.
21. Cf. George Saintsbury, 'The position of the Brontës as Origins in the history of the English Novel'; BST II, pt 9.
22. CB to G. H. Lewes, 18 Jan 1848; SHB II, p. 180.
23. Cf. Sylvère Monod, Introduction to trans. of *Jane Eyre*.

# Selective bibliography

TEXTS

The edition used for the novels of Charlotte Brontë and for
Mrs Gaskell's *Life* has been the Haworth edition edited by
Mrs Humphry Ward and C. K. Shorter (reprinted by John
Murray, 1920-2). (Occasional errors in French (such as
omission of the subjunctive or erroneous use of capital letters
— e.g. 'en Anglais') have been left as in text.) For her
correspondence, *The Brontës, their Lives, Friendships and
Correspondence* Shakespeare Head edition, edited by T. J.
Wise and J. A. Symington, 4 vols, Oxford 1932, has been
used.

The following have also been consulted:

*The Miscellaneous and Unpublished Writings of Charlotte
Brontë and Patrick Branwell Brontë,* Shakespeare Head
edition, ed. T. J. Wise and J. A. Symington, 2 vols, Oxford,
1936-8.

*The Poems of Charlotte Brontë and Patrick Branwell Brontë,*
Shakespeare Head edition, ed. T. J. Wise and J. A.
Symington, Oxford, 1934.

Charlotte Brontë's translation of Voltaire's *Henriade,*
canto i, privately printed by C. K. Shorter, 1919. BM.

*The Twelve Adventurers and Other Stories,* by Charlotte
Brontë, ed. C. W. Hatfield, Hodder & Stoughton, 1925.

*The Spell: An Extravaganza,* by Charlotte Brontë, ed. G. E.
MacLean, O.U.P., 1931.

*Legends of Angria,* by Charlotte Brontë, ed. F. E. Ratchford
and W. C. DeVane, Yale University Press, 1933.


BIOGRAPHICAL AND CRITICAL STUDIES

Bentley, Phyllis, *The Brontës,* Wingate, 1949.
———, *The Brontë Sisters,* Longmans, Green, 1950.

Burkhart, Charles, *Charlotte Brontë. A Psychosexual Study of her Novels,* Victor Gollancz, 1973.

Cecil, David, *Early Victorian Novelists,* Constable, 1934.

Chadwick, Mrs E. H., *In the Footsteps of the Brontës,* Pitman, 1914.

Craik, W. A., *The Brontë Novels,* Methuen, 1968.

Dimnet, Ernest, *Les Soeurs Brontë,* Blond, 1910. *The Brontë Sisters,* trans. Louise Morgan Sill, Jonathan Cape, 1927.

Ewbank, Inga-Stina, *Their Proper Sphere,* Edward Arnold, 1966.

Gérin, Winifred, *Charlotte Brontë. The Evolution of Genius,* Clarendon Press, 1967.

————, *Emily Brontë,* Clarendon Press, 1971.

Gregor, Ian (ed.), *The Brontës, a collection of critical essays,* Prentice-Hall, Englewood Cliffs, N.J., 1970.

Hewish, John, *Emily Brontë,* Macmillan, 1969; St Martin's Press, 1969.

Knies, Earl A., *The Art of Charlotte Brontë,* Ohio University Press, 1969.

Lane, Margaret, *The Brontë Story,* Heinemann, 1953.

Macdonald, Frederika, *The Secret of Charlotte Brontë,* T. C. & E. C. Jack, 1914.

Martin, Bernard, *The Accents of Persuasion,* Faber & Faber, 1966.

Maurat, Charlotte, *Le Secret des Brontë,* Buchet/Chastel, 1967.

————, *The Brontës' Secret,* trans. Margaret Meldrum, Constable, 1969.

Peters, Margot, *Charlotte Brontë. Style in the Novel,* University of Wisconsin Press, 1973.

Ratchford, Fannie E., *The Brontës' Web of Childhood,* Columbia University Press, 1941.

Raymond, Ernest, *In the Steps of the Brontës,* Rich & Cowan, 1948.

Romieu, Emilie and Georges, *La Vie des Soeurs Brontë,* Gallimard, 1929.

————, *The Brontë Sisters,* trans. Roberts Tapley, Skeffington, 1931.

Shorter, Clement K., *The Brontës and their Circle,* Hodder & Stoughton, 1896.

————, *The Brontës. Life and Letters,* 2 vols, Hodder & Stoughton, 1908.

Tillotson, Kathleen, *Novels of the Eighteen-Forties,* O.U.P., 1954.

Traz, Robert de, *La Famille Brontë,* Albin Michel, 1939.

Winnifrith, Tom, *The Brontës and their Background. Romance and Reality,* Macmillan, 1973; Barnes & Noble, 1973.

### ARTICLES IN PERIODICALS, ETC.

For articles in *Brontë Society Transactions,* see chapter notes.
This study was completed when the following article on another Brussels *devoir* appeared in *Brontë Society Transactions:* Lawrence Jay Dessner, 'Charlotte Brontë's Le Nid', an unpublished manuscript; BST XVI, pt 83.

Dunbar, Georgia S., 'Proper Names in *Villette',* *Nineteenth-Century Fiction,* Jun 1960.

Harper, Janet, 'Charlotte Brontë's Heger Family and their School', *Blackwood's Magazine,* Apr 1912.

Heilman, Robert B., 'Charlotte Brontë's "New Gothic" ', in *From Jane Austen to Joseph Conrad,* ed. R. C. Rathbone and M. Steinmann, Jr., University of Minnesota Press, 1958.

Monod, Sylvère, 'L'Imprécision dans *Jane Eyre',* *Études Anglaises,* XVII-I, 1964.

————, Introduction to *Charlotte Brontë: Jane Eyre,* trans. into French and annotated by Sylvère Monod, Classiques Garnier, 1966.

Spielmann, M. H., 'Charlotte Brontë in Brussels', in *Charlotte Brontë. A Centenary Memorial,* ed. Butler Wood, Fisher Unwin, 1916.

Thomson, Patricia, 'Wuthering Heights and Mauprat,' *Review of English Studies,* vol. XXIV, no. 93, Feb 1973.

Ware, John N., 'Bernardin de Saint-Pierre and Charlotte Brontë'. *Modern Language Notes,* XL, Jun 1925.

## CONTEMPORARY FRENCH REVIEWS OF CHARLOTTE BRONTË'S NOVELS

Forcade, Eugène, 'Jane Eyre', *Revue des Deux Mondes,* 1 Nov 1848.
———,'Le Roman Contemporain en Angleterre, Shirley', *Revue de Deux Mondes,* 15 Nov 1849.
———, 'Un Roman Protestant et un Roman Catholique en Angleterre', *Revue des Deux Mondes,* 15 Mar 1855.
Montégut, Emile, 'Charlotte Bronte. Portrait général', *Revue des Deux Mondes,* Jul 1857 (reprinted in his *Écrivains modernes de l'Angleterre,* Ire série, 1885).

## CHARLOTTE BRONTË'S DEVOIRS, TRANSLATIONS AND TRANSCRIPTIONS OF PASSAGES FROM FRENCH AUTHORS (BRUSSELS 1842-3)

*Devoirs*

'La jeune fille malade', 18 Apr 1842; BST XII, pt 62. Trans. Jean P. Inebit. Original in Morris L. Parrish Collection at Princeton University Library.
'Portrait de Pierre l'Hermite', 31 Jul 1842. French text given by Gaskell, ch. XI.
'La Chenille', 11 Aug 1842; BST XII, pt 65. French text and trans. Phyllis Bentley. Original in possession of Heger family.
'La Justice Humaine', 6 Oct 1842; BST XII, pt 62. Trans. Dorothy Cornish. Original in Bonnell Collection, BPM.
'Le Palais de la Mort', 16 Oct 1842; BST XII, pt 62. Trans. Dorothy Cornish. Original in Bonnell Collection, BPM.
'La Chute des Feuilles', 30 Mar 1843; BST VI, pt 34. French text with corrections and comments of M. Heger, introduced by M. H. Spielmann. French text, with M. Heger's corrections and comments, and trans. Phyllis Bentley; BST XII, pt 65. Original in possession of Heger family.
'La Mort de Napoléon', 31 May 1843; BST XII, pt 64. French text and trans. Margaret Lane. Text (incomplete) also given by Mrs Gaskell, ch. XII. Original in Bonnell Collection, BPM.

'La Mort de Moïse, 27 Jul 1843; BST XII, pt 65. French text and trans. Phyllis Bentley. Original in possession of the Heger family.

'Athènes sauvée par la Poésie', 6 Oct 1843; BST XII, pt 62. Trans. Dorothy Cornish. Original in Bonnell Collection, BPM.

Draft of a letter in French, 'Ma chère Jane . . .', unfinished, circa 1843. Bonnell Collection, BPM.

*Translations*

'The Orphans', trans. from the French of Louis Belmontet; SHBP, pp. 72-4. Original MS dated Feb 1843. First published in *The Manchester Athenaeum Album*, 1856, with the exception of the first stanza.

'Napoleon', trans. of Auguste Barbier's 'L'Idole', *Iambes;* SHBP, pp. 229-30. Original MS dated Mar 1843. Fourth stanza has been omitted. Trial lines for part of poem (two versions) are in Bonnell Collection, BPM.

*Transcriptions from French authors*

There are twenty-one transcriptions in the Bonnell Collection, BPM, with headings and usually name of author:

(1) 'La Pauvre Fille' (author not stated, but see p. 26 above).
(2) Chateaubriand: 'Prière du Soir à bord d'un Vaisseau' (*Le Génie du Christianisme,* pt I, book 5, ch. 12).
(3) 'La Prière du Matin' (author not stated).
(4) Chateaubriand: 'Eudore. Moeurs Chrétiennes. IV Siècle' (*Les Martyrs,* book 22).
(5) Chateaubriand: 'Prière du Soir à bord d'un Vaisseau' (Longer version of no. 2 — first two paragraphs identical).
(6) Millevoye: 'La Chute des Feuilles' (*Élégies*).
(7) Chateaubriand: 'La Cataracte de Niagara' (*Atala*).
(8) Hugo: 'Mirabeau à la Tribune' (*Littérature et Philosophie mêlées, Étude sur Mirabeau,* III, VI).
(9) Nodier: 'Du Souvenir chez les Vieillards' (*Souvenirs de Jeunesse, Séraphine*).
(10) Michaut (sic) (Joseph-Francois Michaud): 'Prise de Jérusalem par les Croisés' (*Histoire des Croisades,* book I, 4).

(11) 'L'Espérance' (author not stated).
(12) 'Ruine de Carthage' (author not stated).
(13) Massillon: 'La Médisance' (*Sermons pour le Carême*, book 4).
(14) Frayssinous: 'De la Vérité' (*Défense du Christianisme*, discours 3).
(15) Bossuet: 'La Majesté Royale' (*Politique tirée de l'Écriture Sainte*, book 5, article IV).
(16) Buffon: 'Le Cheval' (*Histoire Naturelle, Les Quadrupèdes*).
(17) Bossuet: 'Le Cheval dompté' (*Meditations sur l'Evangile, La Cène*, pt II, 4).
(18) Hugo: 'Une nuit qu'on entendait la mer sans la voir' (*Les Voix Intérieures*).
(19) Hugo: 'La Pologne' (*Les Chants du Crépuscule*).
(20) Lamartine: 'Épitaphe des Prisonniers Francais morts pendant leur captivité en Angleterre' (*Recueillements Poétiques*).
(21) Barthélemy: 'L'Orage' (*Voyage du jeune Anacharsis en Grèce*, ch. 59).

For connection between the transcriptions and some of Charlotte Brontë's *devoirs*, see chapter 2. There are also some echoes of the transcriptions in the novels. The most significant is the thematic use of 'Le Cheval dompté' in *Shirley*, ch. 27. In the footnote on the penultimate page of the same chapter in the first edition, subsequently deleted, the first verse of Hugo's 'Une nuit qu'on entendait la mer sans la voir' and the opening lines of Barbier's 'L'Idole', translated by Charlotte Brontë in Brussels, are quoted as examples of poems which Louis Moore would have found congenial. There may be a reminiscence in *Jane Eyre* of the passage 'Ruine de Carthage' ('les femmes coupent leurs longs cheveux pour faire des cordages aux machines de guerre') in Rochester's allusion to Blanche Ingram's hair as 'just such as the ladies of Carthage must have had'.

# Index